IFIP Advances in Information and Communication Technology   **587**

Editor-in-Chief

IFIP – The International Federation for Information Processing

IFIP was founded in 1960 under the auspices of UNESCO, following the first World Computer Congress held in Paris the previous year. A federation for societies working in information processing, IFIP's aim is two-fold: to support information processing in the countries of its members and to encourage technology transfer to developing nations. As its mission statement clearly states:

IFIP is the global non-profit federation of societies of ICT professionals that aims at achieving a worldwide professional and socially responsible development and application of information and communication technologies.

IFIP is a non-profit-making organization, run almost solely by 2500 volunteers. It operates through a number of technical committees and working groups, which organize events and publications. IFIP's events range from large international open conferences to working conferences and local seminars.

The flagship event is the IFIP World Computer Congress, at which both invited and contributed papers are presented. Contributed papers are rigorously refereed and the rejection rate is high.

As with the Congress, participation in the open conferences is open to all and papers may be invited or submitted. Again, submitted papers are stringently refereed.

The working conferences are structured differently. They are usually run by a working group and attendance is generally smaller and occasionally by invitation only. Their purpose is to create an atmosphere conducive to innovation and development. Refereeing is also rigorous and papers are subjected to extensive group discussion.

Publications arising from IFIP events vary. The papers presented at the IFIP World Computer Congress and at open conferences are published as conference proceedings, while the results of the working conferences are often published as collections of selected and edited papers.

IFIP distinguishes three types of institutional membership: Country Representative Members, Members at Large, and Associate Members. The type of organization that can apply for membership is a wide variety and includes national or international societies of individual computer scientists/ICT professionals, associations or federations of such societies, government institutions/government related organizations, national or international research institutes or consortia, universities, academies of sciences, companies, national or international associations or federations of companies.

More information about this series at http://www.springer.com/series/6102

Julian M. Bass · P. J. Wall (Eds.)

Information and Communication Technologies for Development

16th IFIP WG 9.4 International Conference
on Social Implications of Computers
in Developing Countries, ICT4D 2020
Manchester, UK, June 10–11, 2020
Proceedings

 Springer

Editors
Julian M. Bass 🆔
University of Salford
Salford, UK

P. J. Wall 🆔
Trinity College Dublin
Dublin, Ireland

ISSN 1868-4238   ISSN 1868-422X   (electronic)
IFIP Advances in Information and Communication Technology
ISBN 978-3-030-65830-4   ISBN 978-3-030-65828-1   (eBook)
https://doi.org/10.1007/978-3-030-65828-1

This Springer imprint is published by the registered company Springer Nature Switzerland AG
The registered company address is: Gewerbestrasse 11, 6330 Cham, Switzerland

Preface

This book presents the collection of papers selected for presentation at the International Federation for Information Processing (IFIP) Working Group 9.4 16th International Conference organized under the banner of the Third European Conference on the Social Implications of Computers in Developing Countries. The conference was hosted in Manchester, UK, by the University of Salford in June 2020.

Research papers published in this volume address ICT-related research challenges in Africa, Asia, and South America, including: Bangladesh, Brazil, Lebanon, Malawi, Myanmar, Nepal, Nigeria, Palestine, South Africa, and Rwanda. Despite being Convened as a European Conference, we were delighted to have facilitated such a global perspective on ICT4D.

We received 29 submissions which were each single-blind peer-reviewed by at least three members of the Program Committee. As a consequence of this process, 14 papers were accepted and selected for presentation at the conference. A further 4 papers were conditionally accepted, subject to refinement using more detailed feedback and advice from reviewers. 10 papers were given detailed feedback but not accepted. The authors of these papers have been encouraged to revise their papers for submission to the next global conference, to be held in Peru during 2021–now postponed to 2022. Sadly, one accepted paper was withdrawn by the authors.

Online Conference

The conference was initially organized as a face-to-face event, to be hosted by the University of Salford at Media City UK in Greater Manchester. However, the COVID-19 pandemic resulted in the UK Government advice to "Stay at Home," along with many countries imposing their own travel restrictions. Consequently, the University of Salford campus was closed and international travel prohibited. In order to facilitate dissemination of the research already submitted, we migrated to an online event.

One consequence of this was that we had to abandon the planned conference dinner in the Manchester United football ground at Old Trafford. Surprisingly perhaps, this sad turn of events did slightly gratify one group of delegates. The local fans of the nearby Manchester City football club were mildly comforted not to have to celebrate the conference dinner at the competing Manchester United ground!

Football rivalries aside and on a more positive note, we were able to retain the conference keynote speakers and workshops, albeit in abbreviated form. Also, the day before the IFIP WG 9.4 event the ICT4D North group of English Universities also held their annual workshop online.

Previous Conferences

The IFIP WG 9.4 First European Workshop on Iterative and Incremental Approaches to ICT4D was held at Robert Gordon University in Aberdeen, UK, in May 2014. The keynote speaker at that workshop was Eswaran Subrahmanian from Carnegie Mellon University, USA.

The second European conference was held in Tirana, Albania, in June 2018, and was organized by IFIP WG 9.4, the UNESCO chair in ICT4D at Royal Holloway, University of London, UK, the European University of Tirana, Albania, and the University of Tirana, Albania.

The IFIP WG 9.4's global conference series has been running for more than 20 years. With the 15th International Conference on Social Implications of Computers in Developing Countries held in Dar es Salaam, Tanzania, in May 2019.

Keynote Speakers

Despite the condensed online format adopted for the third European conference, we were pleased to welcome keynote speakers: Dr. Ciara Heavin, University College Cork, Ireland, and Terrance Fernando, University of Salford, UK.

Dr. Heavin's keynote talk focused on her work on the IMPACT project in Nigeria between 2016–2018. The key findings from the project included identification of isolated rural social agencies that limited the authority and value of centralized initiatives including public health based initiatives. A further important finding indicated that trained healthcare professionals were scarce and that the public health system relied on distributed and informal communities of practice. She emphasized that this meant existing material agencies of rural healthcare centres were not sufficient for deep enactment of agreed healthcare delivery guidelines.

Prof. Fernando spoke on "Technology Enhanced Adaptive Governance for Building Resilient Cities: Barriers and Challenges." His talk drew on the experience of projects that had attracted over GBP £7M over a five year period in areas of disaster response management, disaster risk reduction, and risk sensitive urban design. Drawing on his experience of working in Sri Lanka, Pakistan, and Malaysia, he emphasized the importance of developing a culture of collaboration among stakeholders and building sustainable teams to overcome political instability.

Panels

The first panel addressed "Philosophical Approaches to ICT4D" and was chaired by Dr. Dympna O'Sullivan (Technical University Dublin, Ireland). The panelists were Prof. Sundeep Sahay (University of Oslo, Norway), Dr. David Kreps (University of Salford, UK), and Prof. Silvia Masiero (now with the University of Oslo, Norway).

This panel discussion critically examined the changing ICT4D landscape from a variety of ontological, philosophical, and methodological perspectives. The discussion spanned a variety of topics including the dominance of positivist and interpretivist approaches in the field, the establishment and rapid growth of the HISP project, and the current move towards more critical realist, Southern-based and other indigenous and regional research paradigms and theories. It was strongly argued that such changed methods and philosophical approaches are necessary in order to address the changing nature of the ICT4D field resulting from increasing use of AI and advanced technologies in the Global South and the growing importance of ethical considerations in this work. It was also agreed that we are witnessing the emergence of a new ICT4D 3.0 digital for development paradigm and new approaches are needed to address this.

Prof. Robert Davison, City University of Hong Kong, Hong Kong, and Dr. Pamela Abbott, The University of Sheffield, UK, facilitated the second workshop on "Academic Publishing for Early Career Researchers." The workshop focused on capacity building for researchers from the Global South, to support them in gaining access to high-quality journals for their ICT4D research.

October 2020   Julian M. Bass
                                                                                      P. J. Wall

Acknowledgements

We would like to thank the Program Committee members for their support in reviewing and selecting the submissions. We also express gratitude to all our sponsors: the IFIP WG 9.4 (ifipwg94.org), BCS - the Chartered Institute for IT, Manchester Branch, the University of Salford, UK, and the ADAPT Centre, Trinity College Dublin, Ireland.

We also appreciate the support of Prof. Robert Davison who is chair of the IFIP 9.4 WG and Editor-in-chief of the *Electronic Journal of Information Systems in Developing Countries*. Also, David Kreps, chair of the IFIP Technical Committee 9 on Humans and Computers. Both, not only enabled and supported the event within IFIP, but we were delighted that they attended and contributed to the conference.

Organization

Conference and Program Committee Chairs

Julian M. Bass	University of Salford, UK
P. J. Wall	Trinity College Dublin, Ireland

Program Committee

Pamela Abbott	The University of Sheffield, UK
Rehema Baguma	Makerere University, Uganda
Laurence Brooks	De Montfort University, UK
Suzana Brown	SUNY Korea, South Korea
Jyoti Choudrie	University of Hertfordshire, UK
Regina Connolly	Dublin City University, Ireland
Robert Davison	The City University of Hong Kong, Hong Kong
Christopher Foster	The University of Manchester, UK
Tarek Gaber	University of Salford, UK
G. Harindranath	Royal Holloway, University of London, UK
Andy Haxby	Competa It B.V., The Netherlands
Ciara Heavin	University College Cork, Ireland
Lucy Hederman	Trinity College Dublin, Ireland
Richard Heeks	The University of Manchester, UK
Faheem Hussain	Arizona State University, USA
Ibrahim Inuwa	American University of Nigeria, Nigeria
Muhammadou Kah	American University of Nigeria, Nigeria
Stan Karanasios	The University of Queensland, Australia
Ebenezer Laizer	University of Turku, Finland
Dave Lewis	Trinity College Dublin, Ireland
Arunima Mukherjee	University of Oslo, Norway
Shirin Madon	London School of Economics, UK
Silvia Masiero	Loughborough University, UK
Suvodeep Mazumdar	The University of Sheffield, UK
Brian Nicholson	The University of Manchester, UK
Petter Nielsen	University of Oslo, Norway
Siwel Nyamba	Sokoine University of Agriculture, Tanzania
Dympna O'Sullivan	Technical University Dublin, Ireland
Scarlet Rahy	University of Salford, UK
Ravishankar M. N.	Loughborough University, UK
Jaco Renken	The University of Manchester, UK
M. A. Setiawan	Universitas Islam Indonesia, Indonesia
Mira Slavova	Warwick Business School, UK
Johan Sæ bo	University of Oslo, Norway

Contents

Digital Platforms and Gig Economy

Competing Logics: Towards a Theory of Digital Platforms for Socio-economic Development

Silvia Masiero[1(✉)] and Brian Nicholson[1,2]

[1] University of Oslo, Oslo, Norway
silvima@ifi.uio.no
[2] University of Manchester, Manchester, UK

Abstract. Extant literature on digital platforms is predominantly centred on the Global North, resulting in a paucity of research on the implications of digital platforms for developing countries. Against this backdrop, a recent research stream has focused on digital platforms in developing country contexts, with a view of understanding the affordances and limits of platforms as a route to socio-economic development. This paper seeks to contribute to this nascent literature, unpacking a human-centred development logic as an alternative to the market logic that animates most of the platforms discourse and relying on it to lay the foundations for an emerging theory of platforms for development. Two sub-linkages, centred respectively on platforms' openness and modularity, are conceptualised and illustrated with examples from empirical research. This work has implications for the emerging literature on digital platforms for development, and for theorising platforms in the context of information systems and societal challenges.

Keywords: Digital platforms · Socio-economic development · Institutional logics · Openness · Modularity

1 Introduction

Existing literature on digital platforms is situated primarily in the context of the Global North and seeks to understand business models and market dynamics attached to platformisation (e.g. Gawer and Cusumano 2014; Parker et al. 2016; Constantinides et al. 2018; De Reuver et al. 2018; Rai et al. 2019). Information Systems (IS) literature (Gawer 2009; Evans and Gawer 2016) distinguishes *transaction* platforms (multi-sided markets that connect supply and demand) from *innovation* platforms (which enable the construction of complements from third-party developers). Across the two streams, IS research focuses on innovation in business models and profit generation, observing platform-specific phenomena such as the dialectics of control and openness (Ghazawneh and Henfridsson 2013; Eaton et al. 2015) and monetisation in a predominant business-oriented light. By contrast, significantly less research focuses on the social dimensions of platforms, such as their involvement in solving societal challenges (Majchrzak et al. 2016) and fostering broader goals of human and development.

© IFIP International Federation for Information Processing 2020
Published by Springer Nature Switzerland AG 2020
J. M. Bass and P. J. Wall (Eds.): ICT4D 2020, IFIP AICT 587, pp. 3–13, 2020.
https://doi.org/10.1007/978-3-030-65828-1_1

Against this backdrop, a new stream of research has focused on digital platforms in developing country contexts (cf. Koskinen et al. 2018, 2019; Nicholson et al. 2019). In contrast to previous literature, this stream poses platforms in *explicit* relation to socio-economic development: not only does it observe platformisation outside of the Global North, but openly considers if and how platforms are entrenched in determinate development processes. An important focus of this emerging literature are affordances (e.g. Hatakka et al. 2019) of platforms for development, to be studied in parallel with the constraints that platforms can impose on ongoing development processes. Koskinen et al. (2018, 2019) identify four trends in this nascent platforms-for-development literature: the development potential of platforms; differences between Global North and Global South; the ways in which platforms may exacerbate inequality; public and non-profit alternatives to private platforms.

This paper contributes to the nascent literature on platforms-for-development. Our contribution stems from the observation that, while empirical work on the topic is being conducted, researchers lack a clear mapping of the linkage operating between platforms and socio-economic development. In response to this absence, we observe that a human-centred logic (which we conceptualise drawing on Sein and Harindranath 2004) provides the basis for an alternative to the market logic on platforms, leading to an alternate vision of platforms for development. Our objective is to provide steps towards a theoretical framework that presents platforms as human-centred, illustrating their potential in terms of broader societal objectives that transcend immediate market goals.

To develop such framework we draw on two core properties of platforms, which are characterised by a modular architecture and an open governance structure (Constantinides et al. 2018; De Reuver et al. 2018). Openness and modularity are considered as two defining characteristics of platforms, which differentiate them from other digital objects (Tilson et al. 2010; De Reuver et al. 2018). Drawing on instances of published research on platformisation in developing nations, we examine how each property concurs to enacting a human-centred logic, theorising two sub-linkages which substantiate the connection between platforms and socio-economic development. We also look at the limits of each sub-linkage, which leads us to offer possible reasons for platform-for-development failures.

This paper is structured as follows. In Sect. 2 we illustrate the dominant market logic on platforms, contrasting it with a human-centred logic which expands more on socio-economic development. In Sect. 3 we examine openness and modularity as platform properties, and theorise how these are linked to the enactment of the human-centred logic just explained. In Sect. 4 we observe the limits of each sub-linkage, reading extant cases of platform-for-development failure in their light. In Sect. 5 we conclude, highlighting implications for emerging theories of platforms in ICT4D.

2   Market and Human-Centred Logics

The notion of *institutional logics* is a relevant one to examine the contrasting visions underpinning, respectively, business-oriented platforms and instantiations of platforms for development. Thornton and Ocasio (1999) define *institutional logics* as "the socially constructed, historical patterns of material practices, assumptions, values, beliefs, and rules by which individuals produce and reproduce their material subsistence, organize time and space, and provide meaning to their social reality (1999: 804). Friedland and Alford (1991) conceptualise society as an inter-institutional system where behavior in a context is theorised with reference to societal sectors ("orders") representing sets of expectations for social relations and organisational behavior. Building on these insights, scholars have sought to understand the multiple logics implicit in organisational activity, which can be mutually reinforcing, complementary or in conflict with each other (cf. Besharov and Smith 2014; Thornton et al. 2012).

Rolland et al. (2018) illustrate three perspectives in the literature on digital platforms. These are an engineering ("technical artifacts with a modular architecture consisting of a stable core component and many changing peripheral components"), an economic ("markets that disrupt traditional markets and facilitate efficient interactions between consumers and producers"), and an organisational view ("innovation practices in which actors organise and coordinate innovation enabled by technical mechanisms and social arrangements"). These three perspectives sum up the IS literature on platforms, illuminating its complementary foci on technicalities, organisational aspects and mechanisms of value creation. Underpinning these three is a focus on platforms as profit generators (Parker et al. 2016), which invites questions on business model disruption and its value-generating consequences.

The work by Parker et al. (2016) offers a comprehensive illustration of the market logic implicit in this discourse. Drawing on multiple examples of transaction platforms (Gawer 2009), their book unpacks different instances of business model disruption, highlighting the short business history of actors such as Uber, AirBnB, Google, PayPal or Amazon and pointing out their mechanisms of value-creation. Focus on innovation platforms (e.g. iOS, Android etc.) is limited in this work, and when such platforms appear that is in order to illustrate further profit-generation mechanisms – stemming, for example, from the creation of an apps ecosystem that capitalises on generative properties (Parker et al. 2016). In this work, as in further platform literature in IS and economics, the teleological reason for platforms to exist is that of profit generation, pursued through business model disruption.

To be sure, this paper does not problematise the tenability of the market logic, which is effectively confirmed by multiple works on the profit-generation mechanisms of platforms. It does, however, question the view that a market logic of platforms is "the only" one possible, a view that has arguably dominated platform literature till very recent times. The three perspectives identified by Rolland et al. (2018) all subsume a market logic, only illuminating three different aspects of it (technical, economic and organisational) as applied to platforms. By way of example, recent reviews of platforms literature in lead IS journals barely make a mention of the human, societal or, indeed, development implications of platforms, focusing instead on new trends of platformisation and the relation of platforms with infrastructures (cf. Constantinides et al. 2018; De Reuver et al. 2018).[1].

Against this backdrop, the nascent literature on platforms-for-development (cf. Koskinen et al. 2018, 2019; Nicholson et al. 2019) articulates around a different implicit view of platformisation. As stated in Koskinen et al. (2018, 2019), digital platforms have the potential to create social and economic value in the Global South, meaning that researchers need conceptual tools to understand platformisation outside its common Western-centred focus. Underpinning this is the view that the value of platforms goes well beyond profit generation, and is entrenched into socio-economic development processes aimed at increasing quality of life in resource-constrained settings. If "development" is to be broadly understood as the "enlargement of people's choices" (Sen 1999) through dimensions such as health, education and income, this leaves scope for understanding the role of platforms towards this goal.

Table 1. Digital platforms – market-centred versus human-centred logics

	Market-centred logic	Human-centred logic
Underlying assumption	Platforms as tool for profit generation (cf. Parker et al. 2016)	Platforms as entrenched in "the enlargement of people's choices" (Sen 1999)
Core mechanisms	Business model innovation; disruption of existing industry paradigms	Enabling choices in education, health, and standard of living; building a democratic society marked by involvement, participation and transparency; better management of behavior and customs (Sein and Harindranath 2004)
Type of platforms	Transaction (e.g. Uber, Amazon, AirBnB, etc.) a more limited focus on innovation platforms (iOS, Android etc.)	Transaction (e.g. Uber, Amazon, AirBnB, etc.) but also innovation (iOS, Android etc.) and data platforms (e.g. biometric identification)
Teleology (underlying goal of digital platforms)	Optimisation of business goals (competition; profit-making)	Optimisation of development goals (e.g. life expectancy, education, incomes)

Sein and Harindranath (2004) lay out three core principles that support a "human-centred" logic, complementary (and not necessarily antithetic) to the market one as

---

[1] For example, in Constantinides et al. (2018) there is only one mention of implications of platforms for developing countries, when it is stated that "there are a number of sectors where this (the diffusion of online work) would be highly beneficial, especially for "new-collar jobs" in developing countries". Even this argument has been, however, put into serious question by researchers of digital labour in the Global South (e.g. Heeks 2017; Graham et al. 2017).

illustrated in Table 1. In their analysis of ICTs in national development, they conceptu-alise development processes as "enabling choices in education, health, and standard of living; building a democratic society marked by involvement, participation and trans-parency; better management of behavior and customs" (Sein and Harindranath 2004). While a market logic is inspired by a teleology of profit-generation, it is development in its Senian notion that a human-centred logic is built around, and technologies are seen as entrenched in the making of (or, in some cases, hindering) the forms of enablement that Sein and Harindranath (2004) detail. While a market logic is more squarely focused on transaction platforms, a human-centred logic encompasses different types of plat-formisation such as transaction, innovation and integration platforms (Koskinen et al. 2019).

3   Openness and Modularity: Enacting the Human-Centred Logic

As noted in Constantinides et al. (2018), the architecture and governance of platforms are defining features that differentiate them from other digital objects. In this section we examine *openness* and *modularity* as platform properties, and theorise how these are linked to the enactment of the human-centred logic illustrated above. The two sub-links are articulated as follows.

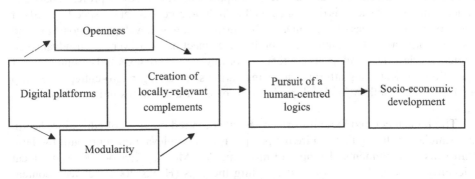

Fig. 1. Digital platforms & socio-economic development – mapping the theoretical link

Openness: Tiwana (2013: 118, cited in Constantinides et al. 2018: 384) defines plat-form governance in terms of "who decides what" with regards to incentive structures, control mechanisms, and the power distribution between the platform's owner and com-plementors. The layered architecture of platforms invites a specific trade-off: that is the balance between owners' control and *generativity*, defined as "the ability of pro-ducing new output without input from the originators" (Zittrain 2008). As opposed to the closed, centralised architecture found in linear value chains (Constantinides et al. 2018: 384), the open architecture of platforms invites forms of governance that allow for generativity, enabling the construction of unfiltered complements on the top of a platform's core. A standard example from IS literature is that of Apple iOS, whose over 140,000 apps built on top of the platforms' core enable contributions from numerous third-party actors (Eaton et al. 2015). Through generativity, openness enables the construction of customised content, enabling third-party actors in developing countries to produce locally-relevant content for their communities.

Modularity: as in Tiwana et al. (2010), platform architecture describes "how the ecosystem is partitioned into a relatively stable platform and a complementary set of modules that are encouraged to vary, and the design rules binding both". Stemming from this, the modularity of digital artefacts (Kalllinikos et al. 2013) is reflected in digital platforms as the recombinability of different modules, predicated on a common platform core and resulting into reprogrammable architectures (De Reuver et al. 2018). The creation of locally-relevant contents, seen in ICT4D literature as a core strategy for filling design-reality gaps (Heeks 2002), is sustained by the creation of the "complementary set of modules" that characterise platform ecosystems as described in Tiwana et al. (2010). In particular, third-party innovators in developing countries can capitalise on the modular basis of platforms to build contents that suit the needs of poor and marginalised users, thus minimising the gaps with their lived reality.

Therefore, as represented in Fig. 1, openness and modularity both feed into the creation of locally-relevant complements, which may transcend the profit-generation goals stated by Parker et al. (2016). These complements are unfiltered, leaving room for grass-root innovation: for example m-Farm, a company running mobile services for farmers in Kenya, runs an Android-based app for crop price information tailored to the needs of local farmers.[2] Similarly, Vula mobile – an app connecting medical professionals and patients in South Africa – is developed on the Android core to meet the specific needs of patients in remote areas of the country.[3] Platforms built with development goals in mind also operate under this remit: Kiva, built for connecting borrowers to disadvantaged lenders worldwide, develops its contents accordingly to its contexts and communities of operation.[4] E-Kutir, a platform connecting farmers sustaining micro-entrepreneurship for farmers in South Asia, develops different modular adaptations in its four countries of action.[5]

The human-centred logic illustrated above is centred on goals of education, health and standard of living that inspire the pro-poor, locally relevant contents built by these platforms. Complements like those of m-Farm, Vula Mobile, Kiva or e-Kutir use local relevance to meet the needs of users, filling the gaps (Heeks 2002) between content design and the reality that users experience. This illuminates the link illustrated in Fig. 1, where the two core features – openness and modularity – feed into a logic of content generation inspired by human development rather than profit-making. It is the open, modular architecture of platforms that enables generative production, a key basis for the grassroot innovation at the root of empowerment in resource-constrained communities.

One clarification is in order here. As noted above, the logics of platforms-for-development is not antithetic, but complementary to the market-centred view: as a result,

---

[2] https://www.mfarm.co.ke/.
[3] https://www.vulamobile.com/.
[4] https://www.kiva.org/.
[5] http://www.ekutirsb.com/.

profit-centred complements are conceivable, and indeed enacted, through the development logic too. For example, Micrograam – an Indian social enterprise operating a platform for microlending – connects socially marginalised borrowers to lenders, generating a profit from interest both for lenders and for the social enterprise.[6] E-marketplaces such as e-Krishi – a platform for farmers to sell their produce at the market price through the Internet – aim at achieving development through profits for members of marginalised communities.[7] Therefore, in a platforms-for-development logic profit making is not "banned", but is seen in a wider human-centred view where profit is a means to greater standards of living (Sein and Harindranath 2004), and in turn to the enlargement of people's choices as in Sen (1999).

4 Limitations

Notwithstanding our description of the platforms-for-development linkage, the literature also engages cases of platforms-for-development which do not function as planned (cf. Koskinen 2020). A reason is that both the sub-links reviewed in our framework can break: openness and modularity enable unfiltered contributions from third parties, but this does not necessarily result in socio-economic development outcomes under the human-centred logic. Below we illustrate how the production of unfiltered contributions may result into perverse effects, ultimately disempowering development subjects rather than resulting in the empowerment (Sen 1999) that inspires the development logic.

So far, we have noted that platforms entail a balance of control and generativity, which enables grassroot innovation by empowering third-party actors (Ghazawneh and Henfridsson 2013). However, following the reasoning in Fig. 1, this process can malfunction in at least two ways: first, openness may be contrasted by control from platform owners that limit the power of local innovators, ultimately disempowering the final users that the platform is meant to empower. Second, modularity can enable complements that do not work towards the intended outcomes, leading to detrimental conditions for the intended beneficiaries of platform-led development efforts. Both cases are illustrated below.

First, platform owners may yield greater power than that assumed by an "open" governance structure. In the case of India's Aadhaar, an identification platform grounded on a large biometric database, complements are constituted by numerous social welfare services, built to "empower the poor" by guaranteeing service access through biometrics (Banerjee 2016). But Aadhaar's openness – enabling providers to build on it – is constrained by the platform's owner, the Unique Identification Authority of India (UIDAI), a government agency that owns and manages the Aadhaar database. Through UIDAI the Indian central government effectively controls Aadhaar-enabled services, resulting into perverse outcomes such as the exclusion of entitled users who fail to authenticate (Khera, 2019). As a result, openness – rather than resulting into empowerment – is contrasted by platform owners, ending up in exclusionary outcomes that harm development subjects (Khera 2019; Masiero and Prakash 2019).

---

[6] https://micrograam.com/.

[7] https://www.ekrishikendra.com/.

Second, modularity enables the construction of grassroot innovations that can empower development subjects, but may also result into perverse effects. Studies of digital lending platforms have shown how, beyond providing loans to the socially disadvantaged, such platforms may strengthen the power of donors and, in turn, the dependency of recipients. In the case of Indian crowdfunding platforms studied by Banerjee (2019), these platforms participate in processes that perpetuate extant practices of development, preserving extant equilibria among actors and crystallising extant relations between non-governmental organisations and their networks.

In sum, emerging stories of failure – or unintended outcomes – in digital platforms for development can be read through the linkage theorised here. First, platform owners can contrast openness by altering the balance of power to the disadvantage of local innovators. Second, modularity can evolve into unfiltered contributions that end up damaging development subjects rather than serving them. The two sub-links theorised above can both malfunction, which contributes to explaining cases of platformisation that do not result into positive development outcomes.

5 Final Remarks

In this paper we have theorised a human-centred development logic as an alternative to the market logic that informs most of the IS literature on platforms. Building on the market logic of theoretical foundations of platform governance and architecture (cf. Gawer and Cusumano 2014; Parker et al. 2016; Constantinides et al. 2018), we have theorised two sub-linkages predicated respectively on digital platforms' openness and modularity. Our framework shows how these properties afford the creation of locally relevant content capable of filling design-reality gaps as in Heeks (2002). We have also observed the limitations of each sub-linkage, showing how platform owners can contrast openness by shifting power equilibria in their favour, and modularity can evolve into unintended outcomes that ultimately result in development failures.

Our paper needs positioning within a broader critique to the limitations of the market logic dominance in digital platforms. For instance, Zuboff (2019) and Taplin (2017) offer an extensive critique of the main global digital platforms (often referred to as the "frightful five") in terms of mass pervasive surveillance, domination of markets without contributing to local tax revenues and acquisition strategies controlling innovation. Others have pointed to the dysfunctional effects on local communities of Airbnb (Dayne 2016) and the damage to local businesses brought by Uber (Elbanna and Newman 2016). Taking stock of this literature, our paper offers a human-centred alternative to the market logic underpinning global platformisation, using it as a lens to study platforms developed with explicit goals of socio-economic development.

Consequently, our theoretical contribution is based on the potential of openness and modularity as a basis for design and evaluation of digital platforms in ICT4D, where profit is not the main purpose. In this domain, meeting the needs of the poor and marginalised and focussing on broader socio-economic development goals is the main underpinning logic. As a result, fundamental platform design building blocks such as "platform monetisation" (Parker et al. 2016) are downplayed relative to the human development logics outlined here through Sein and Harindranath (2004). The reading key offered here views core properties of platforms in relation to this logic, observing their potential to enact it and outlining its principal constraints.

Some final remarks are in order: first, our focus on openness and modularity does not dismiss the affordances of other platform properties for development, such as the ability to connect supply and demand through two-sided markets. While Constantinides et al. (2018) suggest that two-sided markets for digital labour may have positive job creation effects in developing countries, a wide stream of research (cf. Bergvall-Kåreborn and Howcroft 2014; Graham et al. 2017; Chen and Qiu 2019) problematises this view, pointing especially at the exploitative conditions and lack of protection (for example, through unionisation) to which digital workers are subjected. As the perverse effects of digital labour on workers inside and outside the Global South are highlighted, transaction platforms appear as a double-edged sword for development, whose affordances need examination along with their structural drawbacks. In the light of this, the human-centred logic proposed here is offered as a route to undertake this type of research.

The main contribution of this paper is to offer some tentative first steps towards a conceptualisation of the theoretical link between digital platforms and socio-economic development, on which further theoretical development can be built. In line with this, a practical contribution of the framework is to offer advice to designers regarding the governance and architecture of platforms, transcending the insights of prior work that adopts a market logic. Finally, if read as a potential lens to evaluate extant platforms, the framework provides criteria that allow a focus on their suitability for the needs of development subjects, rather than the fulfilment of sheer market purposes.

References

Banerjee, S.: Digitally divided fundraising. the power of online crowdfunding platforms in connecting local NGOs to 'Micro-Philanthropists' in India. Paper presented at the Development Studies Association Conference (DSA), 19–21 June, Milton Keynes, UK (2019)

Banerjee, S.: Aadhaar: Digital inclusion and public services in India. World Development Report, pp. 81–92 (2016)

Bergvall-Kåreborn, B., Howcroft, D.: Amazon Mechanical Turk and the commodification of labour. New Technol. Work. Employ. **29**(3), 213–223 (2014)

Besharov, M.L., Smith, W.K.: Multiple institutional logics in organizations: explaining their varied nature and implications. Acad. Manag. Rev. **39**(3), 364–381 (2014)

Chen, J.Y., Qiu, J.L.: Digital utility: datafication, regulation, labor, and DiDi's platformization of urban transport in China. Chin. J. Commun., 1–16 (2019)

Constantinides, P., Henfridsson, O., Parker, G.G.: Introduction—platforms and infrastructures in the digital age. Inf. Syst. Res. **29**(2), 381–400 (2018)

De Reuver, M., Sørensen, C., Basole, R.C.: The digital platform: a research agenda. J. Inf. Technol. **33**(2), 124–135 (2018)

Eaton, B., Elaluf-Calderwood, S., Sorensen, C., Yoo, Y.: Distributed tuning of boundary resources: the case of Apple's iOS service system. MIS Q. Manag. Inf. Syst. **39**(1), 217–243 (2015)

Elbanna, A., Newman, M.: Disrupt the disruptor: rethinking 'disruption' in digital innovation. In: Mediterranean Conference on Information Systems (MCIS). Association For Information Systems (2016)

Evans, P.C., Gawer, A.: The rise of the platform enterprise: a global survey. Working paper. University of Surrey (2016)

Friedland, R., Alford, R.R., Powell, W.W., DiMaggio, P.J.: The new institutionalism in organizational analysis. New Inst. Organ. Anal., 232–263 (1991)

Gawer, A., Cusumano, M.A.: Industry platforms and ecosystem innovation. J. Prod. Innov. Manag. **31**(3), 417–433 (2014)

Gawer, A.: Platform dynamics and strategies: from products to services. Platf. Mark. Innov. **45**, 57 (2009)

Ghazawneh, A., Henfridsson, O.: Balancing platform control and external contribution in third-party development: the boundary resources model. Inf. Syst. J. **23**(2), 173–192 (2013)

Graham, M., Hjorth, I., Lehdonvirta, V.: Digital labour and development: impacts of global digital labour platforms and the gig economy on worker livelihoods. Transf. Eur. Rev. Labour Res. **23**(2), 135–162 (2017)

Hatakka, M., Thapa, D., Sæbø, Ø.: Understanding the role of ICT and study circles in enabling economic opportunities: lessons learned from an educational project in Kenya. Inf. Syst. J. (2019, in press)

Heeks, R.: Information systems and developing countries: failure, success, and local improvisations. Inf. Soc. **18**(2), 101–112 (2002)

Kallinikos, J., Aaltonen, A., Marton, A.: The ambivalent ontology of digital artifacts. MIS Q. **37**(2), 357–370 (2013)

Khera, R.: Dissent on Aadhaar: Big Data Meets Big Brother. Orient BlackSwan Hyderabad, New Delhi (2019)

Koskinen, K., Bonina, C., Eaton, B.: Digital platforms in the global south: foundations and research agenda. In: Nielsen, P., Kimaro, H.C. (eds.) ICT4D 2019. IAICT, vol. 551, pp. 319–330. Springer, Cham (2019). https://doi.org/10.1007/978-3-030-18400-1_26

Koskinen, K., Bonina, C., Eaton, B.: Digital platforms in the Global South: foundations and research agenda. Working paper at DIODE network (2018). https://diodeweb.files.wordpress.com/2018/10/digital-platforms-diode-paper.pdf

Lee, D.: How Airbnb short-term rentals exacerbate Los Angeles's affordable housing crisis: analysis and policy recommendations. Harv. Law Policy Rev. **10**, 229–232 (2016)

Masiero, S., Prakash, A.: ICT in social protection schemes: deinstitutionalising subsidy-based welfare programmes. Inf. Technol. People (2019, in press)

Nicholson, B., Nielsen, P., Sæbø, J.: Digital platforms for development. Call for papers. Inf. Syst. J. Electron. J. Inf. Syst. Dev. Ctries. (2019)

Ollier-Malaterre, A.: Technology and boundaries between work and life: connectivity, privacy, and self-presentation challenges in Western countries and China. Paper presented at the European Group for Organisation Studies Conference, 4–6 July 2019, Edinburgh (2019)

Parker, G.G., Van Alstyne, M.W., Choudary, S.P.: Platform Revolution: How Networked Markets are Transforming the Economy and How to Make Them Work for You. WW Norton & Company, New York (2016)

Rai, A., Constantinides, P., Sarker, S.: Editor's comments: next-generation digital platforms: toward human–AI hybrids. MIS Q. **43**(1), iii–x (2019)

Sen, A.: Development as Freedom. Routledge, London (1999)

Sein, M.K., Harindranath, G.: Conceptualizing the ICT artifact: toward understanding the role of ICT in national development. Inf. Soc. **20**(1), 15–24 (2004)

Taplin, J.: Move Fast and Break Things: How Facebook, Google, and Amazon Have Cornered Culture and What It Means for All of Us. Pan Macmillan (2017)

Tilson, D., Lyytinen, K., Sørensen, C.: Research commentary—digital infrastructures: the missing IS research agenda. Inf. Syst. Res. **21**(4), 748–759 (2010)

Tiwana, A.: Platform Ecosystems: Aligning Architecture, Governance, and Strategy. Newnes, London (2013)

Tiwana, A., Konsynski, B., Bush, A.A.: Research commentary—platform evolution: coevolution of platform architecture, governance, and environmental dynamics. Inf. Syst. Res. **21**(4), 675–687 (2010)

Thornton, P.H., Ocasio, W., Lounsbury, M.: The Institutional Logics Perspective: Foundations, Research, and Theoretical Elaboration. Oxford University Press, Oxford (2012)

Thornton, P.H., Ocasio, W.: Institutional logics and the historical contingency of power in organizations: executive succession in the higher education publishing industry, 1958–1990. Am. J. Sociol. **105**(3), 801–843 (1999)

Zittrain, J.: The Future of the Internet and How to Stop It. Allen Lane, London (2008)

Zuboff, S.: The Age of Surveillance Capitalism: The Fight for a Human Future at the New Frontier of Power. Profile Books (2019)

Different Approaches to Complementing Software Platforms: A Case Study of Digital Innovation Across 10 Developing Countries

Nilza Collinson[1,2(✉)] ⓘ, Masoud Mahundi[3] ⓘ, and Petter Nielsen[1] ⓘ

[1] University of Oslo, Ole-Johan Dahls Hus, Gaustadalléen 23 B, 0373 Oslo, Norway
`pnielsen@ifi.uio.no`
[2] University Eduardo Mondlane, Av. Julius Nyerere, nr. 3453, Maputo City, Mozambique
[3] University of Dar es Salaam, Dar es Salaam, Tanzania

Abstract. Software platforms offer a foundation for digital innovation and have the potential to take advantage of and leverage the knowledge and skills of distributed and diverse software organizations as 'complementors'. Due to their location far away from platform owners, scarce resources, and limited capacity to hire and retain skilled human resources, organizations in developing countries typically face barriers for participating in digital innovation. This paper aims to improve our understanding of how these organizations can take part in digital innovation. The basis for our research is a case study of software organizations located in different developing countries and their role as complementors related to the DHIS2 software platform, a platform made for the public health sector in developing countries. We contribute by exploring and showing how these organizations differ along multiple dimensions, for instance, the maturity of their software development team, their relation to the platform owners, and their access to resources. Further, we identify and develop a taxonomy consisting of six different forms of digital innovation unfolding in the fringes of a software platform ecosystem and identify contextual factors influencing these different forms.

Keywords: Complementors · Software platform · Fringes · Innovation

1 Introduction

As software platforms permit and require innovations on top of them for their prosperity, to release their economies of scope and scale, the platform owners must ensure that other organizations engage in innovations on top of their platforms. This effort is enabled by the underlying architecture of platforms which is characterised as an 'extensible codebase' [29]. While the objectives and governance of software platforms might be different from one platform to another, they are all defined by their architecture comprising of two parts; one with low variety and high reusability and another with high variety and low reusability [4, 15]. The first part forming the core of the platform while the second forming the periphery, or the fringes [25]. Innovations related to software platforms

© IFIP International Federation for Information Processing 2020
Published by Springer Nature Switzerland AG 2020
J. M. Bass and P. J. Wall (Eds.): ICT4D 2020, IFIP AICT 587, pp. 14–25, 2020.
https://doi.org/10.1007/978-3-030-65828-1_2

thus unfold on two levels: at the core platform to improve its generic features, and on the fringes to serve specific local needs [25]. Being, in the last case undertaken by individuals or organisations, other than the platform owners, commonly referred to as complementors [6, 15, 20, 28], because they develop 'complements' both to the core of the software platform [15, 20] and to the fringes.

Participating in innovations on a software platform requires a considerable amount of resources. Despite that, organizations in developing countries that are not well-positioned, being far from the platform owners, with scarce resources and limited capacity in terms of skills, also participate in digital innovation. We attempted to understand this phenomenon and answer the research question; in what ways do individuals and organisations in developing countries complement software platforms? We respond to this question by engaging in a qualitative case-study method in which we follow ten organisations working and complementing a software platform known as District Health Information System version 2 (DHIS2).

DHIS2 is a software platform meant for managing public health data in different formats. It is currently used in more than 100 developing countries [2], with 15 of them using it as a national standard for health data management. Several other organisations including the US President's Emergency Plan for AIDS Relief (PEPFAR) are also using the platform. DHIS2 is developed and managed by the University of Oslo through an action research network known as Health Information Systems Program, HISP. Founded in the early 2000s [2, 7], HISP built a network of universities, local HISP groups, and individuals actively taking part in the development of health information systems. It, therefore, consists of the platform owner who in this case is the University of Oslo and more than twelve organisations, the HISP groups, serving as complementors to the platform. This study investigates the ways ten of these HISP groups take part in developing innovations related to the platform, as well as the social and technical factors influencing their efforts.

2 Related Literature

Research on software platforms is steadily increasing [3, 21], which is indicative of their role in society. Different studies have addressed several issues related to software platforms. Some have endeavoured to understand what software platforms are [4, 16, 30], others have investigated their architectures [4, 29] and many others have had concerns on how these platforms are managed [17, 28, 29]. Despite this increase in studies, though, studies on approaches and impact of platforms in developing countries are still minimal [21]. Having this in mind, we attempted through the current study, to contribute to this.

2.1 Innovations on Software Platforms

One of the ways to identify the types of innovation is in relation to what other items are connected to the Software Platforms. Hilbolling et al. [20] identify three types on this basis; complements dedicatedly connected to the core only, complements connecting platform and other products, and connecting between platforms or one platform with larger ones. In turn, Gizaw et al. [18] look at innovations in terms of how the global and local contexts are reconciled. As such they introduce the terms *embedding,* referring to how the global context fits into the local, and *disembedding,* referring to the local context influencing the global. In this sense, one form of embedding is what they refer to as appropriation [18], where local developers address their local needs by configuring the platform through the capabilities that the platform owner intentionally built. An advanced form of embedding includes the development of applications on the platform to address needs that the platform owner did not anticipate. Eaton [13], on the other hand, identifies two types of compliments to a software platform; *applications* or apps and *enablers.* While investigating the mobile devices software platform, the last author refers to application type of complements as small software applications that address the immediate needs of the users and, as enablers those software applications which support the development and use of other applications on the software platform.

Several scholars have attempted to investigate the contributing factors of innovations on software platforms, suggesting that these come from both, the platform owners development and working modality (endogenous), and the environment in which the platform works (exogenous) [29]. The recurring endogenous determinant of innovation on a software platform relates to governance. Although the evolution of digital platforms is unpredictable and without control [1, 9, 19] scholars agree that governance of the social and technical components of a software platform can influence the trajectories of its innovation. Ghazawneh and Henfridsson [17] look at governance in light of controlling resources for enabling or constraining third parties in developing innovations on the platform. They, therefore, introduce two contrasting concepts, resourcing and securing. In rudimentary terms, resourcing refers to less control by the platform owners to allow for more innovations while securing refers to more control by the platform owner. Control can also change over time, for example related to what is most strategically sound for the platform owners [26]. Similar to resourcing, Koutsikouri et al. [22] present three triggers to innovations namely adding service value, creating design attractors, and lowering infrastructure barriers. The last two are a direct match to the concept of securing. Rocha and Pollock [27], however, argue that the purpose of the platform is much more determining than its control.

Other studies investigated these factors in a combination of endogenous and exogenous. Mahundi et al. [24], for example, describe three sets of factors influencing innovations; structural support, which is about organisations, technical support that are provided through endogenous support by the platform owner, and process support related to organisations for the sustainability of the introduced innovation.

3 Method

In this study, we attempted to understand reality through the perceptions of actors in their field [12]. We, therefore, employed a qualitative inquiry, which involved practitioners in the selected settings. Since we wanted a detailed understanding of 'how' complementors engage with the platforms and why some ways are more common than others we employed case study approaches [5, 11]. We built the empirical setting around the DHIS2 software platform and the different ways in which individuals and organisations complement it.

3.1 A Data Collection

In qualitative studies, a researcher has a significant impact [12]. Researchers in this study have influenced the collected data following their positions. One of the authors, being a co-coordinator of the development and implementation of DHIS2 at the University of Oslo, has vast experiences in how this platform is managed in different parts of the world. Another author has been working with HISP Tanzania for the last fourteen (14) years in different capacities related to DHIS2, including development, capacity building, and technical support. The third author, working at University Eduardo Mondlane in Mozambique, is currently engaged in research and technical support to the DHIS2 local implementations through the HISP Mozambique. Besides their experiences, researchers also conducted ten semi-structured interviews with practitioners in the field.

We selected HISP groups, to engage in the study and then selected individuals based on the time they have spent in their organisation and the roles they have taken in their teams. From Africa, the study included HISPs Tanzania, Mozambique, Malawi, Rwanda, Uganda, Nigeria, and the HISP Western and Central Africa, whereas from Asia the study benefitted from experiences of HISPs India, Bangladesh, and Vietnam. Most of the interviews were audio-recorded and transcribed verbatim into different text files, except for three, which experienced some technical constraints. We gathered information related to the organization, financing, and extension of their operations.

3.2 Data Analysis

We employed a theoretical thematic analysis [8, 10, 23] as a guide to the data analysis process in which we strictly observed the six phases of analysis that Braun and Clarke [8] suggest. In phase one, we familiarised ourselves with the data by listening to the audio files and later transcribing them, verbatim. This gave us an idea of the contents in the interview as well as interesting findings. We could also clearly establish the different characteristics features of the HISP nodes which were a part of our study. We understood how they are organized, how they interact with DHIS both in the field and in their development sites and other innate features. Following, in the second phase, we picked two issues of interest for our research question; *ways/forms of engagement* and *influencing factors*. We then listed the codes related to the issues and identified others as potential issues to explore further. These codes included; *configuration, hacking, customisation, scaling, extending, integration, interoperability, application to the core, local application,* and many others. During phase three and four we embarked on an iterative process of suggesting themes and discussing them among ourselves, in a process which helped us to refine our understanding of the process of innovation. It was through these iterations that we were also able to establish relationships between codes and their patterns and eventually started charting relevant themes. In stage five we defined the resulting themes that we had finally agreed upon and, in phase six we documented them as present in the findings section.

4 Case Description: The HISP Groups

The organizations we focus on in this paper are all HISP groups that have a history of support from the University of Oslo (UiO) from their inception. These, either based in local universities or as independent organizations, typically with a close relationship with the Ministry of Health (MoH) through research and development projects. Many of the lead local experts in these organizations are graduates with a Ph.D. from UiO. Table 1 lists the HISP Groups involved in the study,

Table 1. The main target of support from the HISP Groups selected for the study.

HISP group (team size)	Country/Region supported
Western and Central Africa (23)	16 countries in the region and 5 countries in other African regions
Tanzania (19), Uganda (16) and Rwanda (5)	East Africa/Consortium
Mozambique (15)	Lusophony countries in Africa
Vietnam (10)	4 countries in South East Asia
Malawi (5), Nigeria (8), India (45) and Bangladesh (6)	Own country

While some of these organizations are non-profit, by nature, all share similar support mechanisms based on projects and contracts with MoH, Universities, or donors. Due to limited funding, most of them experience human capacity constraints, and with the need for continuous development of local competence, the teams rely on support from UiO employees.

The HISP groups are actively involved in capacity building and training locally and abroad, involving team members, health practitioners, and students from the Universities related to the local projects. In a collaboration between them, HISP groups organise international academies, sometimes with the support and involvement of the core development team at UiO. These training activities are conducted in different languages, for instance in French, Portuguese, and English by HISP Western and Central Africa, HISP Mozambique, and HISP Tanzania, respectively, and according to the actual needs and maturity of the local users.

Besides academies, HISP groups also closely collaborate through cross-country projects. The language here plays a significant role, for instance, the Eastern Consortium that connects the HISPs Tanzania, Uganda, Rwanda, Malawi, and others are English speaking. HISP Mozambique, on the other hand, supports implementations in three Portuguese speaking countries within the region covered by the HISP Western and Central Africa. Sometimes collaborations are intercontinental where HISP groups in Asia have had several collaborations with HISP West Africa.

Each HISP group maintains its profile. For example, some only work with NGOs that support the government, like HISP India, while others do not limit their relations and work with private and other non-governmental organizations as well, like HISPs Uganda and Nigeria.

The organizations selected for this study are in different stages of maturity, with HISPs India, Bangladesh, Western and Central Africa, Tanzania, Uganda, Rwanda, and Mozambique being the more mature. HISP Vietnam, Nigeria, and Malawi are still in a phase of capacity building. The different HISP groups typically have a staff of technical DHIS2 experts, public health experts, implementers and project managers. Some of the HISP groups have a stronger technical capacity and is thus more involved in software development.

5 Ways Local Organisations Complement DHIS2

We have seen before that individuals or organizations can be considered 'complementors' if they develop 'complements' to a software platform. In our case study, the activities related to this complementing have continuously transformed the DHIS2 platform in many different ways. We define complementing as engaging in activities to improve the working or usefulness of a platform by developers other than the platform owner. We identify, through analysis of our empirical data, six ways through which organisations from developing countries take part in the innovation of a software platform. We classify these ways into three, *hacks and customisation*, *requirements translation* and *development*. Subsequent sections describe these ways in detail.

5.1 Hacks and Customisation

Complementors in this category attempt to customise and hack the software platform to fit the contextual requirements. The first way in this category is *customisation*. Through customisation complementors with a fair understanding of how the platform works incorporates the local requirements into the platform. In Tanzania, for example, the first official use of the DHIS2 involved three data collection tools related to HIV in 2009. The HISP team kept defining more tools as needs were arising and this is a common exercise in the organisation since then. The national rollout of the system with the DHIS2 platform was done in 2014 with fifteen (15) data collection tools defined in the platform.

Complementors also engage the software platform by *extending the use-domain*. In this, complementors use the same platform to address the system requirements in the domain other than the intended. Compared to customisation, this engagement required more support from the platform owners as it involved both, hacks by the complementors and generalisation of some features by the platform owner. In Table 2 we list a few examples of were to different HISP teams have been extending the use-domain of DHIS2.

The third way of complementing is through *integration*. Software platforms often meet other systems in local contexts. Some of these existing systems are deeply institutionalised and therefore not easy to change. A way to work with them is by integrating them into the new platform or communicating data between them and the platform. HISP Mozambique presents a good example of this. They worked to connect a system from COVIDA, with the dashboards in DHIS2. So while stakeholders were managing data in their system, reports and visualisations were managed through DHIS2. They further developed mechanisms to connect DHIS2 with the data from an ODK server.

5.2 Requirements Translation

In this way, complementors do not develop the innovation but, instead, structure the requirements and serve as clients to the platform owner who then develops the innovation. A member from HISP West and Central Africa stated, generically, that;

Table 2. Examples of other domains the DHIS2 platform had been implemented.

New domains	Countries
Education	Gambia, Malawi, Guinea Bissau and Mozambique (in discussions)
Agriculture (with Forestry and Veterinary)	Rwanda, Mozambique, and Tanzania
Environmental Health	Uganda
Water points management	Tanzania and Mozambique
Road safety	Tanzania

"At the same time, we have also been pushing for some features coming from the field and those features have been another part of DHIS2 core, although we cannot claim that it is only from our side but we also express this demand" HISP West and Central Africa, June 2019

This also happened in Bangladesh;

"… so [in 2011] we build dashboard into DHIS2 with the framework and that idea was quite good, and I think that triggered the need for the dashboard and introduced it to the DHIS2, so that's actually our idea..." HISP Bangladesh, February 2020

5.3 Development

Through this, complementors develop software solutions on software platforms. First complementors can engage in *local application development*. This happens when users of a platform face a challenge that the existing platform cannot address and it is not in the priority of the platform owner. As exemplified in Table 3, complementors then resort to developing applications on the platform as a solution to the challenge. Stressing on this necessity, a HISP Vietnam team member explains that;

Table 3. Examples of local application development.

HISP group	Example local applications
HISP West and Central Africa	Predictor functionality in DHIS2 to support eLMIS
HISP Tanzania	USSD Manager: an app that enables the configuration of USSD forms in DHIS2 by non-programmers

"It depends on the requirements, one of the things is… if everything can be solved in DHIS2, we just … use the DHIS2, writing any new code or any new app, maintenance and all the different things is a long time commitment, so that is the

one thing which we want to avoid most of the time" HISP Vietnam, November 2019

Complementors can also engage in *cross-setting development*. This resembles local application development but differs in that the resulting application becomes useful in other settings. It requires not only programming skills but an accurate understanding of the platform core. Once in every year, the UiO organises week-long conferences attended by DHIS2 stakeholders from all over the world to promote this kind of engagement, among other things. Table 4 lists some examples of applications that later formed part of the core,

Table 4. Some of the contribution of the HISP Groups to the software platform

HISP group	Application
HISP West and Central Africa	Minimize data collection tools to reduce overlap data Extend the predictor functionality to create specific Indicators
HISP Tanzania	i. Bottleneck analysis (BNA) application. HISP Tanzania had the development roles while systems analysis was managed by HISP Uganda ii. Function maintenance: an application meant to help with all the computations which the DHIS2, by default, is not supporting iii. Interactive Dashboard: A dashboard that presents data from the DHIS2 database but allows dynamic changes in the options of presentation

6   Discussion

Literature shows a variety of forms and types of innovations on a software platform [13, 18, 23]. This study focused on understanding how individuals and organisations in developing countries take part in contributing to the innovations of a software platform. Our empirical data reveals six ways through which these third party organisations contribute to the progress of software innovation. These include *customisation, extending use-domain,* and *integration*. Others are *requirements translation, local application development,* and *cross-setting development*. We, further, grouped these ways into three classes; customisation and hacks, requirements translation, and development.

This study is significant for two main reasons, among others. First, it systematically identifies the different ways of engaging in the innovation process. Several other studies have listed a few ways of engaging with the software platform in a manner we found not comprehensive. Eaton [13], for example, lists apps development to mean small apps and enablers' development to mean bigger apps that support others. This partly coincides with one category of ways in which we identified development. We found out that development can be in two forms, either developing applications for local use or developing applications that can also be used in other contexts. Gizaw et al. [18] to the former as embedding where developers attempt to fit the global artefact into a local context, and the former as disembedding which means local contexts abstracted for use in the global. The effort, we found, is not on the size but the context of use. Second, our analysis highlights the need to consider what exists already. One of the ways of engagement, we found, was *integration*. Software platforms are not installed in vacuum. They often meet existing systems in the different settings they arrive at. One of the innovations on these platforms is that of connecting them to the existing, well-rooted electronic systems, either for permanent or temporary use.

This study also found different factors influencing these innovations. Some related to the architecture of the platform, others related to the platform owners conduct, while others related to the capacity of the complementor. The strength of the community of complementors is also another factor.

The architecture of the platform itself determines how much the platform supports innovation. While the generic architecture of platforms is by default to allow innovations, some allow more than others. This is congruent with what Ghazawneh and Henfridsson [17] describes in terms of control over a software platform. They cite two forms affecting how much a platform can allow innovations. Resourcing and securing, where the former means giving more control, technically, to complementors and the later means less control to complementors. A member of HISP Mozambique declares that;

"What enablers, to individuals [who are] developing... first is what the DHIS2 provides, when they start to open up a friendly API so that people can do local development, I think this is the one that enables individuals to start thinking on how to develop... and the second one [enabler] is the possibility of having these academies where you teach individuals how to use the API... so now we know that I can use the API to develop my local applications" HISP Mozambique, November 2019

One particularity of the open software platforms, such as DHIS2, is the possibility to attract independent complementors. While it allows for extension through scaling or chartings and does not pressure the platform owner with dependencies of the complementors. The platform owner, also, has so much influence over how innovations on platform progress. The UiO as platform owners devised several mechanisms to promote innovations on DHIS2. They, for example, organise annual meetings to show-case innovations, they train complementors on the platform through technical systems as well as postgraduate educations. Many individuals in the complementor organisations are graduates from the UiO. The UiO also plays an intermediary role where international institutions channel their requirements for development to them and the UiO connects the different nodes for development. Importantly, the UiO modality of working with stable institutions was one of the driving forces. HISP West and Central Africa started as a UiO initiative to support Sierra Leon 2008, with locals from Togo who had an affiliation with the UiO. Later, in 2012, the locals with support from the UiO formed the HISP West and Central Africa. HISP Tanzania, on the other hand, started as a project within the UDSM, but later registered HISP Tanzania as an incorporated company that now works in complementarity with the UDSM.

Several factors are related to the complementor organisation. Such factors include their setup which is not antagonistic with the existing government structures. Irrespective of the size and maturity of the team, the endorsement of DHIS2 by the government has positively influenced innovations on the platform. One HISP manager declares their strength to be;

"... that we have a good relationship with the government and we are working with the government so this is a very big strength because we do not need to convince the ministry to do work with us, they are relying on us and this trust and understanding is our major strength" HISP Manager, Bangladesh, February 2020

7   Conclusion and Recommendations

There is a considerable body of literature on the architecture of software platforms and how that architecture influences innovations. It is, further, clear that for an increase in the economies of scale and scope, third party developers have to contribute to the progress of a software platform through innovations. Not much is known, though, on the ways through which these third parties situated in Developing Countries take part in the innovation processes. In this study we attempted to respond to the research question: in what ways do individuals and organisations in developing countries complement software platforms? We engaged this question by examining how ten (10) members of the HISP network complements the DHIS2 software platform through innovations. We were motivated by the fact that these organisations work from the developing countries and, therefore, not well-positioned in terms of funding, skills, and other resources.

We identified six ways through which these organisations complement to the DHIS2 software platform. Such ways include customisation to fit the contextual requirements, extending features to address, developing local applications, developing functionalities for the core platform, integration with the existing software systems, and rationalising requirements. We, further, identified the social and technical factors influencing third party actors into complementing the software platform. These factors include those related to how the platform owner motivates innovation. In our case study, the platform owner has been very active in supporting third parties in development. These have been through organising training academies and annual meetings. We also found that some of these factors are related to the software platform itself, how its interfacing features like API support innovation. Other factors included the organisation of the third party institutions, and how the community of practice around the platform promoted complementing by these complementors. Clarity on the ways of engaging in innovation by third parties, and the different factors influencing that is beneficial to platform owners and third parties in furthering the use of software platforms.

Further research could focus on if and how these factors are also relevant related to other software platforms and in other contexts, establishing quantitatively how each of these factors influences the process of innovation and through which of the six ways we have identified.

References

1. Aanestad, M., Grisot, M., Hanseth, O., Vassilakopoulou, P.: Information infrastructures and the challenge of the installed base. In: Aanestad, M., Grisot, M., Hanseth, O., Vassilakopoulou, P. (eds.) Information Infrastructures within European Health Care. HI, pp. 25–33. Springer, Cham (2017). https://doi.org/10.1007/978-3-319-51020-0_3
2. Adu-gyamfi, E., Nielsen, P., Sæbø, J.: The dynamics of a global health information systems research and implementation project. In: Proceedings of the 17th Scandinavian Conference on Health Informatics, Oslo, Norway, pp. 12–13 November 2019 (2019)
3. Asadullah, A., Faik, I., Kankanhalli, A.: Digital platforms : a review and future directions. In: PACIS Proceedings, Yokohama, Japan, pp. 1–14 (2018)
4. Baldwin, C.Y., Woodard, C.J.: The architecture of platforms: a unified view. In: Gawer, A. (ed.) Platforms, Markets and Innovation, pp. 19–38. Edward Elgar Publishing (2011)
5. Baxter, P., Jack, S.: Qualitative case study methodology: study design and implementation for novice researchers. Qual. Rep. **13**, 544–559 (2008)
6. Boudreau, K., Jeppesen, L.B.: Owners on both sides of the deal: mergers and acquisitions and overlapping institutional ownership. Strateg. Manag. J. **36**, 1761–1777 (2015)
7. Braa, K., Nielsen, P.: Sustainable action research: the networks of actions approach. In: Proceedings of the 13th International Conference on Social Implications of Computers in Developing Countries, Negombo, Sri Lanka, pp. 331–343 (2015)
8. Braun, V., Clarke, V.: Using thematic analysis in psychology. Qual. Res. Psychol. **3**(2), 77–101 (2006)
9. Ciborra, C., Hanseth, O.: Introduction: from control to drift. In: Ciborra, C. (ed.) The Dynamics of Corporate Information Infrastructures, pp. 1–11. Oxford University Press (2001)
10. Clarke, V., Braun, V.: Teaching thematic analysis: overcoming challenges and developing strategies for effective learning. Psychol. **26**(2), 120–123 (2013)
11. Creswell, J.W.: Research Design Qualitative Quantitative and Mixed Methods Approaches. Laughton, C.D., Novak, V., Axelsen, D.E. (eds.) SAGE Publications. International Educational and Professional Publisher (Second), London (2003)
12. Creswell, J.W.: Designing a qualitative study. In: Creswell, J.W. (ed.) Qualitative Inquiry and Research Design: Choosing Among Five Approaches. Sage, Thousand Oaks (2007)
13. Eaton, B.D.: The dynamics of digital platform innovation: unfolding the paradox of control and generativity in Apple's iOS. PhD thesis, The London School of Economics and Political Science (LSE) (2012). https://urldefense.proofpoint.com/v2/url?u=http-3A__etheses.lse.ac.uk_463_&d=DwIFAg&c=vh6FgFnduejNhPPD0fl_yRaSfZy8CWbWnIf4XJhSqx8&r=RF5ZusSfL-zo6cJvDnfZWKY3eU00jY410Ja_afMJGvioF_jurx7CclQLvdlk9M0l&m=afF1PCf44RXy4xXJxWxy0mSw0KcnlV9wFAg6cKhe9Q0&s=qIpugzPvAgUkEUqtR9GcOQOAqqzGnQ3Db_WnUehyQ7Y&e=
14. Gawer, A.: Platforms, markets and innovation: an introduction. In: Gawer, A. (ed.) Platforms, markets and innovation, pp. 1–396. Edward Elgar Publishing, Gloucestershire, England (2009)
15. Gawer, A.: Platforms, Markets and Innovation. Edward Elgar Publishing, Cheltenham (2009)
16. Ghazawneh, A., Henfridsson, O.: Balancing platform control and external contribution in third-party development: the boundary resources model. Inf. Syst. J. **23**(2), 173–192 (2012)
17. Gizaw, A., Bygstad, B., Nielsen, P.: Open generification. Info Syst. J. **27**, 619–642 (2017)
18. Hanseth, O., Monteiro, E.: Understanding Information Infrastructure, (1998)
19. Hilbolling, S., Berends, H., Deken, F., Tuertscher, P.: Complementors as connectors: managing open innovation around digital product platforms. R D Manage. 1–13 (2019)
20. Koskinen, K., Bonina, C., Eaton, B.: Digital platforms in the global south: foundations and research agenda. In: Nielsen, P., Kimaro, H.C. (eds.) ICT4D 2019. IAICT, vol. 551, pp. 319–330. Springer, Cham (2019). https://doi.org/10.1007/978-3-030-18400-1_26

21. Koutsikouri, D., Henfridsson, O., Lindgren, R.: Building digital infrastructures : towards an evolutionary theory of contextual triggers. In: Proceedings of the 50th Hawaii International Conference on System Sciences, pp. 4716–4725 (2017)
22. Maguire, M., Delahunt, B.: Doing a thematic analysis: a practical, step-by-step guide for learning and teaching scholars. All Ireland J. Teach. Learn. High. Educ. **3**, 3135–3140 (2017)
23. Mahundi, M.H., Nielsen, P., Kimaro, H.: The social and technical conditions enabling innovations in information infrastructures: a case study from public health in Tanzania. Afr. J. Sci. Technol. Innov. Dev. **11**(7), 795–805 (2019)
24. Msiska, B., Nielsen, P.: Innovation in the fringes of software ecosystems: the role of socio-technical generativity. Inf. Technol. Dev. **24**(2), 398–421 (2018)
25. Nielsen, P., Aanestad, M.: Control devolution as information infrastructure design strategy: a case study of a content service platform for mobile phones in Norway. J. Inf. Technol. **21**, 185–194 (2006)
26. da Rocha, F.N., Pollock, N.: Innovating in digital platforms: an integrative approach. In: International Conference on Enterprise Information Systems, Heraklion, Crete, Greece, pp. 505–515 (2019)
27. Schreieck, M., Wiesche, M., Krcmar, H.: Design and governance of platform ecosystems – key concepts and issues for future research. In: The European Conference on Information Systems (ECIS), İstanbul, Turkey (2016)
28. Tiwana, A., Konsynski, B., Bush, A.A.: Platform evolution : coevolution of platform architecture, governance, and environmental dynamics. Inf. Syst. Res. **21**(4), 675–687 (2010)
29. Yudina, T., Geliskhanov, I.: Features of digital platforms functioning in information-digital economy. In: IOP Conference Series: Materials Science and Engineering, vol. 497 (2019)

Risks and Risk-Mitigation Strategies of Gig Economy Workers in the Global South: The Case of Ride-Hailing in Cape Town

Tatenda Mpofu[1] ⓘ, Pitso Tsibolane[1](✉) ⓘ, Richard Heeks[2] ⓘ,
and Jean-Paul Van Belle[1] ⓘ

[1] Centre for Information Technology and National Development in Africa, University of Cape
Town, Cape Town, South Africa
mpftat003@myuct.ac.za,
{pitso.tsibolane,jean-paul.vanbelle}@uct.ac.za
[2] Centre for Development Informatics, University of Manchester, Manchester, UK
richard.heeks@manchester.ac.uk

Abstract. Fast growth of the gig economy in the global South has brought with
it both hopes and concerns about this new form of digitally-enabled employment.
Relatively little work has so far looked at the risks of such work; risks shaped by
the particular context of developing countries. This paper undertakes an inductive,
interpretive study of risks endured and risk-mitigation strategies adopted by ride-
hailing drivers in Cape Town, South Africa, drawing from the perspective of
ride-hailing drivers working for Uber and Bolt in Cape Town. A thematic analysis
of eighteen (n = 18) semi-structured interview data shows three main perceived
risks; inadequate income, personal safety, and deactivation from the platform.
The severity of these risks means most drivers seek to mitigate them and we
identify three types of mitigation strategy; initiated by the platforms (e.g. panic
buttons), by the drivers individually (e.g. techniques for handling risky riders or
locations), or by driver groups (e.g. rotating savings schemes). Platform design
and business decisions mean it is individual workers who bear the majority of risks
and individual workers who have to take responsibility for the majority of risk-
mitigation strategies. Based on these new insights into digitally-enabled work, we
suggest some directions for improved risk mitigation and for future research.

Keywords: Gig economy · Platform economy · Ride-hailing · Risk · South
Africa

1 Introduction

Gig work – tasks done for money and managed via digital platforms that are marketplaces
bringing together buyers and sellers [adapted from 12] – already employs up to 40 million
people in the global South – some 1.5% of the workforce – and growth rates are rapid
[15]. Alongside high hopes around job creation and worker perceptions of benefits of

© IFIP International Federation for Information Processing 2020
Published by Springer Nature Switzerland AG 2020
J. M. Bass and P. J. Wall (Eds.): ICT4D 2020, IFIP AICT 587, pp. 26–38, 2020.
https://doi.org/10.1007/978-3-030-65828-1_3

such work, there have also been concerns that such work is precarious and risky [10, 14]. While there has been some research on gig work risks [4, 8] little of it has focused on developing countries, and we found no research yet focused on risk-mitigation strategies. Yet such strategies are vital given the dangers with, for example, riders and drivers dying in the global South on a regular basis [7, 26].

To investigate these issues in more detail, the research reported here undertook an inductive, interpretive study of risks endured and risk-mitigation strategies adopted by ride-hailing drivers in Cape Town, South Africa. Following a short literature review, and an explanation of case methodology, the paper presents two sets of findings – on risks and on risk-mitigation strategies. We end with some recommendations and ideas for future research.

2 Literature Review

As noted above, the gig economy in the global South is already sizeable, providing work for tens of millions of workers with employment growth rates estimated at up to 30% per year [14]. There are many benefits brought by the growth in gig work: it seems likely to be increasing the quantum of employment in the global South; it is improving services and reducing costs for clients; and it can provide work for those excluded from other forms of employment [16].

But there have also been many concerns about the rapid growth in this form of employment; especially in comparison to traditional, formal-sector employment [13]. In particular, that the mediation of digital platforms exacerbates labour market inequalities; notably those between capital (i.e. the platforms) and labour (i.e. the workers) [14]. These inequalities can be understood in various different ways: for example, inequality in capture of the financial benefits of gig work, or information inequality comparing the panopticon-style understanding of the platform compared to the porthole-style understanding of workers.

We could also see a potential inequality of risk, if the risks of work are being loaded by platforms onto workers, and if platforms are taking few responsibilities for mitigating risks or for responding when risks materialise [14]. This is something of an issue for digital gig work, defined as location-independent digitally-centred activity such as data entry, translation and web development via platforms such as Amazon Mechanical Turk, Upwork and Freelancer. Risks reported by global South digital gig workers include discrimination by clients who prefer to employ workers from the global North, over-work, or clients refusing to pay for work [12, 18].

Risks are much greater, though, for physical gig work, defined as location-bound physical activity such as taxi driving, food delivery and house cleaning via platforms such as Uber, Deliveroo, Rappi and GoJek. As noted above, at its most extreme, physical gig workers in developing countries are at risk of dying during their work. Other risks identified include "accidents, breakdowns, robbery, traffic tickets", lack of income and being stuck in traffic [11] and "fatigue, stress, hunger and sleep deprivation" [17]. These risks are undoubtedly greater within developing countries; impacted by a context of, for example, greater insecurity and crime in terms of personal risk; and a context of lack of unemployment benefits and other protections in terms of financial risk. One must take care when enumerating the risks of gig work in developing countries to ask what the comparison is – the alternative for many gig workers is not well-protected formal employment but equally-risky work in the informal sector or even black economy. However, this does not reduce the risks of gig work or the need to do something about them.

It is the "do something about them" that has been little researched to date: we were unable to identify any previous work focused on gig work risk-mitigation strategies. It is this knowledge gap that motivates the current study.

3   Case and Methods

We chose to focus our study on ride-hailing in South Africa for two reasons. The gig economy in the country is relatively important. One estimate puts the number of physical gig workers at 30,000 [15] with up 100,000 active digital gig workers [14, 25] While many of the latter will not be full-time, this still suggests gig work touches at least 1% of the workforce and, as noted above, growth rates are high. Second, this sector reflects wider patterns of the global South gig economy with risks and materialised dangers being a constant theme [2, 6]. At the time of research, there were two main platforms operating in South Africa: Uber which has nearly three-quarters of the market with just over five million registered users and Bolt which has just over a quarter of the market with around two million users [9]. There was also a recent arrival – In-Driver – which was in process of trying to break into the market.

Because of the lack of prior work on risk mitigation and of understanding risks from a worker perspective, it was decided to follow a relatively inductive and interpretive research design. While sensitised to typical gig work risks and to some of the key issues to understand when identifying risk and mitigation strategies [27], this allowed drivers to represent their own lived experiences and for the researchers to then analyse and structure those experiences. The research complied with the University of Cape Town's prescribed code of ethics and obtained the necessary permission. Eighteen (18) semi-structured, face-to-face interviews were conducted with a random/convenience sample of drivers, contacted through a combination of Uber/Bolt ride-booking and snowballing. The interview method was chosen because the objectives of this research centred on understanding experiences, opinions, attitudes, values, and processes relating to driver risk mitigation strategies. Data analysis followed a thematic analysis protocol: familiari-sation with data, searching for and review of emergent themes (in this case, both risks and risk-mitigating strategies), definition and naming of themes [1].

All drivers were men, reflecting the gender-skewed profile of ride-hailing in South Africa (and most of the global South). As summarised in Table 1, two-thirds were from Zimbabwe, three were from South Africa, and three from other African countries (DRC and Zambia); reflecting the heavy presence of immigrant workers as riders and drivers in South Africa's gig economy. Seven of the eighteen owned their vehicle; two were on a rent-to-own financing deal; the remaining nine were renting from an owner. The great majority (14 of the 18) said they were the main breadwinner for their household. Ten drivers worked only for Uber, three only for Bolt, and five worked for both platforms. Two drivers had registered with In-Driver but the novelty of the platform and lack of work meant it did not impinge on their responses. On average, they had worked for a ride-hailing platform for two years (the range was two months to four years).

Table 1. Overview of interviewees

No.	Country of origin			Platform				Ownership		
	Zimbabwe	SA	Other	Uber	Bolt	Both	In-driver	Owner	Renter	Rent to own
1			✔	✔				✔		
2	✔					✔		✔		
3	✔			✔					✔	
4	✔					✔				✔
5		✔			✔		✔	✔		
6	✔			✔				✔		
7	✔			✔						✔
8	✔			✔			✔	✔		
9			✔	✔				✔		
10	✔					✔		✔		
11		✔		✔				✔		
12	✔			✔				✔		
13			✔		✔			✔		
14	✔				✔			✔		
15	✔					✔		?		
16	✔					✔		?		
17	✔			✔				✔		
18		✔		✔				✔		

4 Findings

4.1 Risks

We categorised the risks identified by drivers into three main themes/issues: income, safety and deactivation.

Income
Given their role as main breadwinners for their households, drivers felt a strong need to earn a certain level of income. This was exacerbated for many because they had other required payments: financed loans in the case of some of those who owned cars; weekly payments to owners of R2,000–R2,700 (c.US$130–180) in the case of those who were renting their vehicles. Meeting these multiple demands was jeopardised in various ways.

Though not a risk but an integral part of ride-hailing, drivers resented the percentage of client payments taken by the platforms: 20% by Bolt plus a 5% booking fee; 25% by Uber plus a 3% booking fee at the time of writing [19]:

> "we feel like Uber is ripping us off; 25% is too much. 1 feel like they are taking advantage of the situation in South Africa about unemployment and then now they just dictate it's going to be 25% ... if you don't want the 25% to be taken what else are you going to do?" (D10[1])

Dynamically, and because of their ability to control entry into the marketplace, platforms have increased the supply of cars/drivers on the platform over time. This has led to over-supply compared to demand, and drivers have thus faced falling income [3] and concerns that platforms should stop adding cars in order to enable drivers to make enough income (D14). Further growth of supply and competition is a key part of income risk.

A central element of platforms' strategy has been to avoid regulation [16] and part of this has been to allow drivers to work without a taxi license, which the majority of drivers do: "You see I'm operating this car; it has no taxi operating license as you can see it only has one disc there for the vehicle" (D12). This therefore opens the drivers up to police impounding their vehicles and fining them. We estimate at least a 20% chance of being caught each year in Cape Town, with fines for repeat offences escalating up to R15,000 (just under US$1,000) and with drivers then unable to work while the police hold their car.

Safety
By far the main safety-related risk is the danger of robbery, including violent robbery:

> "I was robbed. Someone requested when I was in Bellville and those guys were good looking; you can't even think that they can rob you. So their requesting was saying they are going to Bellville South, there were three; I drove them to Bellville South. So when we were almost close to the place of destination so they said don't mind that map we will direct you to the place we want to go, so they kept on saying turn right, turn left and go straight this and that until we got to a place which is a bit quiet and dull and the next thing they started pulling off their guns and they said I should with my phone give us the password so myself I had no choice I have to give them, bring that pocket and bring the next pocket pull it out and ... then they took everything which I had." (D15)

Drivers explained why they face these risks. When ride-hailing first launched in South Africa, it followed a global North model of payment via credit card but client demand led to cash payment options then being added, meaning criminals assume drivers carry cash. By definition, gig work also requires that they have a phone:

> "So they just want the money; they know every Uber driver has a smartphone and they think we carry money all the time." (D4)

---

[1] This refers to driver interview no. 10; other interviewee references in the text follow a similar format.

"Like I have a nice phone, I'm risking again because if you have a cheap phone it doesn't work here. Because this phone costs R1,800 and the thief will sell it for R500." (D14)

Like many global South cities, Cape Town is heterogeneous in terms of its areas, with a number of high-crime locations that drivers may be asked to pick up from or drop off to, increasing the risk that they will be victims of crime:

"You see on Bolt, most of the Bolt clients use cash trips so and normally they go to those dangerous locations; Mitchells Plain, Hanover Park." (D4)

The concern over cash-paying clients arises because the level of client identification is lower than for those paying via credit cards; making it possible for criminals to more-easily create fake accounts. This was even more of a problem on Bolt because the platform provided few details:

"I mean you get a request and you don't know whom you are picking ... where they want a ride, or they want to rob you. You can't tell." (D5)

A secondary safety risk arises from the danger of altercations with traditional meter taxi drivers who have been vehemently and sometimes violently opposed to the arrival of ride-hailing platforms in South Africa [21]:

"I also faced another that I was in Kuils River and I wanted to pick a rider ... The moment the rider came to my car a taxi driver came to me he threatened me: 'Hey you Uber, who told you can pick up people here I am going to kill you' ... I quickly picked up the rider and drove away ... he was following me, but I just drove quickly off the place." (D12)

Deactivation
Very much related to concerns about earning enough income, drivers were concerned about the risk of deactivation from the platform which of course would mean they would be unable to work or earn. This could typically occur if their rating on the platform fell below a certain level and/or if a client made a complaint against them. This puts a lot of power into the hands of the client:

"I should exercise my rights as a driver; I can be an Uber driver and I'm still human, I have the right to express myself. But with this Uber app everyone who requests automatically becomes my boss or dictator or something. Someone comes into my car they start telling me can you do this, do that; they call it service but to us, on the other hand, it's a form of abuse and people take advantage of and tell us if you don't do this I will rate you and Uber will deactivate you." (D10)

It also puts a lot of power and information in the hands of the platform, as the same driver related:

"Whenever a client is treating you badly, they know they have Uber at their back. Tomorrow Uber is going to support the client, of course they don't say that but that's the issue. We find our riders are becoming abusive to the drivers, they become rude, they don't treat us well, of course, we have no choice. For example, this is the only job that I have so now I'm forced to take what I don't want. I have an example one of the days they send me an email and they tell me that a rider complained; that a rider said I behaved in an inappropriate manner. Because that didn't go well with me I wrote an email back asking okay fine I got the email and they tell me that they can deactivate my account. I asked them if they could provide the details like which details were that, so that I take legal action if there's need. For me this was like defamation of character that client has taken advantage of me; because I'm not there and I have no room to defend myself they said whatever they liked about me, because now my job is at risk I don't know what you think about me also one thing that if tomorrow there's another complaint that means they are two and I might get deactivated. They told me because of their policy they don't provide details. These are things that we face. This was the end of the story there is nowhere I can go; I cannot face them if they can just block me and that's the end of my job. … My man, I feel like being oppressed; I have no more rights I can say ever since I joined Uber it's difficult for me to express my rights especially when I'm doing the job." (D10)

4.2 Risk-Mitigation Strategies

Before discussing risk-mitigation strategies, we must first note the number of drivers who do not adopt such strategies. In particular, the pressure to earn income – exacerbated by the platform's management of the market to create an excess of supply (drivers) over demand (riders) – has led drivers to engage in high-risk behaviours. Some simply hope or believe that nothing bad will happen to them; others turn to higher powers: "Like I said its God who protects me" (D1). But this is not enough: as an example, drivers still go to Nyanga at night: a district notorious as the "murder capital" of South Africa [23]. Predictably, there have then been repeated incidents of drivers murdered during robberies and hijackings [5, 24].

Of the risk-mitigation strategies reported by the drivers, we identified three different themes/types: platform-initiated, driver-initiated, and driver group-initiated.

Platform-Initiated Risk Mitigation

Platforms may mandate certain risk-mitigation strategies. For example, "You can't drive on Uber without insurance" (D4): there is a check to ensure that all cars registered on the platform have vehicle insurance to avoid major financial loss in case of an accident.

Platforms may also provide risk mitigations themselves. Both Uber and Bolt provide a panic button as part of their app: interviewees were able to demonstrate its presence but were somewhat dubious about its value: "That one [panic button] doesn't work because in a robbery that's [phone] the first thing they will grab before you do anything in the car" (D4). Uber, alone, provides two other mitigations against loss of income. "If this car gets impounded by the traffic cops, Uber, they pay the amount to get back the vehicle but Bolt doesn't pay the amount" (D12). Uber will also pay the driver to cover the costs of riders who run off at the end of a journey without paying.

Individual Driver-Initiated Risk Mitigation

By far the largest number of strategies identified were the responsibility of individual drivers.

Income Mitigation

To mitigate the risk of not achieving the required level of income, drivers work very long hours:

> "It's not easy; the thing is like if you're working for someone, you need to pay the R2,500 a week [to the vehicle owner]. For you to pay that, to get that R2,500 a week you must be working; so you need R2,500 to pay the car first, money for your petrol, and money for yourself, so you must be on the road for long. That's why you see so many of the guys don't even go home, that's why they stay on the road." (D8)

The average working day for drivers was just over 12 h. Given they typically work six days a week, that means on average more than 72 h per week; 60% longer than the maximum 45-h working week set out in the country's Basic Conditions of Employment Act [28]. Another platform-mandated risk mitigation is the imposition of a 12-h maximum working day. However, workers get around this by registering on, and working for, more than one platform: hence D5 reported working up to 17 h per day. Workers also register on multiple platforms in order to avoid the risk of under-earning; taking rides on one platform if business is slack on the other.

There are also very situation-specific strategies. On Bolt, which does not compensate for rider non-payment, drivers reported "we sometimes take their [rider's] belongings so that we can recoup the money we used for our petrol" (D9) if the rider says at the end of the journey that they cannot pay. The intention is that the items are just held temporarily while the rider goes to get money for payment, to reduce the risk of non-payment.

Safety Mitigation

To mitigate risks to personal safety, drivers undertake rider screening. Some of this is platform-assisted: drivers will look at the rider's rating on the platform and may refuse those with low ratings:

> "You know we have this rating. When I see a 3 that person is in trouble and when I see 4 I don't doubt until 4.9. If it's 3, I doubt especially their attitude, 5 stars they are probably new, I don't trust them also." (D17)

They may also refuse those seeking to travel to or be picked up from locations with high-crime reputations; and they may refuse those who are seeking to pay cash, particularly when travelling at night. In addition, on arrival at the pick-up, drivers assess the rider(s): and may drive off if they perceive the rider is drunk, or if the riders are a group of men. Again, these rider-refusal behaviours are more likely at night. Of course this all comes at a cost: not just loss of income but also algorithmic downgrading due to turning down rides; but those costs are seen to be outweighed by the benefits of risk mitigation.

Drivers also undertake various location-specific risk-mitigation strategies if they are driving in an area they consider to be dangerous. If picking someone up from such a location, they may avoid stopping until the rider is ready to quickly jump into the car:

> "For me when I gets to the dangerous places, I don't stop my car when I get to the pick-up point. I just patrol there like someone patrolling while I inform the rider." (D11)

When picking up someone to go to these areas, they may agree only to take the client to a safe place:

> "If he or she is going to Gugulethu … I don't mind going there but at this time I don't feel safe so I give the client options … either I take him halfway down when I get to this point or I drop you near the police station." (D5)

They may share details of the trip with family members or with other drivers, and they may get riders to pay prior to reaching the destination so that at the drop-off, the driver can just drop them very quickly and leave immediately.

Lastly in terms of safety, drivers adopt various personal protection measures. They avoid wearing seatbelts at night so that they can quickly turn around or get out of the vehicle if necessary. Platform policy is that "we are not allowed to carry any weapon in the car" (D4) but one did admit to having a can of pepper spray, and another stated that, while he himself did not have a weapon, others did:

> "maybe they have weapons in their cars: that's the best way they can protect themselves. If you attack them [the driver] then they attack you if they have a chance to." (D5)

There are certainly reports of drivers using weapons they were keeping their cars [22].

Deactivation Mitigation
The main strategy that drivers adopted here was 'making nice' with clients. As D10 noted above, when a rider says "do this, do that" then drivers feel obliged to comply in order to avoid getting a bad rating and risk being deactivated: "we have no choice".

Driver Group-Initiated Risk Mitigation
To help address some of the income challenges they faced, some drivers had joined what is locally known as *Stokvels* - rotating savings and credit schemes [20]. These have a general intention to encourage drivers to save their earnings, enabling them to make more effective use of their income and therefore reduce the need to accept high-risk trips or riders. They have also been used more specifically to help drivers buy their own car; something which increases income relative to having to rent a car, and thus addresses both income and safety risks, again by reducing the need for high-risk trips:

> "Yah especially us Zimbabweans, that's how we bought our own cars. We always do the groups like Stokvel; put the money together until its fine for one person to buy and then the next [time] we buy for someone else."(D7)

On a more day-to-day basis, drivers share information either via WhatsApp groups or by meeting up in some set locations in-between trips or when waiting at the airport. Information shared includes locations where the police are impounding license-less vehicles, or where crimes have been committed, or other experiences which can alert drivers to implement risk-mitigation strategies. As well as being a mechanism for 'horizontal' sharing between peers, this was also acting in a more 'vertical' manner to help new drivers learn quickly about key risks and ways to avoid them.

5 Discussion and Conclusions

Clients face risks in using ride-hailing services: there are occasional reports of robbery or attack or they may be caught up in accidents. Likewise, platforms themselves also face risks such as lawsuits or bankruptcy. However, overall, and as proposed in the literature [14], this research exposed a strong asymmetry of risk between the stakeholders of gig economy platforms in the global South. It is the workers who bear the lion's share of the risks; many of which arise from the specifics of the South Africa context: risks of not earning enough to cover necessary outgoings; risks to personal safety up to and including death; risks of losing their job through deactivation. While these are risks identified in the literature, it is valuable to receive bottom-up corroboration from gig economy workers.

Just because it is workers who must face the greatest risks, there is no necessity for workers to have to undertake most of the risk mitigation; a topic about which the literature has so far told us little. Yet this was the situation here. Digital platforms could take on more risk and more responsibility for risk mitigation, but they do not do so because their business model requires them to treat workers as 'independent contractors' and not as employees:

> "Uber does not want to come as an employer, it comes out as a service provider by providing us with the application. For example, when it comes to an accident, Uber does not involve itself, they do not compensate hospital or funerals as there are a lot of drivers who have passed away from this." (D18)

Similarly, it could easily design away the current information asymmetries between clients and workers; for example, requiring more details from clients when they register, and providing drivers with full information about clients. Both of these would reduce risks. It could also 'red-line' certain areas of the city where drivers have been repeatedly attacked and stop drivers having to travel there. Again, this would reduce risks. It does none of these things because they would potentially reduce business, and platforms themselves are under the pressure of high levels of debt to maximise income and profit.

The result, then, is that responsibility for risk mitigation is laid largely at the door of the individual worker; consistent with the gig economy view of an atomised, individualised workforce, and with the idea of risk inequalities between platforms and workers. To some extent, workers accept this, trading off the risks against the benefits of an income and the autonomy and flexibility they perceive such work to offer [see also 8]. But this should not be seen as a free choice. The developing country context shapes not just risks and, hence, risk-mitigation strategies but also acceptance of risk and adoption of risk mitigation. As noted, many of these workers are immigrants who move to South Africa due to lack of employment opportunities in their home countries but then find a similar lack of options other than gig work, as two of the Zimbabweans commented: "there are no jobs here in South Africa" (D12); "It's not just like all about that Zimbabweans will just accept any rate that comes up, but the situation is the one that can force us" (D15). Once within the sector, and notwithstanding risk-mitigation strategies, the way in which platforms have constructed the market creates pressure from supply—demand imbalance and leads drivers to undertake high-risk strategies; sometimes at the cost of their own lives.

In terms of recommendations, one would say that there should be more risk-bearing and risk-mitigation by the platform. With workers literally dying for Uber and Bolt there is at least a moral argument for this. Yet there are dangers of things moving in the opposite direction: in early 2020, the South African platforms were under fire for increasing their commission rates, continuing to add new cars and drivers to the platform, and removing driver access to advance rider and trip details [19]. Each of these will increase not decrease risks. This creates an urgent need to place a greater emphasis on workers and their perspective, as outlined in this paper. That, for example, is the aim of the Fairwork Foundation, which has been active in South Africa for the past two years. It rates platforms against decent work standards that include their risk-mitigation actions, and seeks to use public, client and government pressure to make platforms improve [10]. Similar initiatives are needed to pressurise platforms to do more to reduce worker risks.

A second recommendation would relate to worker groupings. It is notable that one time-honoured group-initiated risk-mitigation strategy is not much in evidence in South Africa: the formation of trade unions or even of worker associations. The South African e-Hailing Association in Cape Town and The Movement in Johannesburg have both sought to collectivise workers, but with only limited success. One problem – reflected in views of those interviewed here – is that many drivers have bought into the 'independent contractor' identity and regard themselves as entrepreneurs or proto-entrepreneurs; an identity at odds with membership of any formal worker association. Sadly, it may take greater materialisation of the risks to change this.

Finally, we can note some directions for future research. The first will be a more general repetition of this work in other cities, countries and gig economy sectors to get a broader and more systematic understanding of risk and its mitigation; perhaps using the categorisation of risks presented above as a basis for deductive enquiry. The second would arise from some sense of differentiation that emerged in the interview data e.g. that younger drivers may take more risks, or that Bolt drivers faced more risks than those driving for Uber. Future research could therefore investigate various possible dimensions of difference in terms of risk profiles and risk-mitigation strategies: older vs. younger workers; men vs. women; immigrant vs. local workers; owners vs. renters; and between different platforms.

References

1. Braun, V., Clarke, V.: Using thematic analysis in psychology. Qual. Res. Psychol. 3(2), 77–101 (2006)
2. Burke, J.: Violence erupts between taxi and Uber drivers in Johannesburg. Guardian (2017)

3. CCSA: Market Inquiry into Land Based Public Passenger Transport: Metered Taxis and E-Hailing Services, Competition Commission South Africa, Pretoria (2020)
4. Christie, N., Ward, H.: The health and safety risks for people who drive for work in the gig economy. J. Transp. Health **13**, 115–127 (2019)
5. Daniels, N.: Cops offer to escort e-hailing drivers to Nyanga after murder. Independent Online (2019)
6. de Greef, K.: Driving for Uber when you can't afford a car. Atlantic (2018)
7. de Greef, K.: One more way to die: delivering food in Cape Town's gig economy. N. Y. Times (2019)
8. De Stefano, V.: The rise of the just-in-time workforce: on-demand work, crowdwork, and labor protection in the gig-economy. Comp. Labour Law Policy J. **37**, 471–503 (2015)
9. de Villiers, J.: Taxify scraps ad that claims drivers earn R8000 a week. Business Insider (2019)
10. Fairwork: Fairwork: Labour Standards in the Platform Economy. University of Oxford, Oxford (2019)
11. Gomez-Morantes, J.E., Heeks, R., Duncombe, R.: A multi-level perspective on digital platform implementation and impact: the case of EasyTaxi in Colombia. In: Nielsen, P., Kimaro, H.C. (eds.) ICT4D 2019. IAICT, vol. 551, pp. 195–206. Springer, Cham (2019). https://doi.org/10.1007/978-3-030-18400-1_16
12. Graham, M., Lehdonvirta, V., Wood, A., Barnard, H., Hjorth, I., Simon, D.P.: The Risks and Rewards of Online Gig Work at the Global Margins. Oxford Internet Institute, Oxford (2017)
13. Graham, M., et al.: The Fairwork Foundation: strategies for improving platform work in a global context, Geoforum, advance online publication (2020)
14. Heeks, R.: Decent Work and the Digital Gig Economy, GDI Development Informatics Working Paper no. 71, University of Manchester, UK (2017)
15. Heeks, R.: How many platform workers are there in the global South? ICT4DBlog, 29 January 2019
16. Heeks, R., Eskelund, K., Gomez-Morantes, J.E., Malik, F., Nicholson, B.: Digital platforms and institutional voids in developing countries: labour markets and gig economy platforms. Paper presented at IFIP WG9.4 European Conference on the Social Implications of Computers in Developing Countries, University of Salford, 10–11 June 2020
17. Kashyap, R., Bhatia, A.: Taxi drivers and taxidars: a case study of Uber and Ola in Delhi. J. Dev. Soc. **34**(2), 169–194 (2018)
18. Malik, F., Nicholson, B., Heeks, R.: Understanding the development implications of online outsourcing. In: Choudrie, J., Islam, M.S., Wahid, F., Bass, J.M., Priyatma, J.E. (eds.) ICT4D 2017. IAICT, vol. 504, pp. 425–436. Springer, Cham (2017). https://doi.org/10.1007/978-3-319-59111-7_35
19. Malinga, S.: Uber, Bolt drivers plan shutdown of ride-hailing services. ITWeb, 20 February 2020
20. Menze, A., Tsibolane, P.: Online Stokvels: the use of social media by the marginalized. In: CONF-IRM 2019 Proceedings, p. 26 (2019)
21. Mitchley, A.: Uber and meter taxi feud claims life of driver. News24 (2017)
22. Mlambo, S.: How Durban man's 38th birthday ended with death in a Taxify ride. Independent Online, 21 April 2019
23. Mlamla, S.: Crime stats. Independent Online, 12 September 2019
24. Nwokocha, F.: Tragedy as second Nigerian taxi driver Joseph Ajouna murdered in South Africa within a week. Niger. Serve (2019)
25. Onkokame, M., Schoentgen, A., Gillwald, A.: What is the State of Microwork in Africa? Research ICT Africa, Cape Town (2017)
26. Phillips, D.: Murder of Uber drivers may be Brazil gang leader's 'revenge' for cancelled ride. Guardian (2019)

27. Rogers, R.W., Prentice-Dunn, S.: Protection motivation theory. In: Gochman, D.S. (ed.) Handbook of Health Behavior Research 1, pp. 113–132. Plenum Press, New York (1997)
28. RSA: Basic Conditions of Employment Act 1997. Republic of South Africa, Cape Town (1997)

Theory and Open Science

The Potential of Open Science for Research Visibility in the Global South: Rwandan Librarians' Perspectives

Pamela Abbott$^{(\boxtimes)}$ ⓘ and Andrew Cox ⓘ

University of Sheffield, Sheffield S1 4DP, UK
{p.y.abbott,a.m.cox}@sheffield.ac.uk

Abstract. The weak visibility of African research outputs and scholarship in established global publication outlets and research networks is often the subject of debate. Encouragingly, some discourses around open science appear to offer a solution for this issue. In this paper we explore whether and how open science can help in addressing the inequities that seem to hinder African scholarship, by taking a closer look at the research environment of one particular country, Rwanda. We drew upon the experiential knowledge of four senior librarians in Rwandan higher learning institutions through a week-long data gathering and engagement workshop. We then analysed this data and compared it to three literature-based perspectives on the issues underlying the perceived invisibility of African scholarship. From our findings, we conclude that research contexts may be systemically and structurally constituted and that open science initiatives may only offer partial solutions when considered within a broader appreciation of these constraints. We offer support to decolonial approaches in reframing these efforts.

Keywords: Open science · African scholarship · Cognitive injustice · Rwanda · Research lifecycle

1 Introduction

Open science is an important new development in the governance and practice of research (LERU 2018). Originating in the Global North, it encompasses a number of different discourses (Albagli 2015), but as an idealistic movement to reform science, there is an expectation that it should be able to address inequities in how science works and improve opportunities for all scholars (Levin et al. 2016). One notable documented inequity in the practice of scholarship is the weak global visibility of African research (Chan and Gray 2013). An oft-quoted statistic is that sub-Saharan Africa produces less than 1% of the world's research output (e.g. Fonn et al. 2018; Ngongalah et al. 2018). We will suggest in this paper that the apparent weak visibility of African scholarship can be centred around three conflicting perspectives.

A number of authors are optimistic that open science offers some scope to address these endemic challenges to the visibility of African scholarship (e.g. Raju et al. 2015;

© IFIP International Federation for Information Processing 2020
Published by Springer Nature Switzerland AG 2020
J. M. Bass and P. J. Wall (Eds.): ICT4D 2020, IFIP AICT 587, pp. 41–53, 2020.
https://doi.org/10.1007/978-3-030-65828-1_4

Ahinon and Havemann 2018). This paper will engage with this debate by exploring its potential in a particular research context in the Global South, that of Rwanda in East Africa. With its historical and colonial legacies, Rwanda presents a unique and illustrative case through which these issues can be examined. The perception of the key enablers and constraints of the Rwandan research context through data collected from Rwandan librarians provided a basis on which to consider the potential of open scholarship as a change agent in their situation. The paper seeks to answer two research questions: *1. What are Rwandan librarians' perceptions of the challenges for research in their country? 2. How is open scholarship relevant to addressing these challenges?*

Next, we present in the literature review existing perspectives on open science and explore debates about the invisibility of research outputs from the Global South, specifically African scholarship. We then explain the methodological approach used for the study, the results of which we present in the findings section. We discuss these findings and explore the implications of open science for addressing the identified challenges. We conclude with implications of this study.

2 Literature Review

2.1 Open Science/Open Scholarship

There is growing momentum in policy and practice in the Global North around the concept of open science or more broadly open scholarship. Open science adheres to ideologies pertinent to "openness" as a social movement (LERU 2018). Here, openness is meant to refer to democratisation of knowledge and therefore links to ethical and moral standpoints privileging public access to, and participation in, knowledge production (Albagli 2015; Fecher and Friesike 2013). Open science initiatives are thus part of a long-standing tradition to "open up" the products and processes of scientific practice to all (David 2008). At the simplest level, this is about the open sharing of resources and ideas. Examples include: open access journals where content is freely available to any reader without subscription; also, use of open access repositories which enable researchers costless access to published papers. Some of these are based on subject area, while others are run by institutions, for all the outputs of all their authors. Sharing of a version of research data or coding underlying results in a data repository, is another aspect of open scholarship.

The benefits of such openness include ensuring rigour and reliability of research, increasing the speed and reach of dissemination, broadening participation in research, and better resource usage (National Academies of Sciences 2018). Acknowledged barriers are the costs and infrastructure needs; the current scholarly communications system; lack of the appropriate culture; various privacy or security issues; and disciplinary differences (National Academies of Sciences 2018). Key to the concept of open scholarship is that it includes but extends beyond mere access. Opening up the practice of scientific knowledge production in these ways necessarily affects the research process since each stage of a typical "research lifecycle" will be affected. Thus, accounts of open science suggest the need to refer to a significantly wider range of open practices. Grigorov et al. (2016), amongst others, for example, have mapped various different open scholarship interventions to the research lifecycle.

Much of the rhetoric around open scholarship, as with open access before it, revolves around the equity and integrity of scholarship but it rarely engages explicitly with the issues challenging research in the Global South. Limited research on the relationship between the open movement and development outcomes has sought to examine how open science could be harnessed to enrich local research environments (Chan et al. 2015; Hillyer et al. 2017). These arguments suggest that through strengthening the research environment, the local research community would be better able to leverage knowledge to address local problems (e.g. Guerrero-Medina et al. 2013). Actual research into how open science *does* influence these local research environments is scarce, however (Rappert and Bezuidenhout 2016). In considering whether and how open scholarship can help in addressing the inequities that seem to hinder African scholarship, we first take a look at three perspectives from the literature on this topic.

2.2 Perspective 1: Open Scholarship and Inequalities in the Scholarly Communication System

One perspective on the relative invisibility of African research is to locate the problem firmly within the scholarly communication system as currently constituted (Chan and Gray 2013). This system is dominated by a number of powerful commercial publishers based primarily in the USA and UK, and publishing in English (Chan 2018). Run on for-profit grounds, the journals they publish are relatively expensive to license, especially for resource-constrained contexts and the costs have historically spiralled upwards (Milne 1999). Journal impact factors, which operate as a means of measuring research significance within this system (Hecht et al. 1998), reinforce their legitimacy by effectively encouraging citation frequency within this same network of journals. Material published outside the system is invisible and so effectively has no impact (Chan and Gray 2013). The way the publishing industry works places authors in the Global North in a powerful positon to dominate academic knowledge (Haider 2018). The research agenda is often set by issues defined in the Global North (Gwynn 2019). A large proportion of papers published about the Global South are not co-authored by researchers from the Global South (Boshoff 2009).

Open scholarship is positioned to address key issues within the scholarly communication system, though its efficacy is open to question. For example, it assumes that everyone has a network connection and the digital skills to locate and use open material. Given the greater scale of research in the Global North, openness could reinforce its dominance, i.e., those in a position to benefit from open infrastructures would be the primary beneficiaries, which unfortunately does not include most lower middle income countries (Herb and Schöpfel 2018). There are also fears that scholars in the Global North use their infrastructural advantages to access and exploit data produced in the Global South (Rappert and Bezuidenhout 2016). There are certainly other problematic aspects of the scholarly communication system that do not seem to be addressed via dominant discourses of open scholarship. For example, the problem of "linguistic imperialism" (Canagarajah and Ben Said 2011), due to the dominance of English as the language of science, is not addressed.

2.3 Perspective 2: Open Scholarship and Deficits in the In-Country Research Environment

An alternative perspective on the relative invisibility of research outputs from sub-Saharan Africa, could be dubbed the "country deficit" perspective. This places centre stage a web of in-country issues which are assumed to create research environments that function poorly when compared to those of the Global North. This perspective emphasises what the country lacks and how it can "catch up" to more developed country research contexts, without necessarily positioning these issues within broader systems of imbalance such as the inequalities created by the international scholarly communication system. Rather, it focuses on the way that a weaker in-country environment for research makes it more difficult to perform research on par with scholars in the Global North. Some of the key issues highlighted within this perspective are briefly reviewed here.

Inadequate investment in research and higher education is often cited as a central issue leading to, and often led by, dependency on foreign aid organisations, like the World Bank, and their development agendas (Fonn et al. 2018; Beaudry et al. 2018; Collins and Rhoads 2010). Another issue often highlighted in this perspective is the lack of support at the institutional and supra-institutional levels for researcher development (Beaudry et al. 2018; Ngongalah et al. 2018) including lack of alignment of research policy to local contexts (Boshoff 2009). Yet another common issue identified is inadequate development of research support infrastructures (Gwynn 2019), like institutional repositories, for example (Dlamini and Snyman 2017), and support for open science (Nwagwu 2013). Reinforcing the in-country deficit view is the migration of trained scholars (Ondari-Okemwa 2007), seen to be as much as 30% in the 1980s and 90s (Beaudry et al. 2018), leading to human capacity issues.

These in-country deficits spill over into the development of open initiatives, thus complicating any ameliorating effect that open scholarship could bring to this situation. Low investment in higher education leads, for example, to lack of access to licensed content and insufficient funding for some open access routes. Lack of support for research development and infrastructure could mean that even where open access content is available, scholars may lack the bandwidth or digital and information literacy skills to access the content. Lack of support for running repository infrastructures efficiently would contribute to further invisibility of African scholarly publications.

2.4 Perspective 3: Open Scholarship and Cognitive Injustices

A third perspective can be seen emerging which potentially underlies both the scholarly communication system and country deficit perspectives, but locates the fundamental issue in neo-colonialism and the diminution, even erasure, of African ideas within human knowledge systems dominated by the Global North. We follow Nkoudou (2015) and Piron et al. (2016) in labelling this the cognitive injustices perspective.

Nyamnjoh's (2012) analysis traces the deprecation of African knowledge, as epistemicide, to the violence of colonialization when endogenous knowledge was seen as inferior and primitive. This has resulted in African education retaining vestiges of "epistemological xenophilia and knowledge dependency" Nyamnjoh (2012: 143) with scholars trying to make sense of local problems through the Global North's knowledge system, rather than develop their own theory (Andrews and Okpanachi 2012).

In the African open scholarship context, this argument is most recently articulated by Nkoudou (2015) and Piron et al. (2016) through identifying eight, inter-related "cognitive injustices" that beset African scholarship. Nkoudou (2015) identifies both endogenous and exogenous cognitive injustices. Endogenous factors include the continuing neo-colonialism of African education which is directed to reproducing local elites and is based on the assumption that local African knowledge is inferior to the knowledges of the Global North. The lack of policy and infrastructure to support research in African countries is seen as a further endogenous, cognitive injustice arising from this sense of inferiority. A further effect of the dependence on ideas originating in the Global North is to alienate African citizenry from research, reinforcing a strong barrier between science and society (Nkoudou 2015).

Central to exogenous epistemic injustice is the impact of the for-profit scientific publication system (Piron et al. 2016). This is premised on the purpose of research being to promote economic growth, a perspective found pervasively in policy justifications of open science. But the authors argue that this is an alien model of development because it does not fit Africa's needs. The for-profit publishing system effectively restricts access to the apparatus of scholarly publishing, both to publish and to read.

Ultimately, within this argument, minor reforms to how science works now are unlikely to address the underlying issue that African knowledge remains unvalued. Open science is often explained as a return to fundamental principles found in the early centuries of Western science in Europe (e.g. National Academies of Sciences 2018). This makes the assumption that Western science is the model for all knowledge creation. Just as open access has not evolved in an afro-centric direction (Nwagwu 2013), there is a risk that open scholarship as defined in the Global North will fail to reflect African realities, and so may not therefore bring the hoped for benefits, despite the often good intentions. Thus Nkoudou (2015) and Piron et al. (2016) do see benefits in open science, but only if it is defined as the democratisation of access to science, not if it is understood as a means to accelerate scientific productivity or for economic growth.

We summarize the three perspectives. Taken from perspective one, the problem of invisibility of African scholarship is systemic; dominant actors from the Global North effectively exclude participation from Global South scholars. Open science can bring visibility through disrupting aspects of the research process towards more open, inclusive and collaborative approaches. From perspective two, the problem is due to in-country research environment failure; state and institutional actors create a weak environment for scholarship in general. Open science could face implementation barriers and therefore be ineffective in providing solutions. From perspective three, the problem is due to the entrenched epistemic injustices legacy of colonialism, which is also implicated in perpetuating aspects of perspectives one and two. Open science would need to be positioned as a liberating force, but may be unable to unseat the status quo. The three perspectives therefore give conflicting views on the role open science could play.

Given this, we decided use the research lifecycle (e.g. Grigorov et al. 2016) as an orienting framework for understanding research challenges in Rwanda and to assess, in the light of the three perspectives, the transformative potentials of open science.

3 Methods

Data for this paper were collected as part of a project engaging with the higher learning institution (HLI) librarian community in Rwanda. We collaborated with 4 librarians from 3 HLIs in Rwanda: University of Rwanda (2 participants), University of Lay Adventists of Kigali (1 participant) and Ruhengeri Institute of Higher Education (1 participant). All participants were directors of their respective libraries, at either a specific campus or serving the entire institution. During a six-month period, we conducted quasi-monthly video-conference meetings with the participants to plan a week-long engagement workshop with them at the Information School, University of Sheffield, UK. The participants devised questionnaires and conducted informal enquiries in their institutions about the research practices of their academic user base. The areas of enquiry were: Rwandan researchers' main publishing challenges (globally and locally), issues related to English language publishing, literature search, sharing data and dealing with digital research outputs.

During the week-long workshop, we conducted daily data gathering activities involving the participants including: 3 group interviews and discussions, a "rich picture" collaborative group exercise (similar to Walker et al. 2014), 1 panel discussion and 1 focus group. Altogether, we collected around 12 h of recorded material over the week-long period supplemented by 6 "rich pictures", 10 flipcharts representing discussions and 30 A4 pages of notes. The collected data were discussed by the two Information School researchers in 4 meetings for which each researcher prepared by reading the notes related to the engagement workshop and reviewing the audio-visual and physical materials produced. The researchers discussed and agreed upon broad themes emerging from the data and an analytical framework to structure the themes. This framework was then used for systematic analysis of the data to prepare the results matrix shown in Table 1. These approaches are based on qualitative inductive analysis methods (Miles and Huberman 1994).

The results matrix organised the data along two dimensions: (1) the research lifecycle, taken here as the stages *idea generation*, *data collection and analysis*, *dissemination of results* and (2) broad contextual factors from the emerging thematic areas. The research lifecycle stages were further subdivided by emerging categories from the data such as *motivation*, *access to literature* (idea generation aspects) and *local publication*, *publication in international journals*, *open access* and *dissemination to the public* (dissemination of results aspects). The contextual themes were categorised as: *researcher position*, *costs*, *national and institutional support infrastructure*, *skills* and *access*. For each stage/sub-category of the research lifecycle, these factors were elaborated on, so as to relate the issues found in the context to that specific research stage. The resulting matrix thus effectively formed a representation of the librarians' perceptions of the Rwandan research context.

4 Findings: Challenges for Researchers in Rwanda

We discuss the five interconnected contextual themes emerging from the data and represented in Table 1. The first theme revolved around the motives and challenges for

Table 1. Matrix representing a map of Rwandan librarians' perceptions of the local research context.

Research lifecycle	Idea generation	Access to literature	Data coll. & analysis	Dissemination of results			
				Local publication	Publication in international journals	Open access	Dissemination to the public
Themes	Motivation						
Researcher position	Publish or perish model I Limited funding for research, mostly from external funders, disconnected from local agendas I Teaching loads			International journal publication needed for promotion	High rejection rates Predatory publishers	Lack of institutional open access mandates	External funders drive the research agenda – disconnect to in-country need
Costs	Lack of financial motive to do research I Doing extra teaching is easier than doing research	High cost of access to literature content	Lab costs I Data collection costs – paying participants' travel or fees		Publication costs: reviewing costs, APCs (notwithstanding discounts)		

(continued)

Table 1. (*continued*)

Research lifecycle	Idea generation	Data coll. & analysis	Dissemination of results		
National and institutional support infrastructure		Poor technical infrastructure: electricity, computer ownership, bandwidth, software and IT support • ICT support staff leave quickly when they have been trained Hard to work from home because of network cost • Librarians low status		No robust open access infrastructure at institutional level • Lack of skills to maintain open access infrastructure	Internet connectivity is limited and expensive
Skills	Lack of reading habits • Lack of search skills • Low English skills		Low English skills Lack of academic writing skills • Lack of understanding of publishing process	Little understanding of IPR in publication context	
Access	Lack of local content • High cost of subscriptions		Rwanda has graduated out of Research4Life		Scholars publish in international journals in English, not for local audiences, including policy makers

the researcher. Researchers were subject to a "publish or perish" model: in which the motivation to undertake research was to gain funding, build reputation and publish in international journals. But this was highly problematic because research funding is very competitive with success rates at 2–5%. It also skewed research towards quite a narrow research agenda, so that 70% of publications came from just one sector: health. What funding there was came from external funders, so they drove agendas, not researcher interest or in-country need. Participants felt strongly that external funders were not aware enough of in-country needs. The result was a disconnection between research and policy. This was further reinforced by funders' preference for publication in international journals that local policy makers would be very unlikely to access. Teaching loads made doing any research hard. Most contracts stated that 50% of time was for teaching (30% research; 20% administration). But class sizes were very large, so that in reality there was little time for research. Getting published was also hard, because again rejection rates were high.

The second theme was the financial issue. The motive to undertake research was weak financially: salaries were low but typically academics found it easier to do extra teaching at another institution if they needed to make more money. There was no shortage of such work. At the same time, there was a sense of the many expenses throughout the research lifecycle: subscription costs, lab costs, data collection costs and later publication costs, such as for translation and proofing work and for APCs.

A third issue was the infrastructure, including ICTs. At both national and institutional levels there were issues with basic electricity supply, computer access and ownership, bandwidth, software and IT support. There were not enough computer labs; not all researchers have computers. Once IT support staff are trained they tend to leave. There was also a sense that the skills to maintain an open access infrastructure were lacking within institutions.

Fourthly, another challenge was researchers' skills, which were lacking across a range of critical areas, including writing, particularly in English, but also information searching and understanding the publishing process. One underlying factor seemed to be language. Rwandan culture is mainly oral, with most day-to-day interactions based on Kinyarwanda which is not used much in education or research. The driver to publish research results in English language international journals effectively makes results inaccessible, because public access to knowledge is mainly oral and English is not the natural language of communication. Research outputs were thus disconnected from citizens and policy makers. Furthermore, many Rwandans have learned French as a second language; the introduction of English as a language for teaching or publication is relatively recent. Like many non-native English-speaking researchers, translating their ideas into English for publication in international journals thus incurred additional costs and effort.

The fifth challenge was access to content, which from international journals was expensive. Researchers often had to find money for journal subscriptions themselves. Research4Life had been very useful, but publishers now consider Rwanda's GDP to be high enough to be able to afford the content. In reality this is not the case, therefore full text access has been lost. Government and consortia efforts to acquire content had failed, resulting in a lack of access to key material for scholars. Equally, local content about

Rwanda was lacking, making it harder to establish a baseline of knowledge on which to build research. The local publishing industry was hardly developed. Many materials used in learning were not adapted to the local context, because they were produced outside the country. Library collections focussed on printed material; there were problems collecting and organising local cultural materials. Researchers were not motivated to report results in ways to have an impact on policy.

5 Discussion and Conclusion

Regarding the first research question, we find that the Rwandan librarians' perceptions of the research challenges for Rwanda appear to align quite strongly with the in-country deficit perspective, recognising the role of weak researcher motivation and support, and poor infrastructure. Most of the findings emphasize the material (e.g. resources and finance), human capacity, infrastructural and institutional barriers for African scholarship to engage with global research networks. Such a view suggests that there is something specific about the Rwandan context that can account for a lack of engagement in research in-country and in broader networks. Furthermore, there is an implication that the solution would be that of addressing such shortfalls in-country. It apportions the 'blame' to the country itself. It is important, however, to determine if the problem is situated locally or is part of a more systemic issue, within which this context can be placed. In the case of Rwanda, the participants highlighted certain cultural norms and language policies that could be seen as specific to Rwanda and influential on the development of the research context, and they are non-trivial. The extent of their influence, however, could also be seen as part of broader systems and structures influencing Rwandan scholarship. The colonial heritage of this country, for example, to some extent has exacerbated issues related to learning and publishing in the English language.

Less obvious from these findings were the systemic and structural considerations of the imbalances in the scholarly communication system and continuing neocolonialism. As librarians, participants were certainly aware of the inequities of the scholarly communication system although their roles placed them in the paradoxical position of having to promote access to international literature despite the obvious barriers this presented. Within their institutions, they also faced systemic pressures of "low status", which translated into an inability to change the status quo, and powerlessness to satisfy their user community, e.g., in gaining access to Research4Life articles behind the paywall.

Amongst the data we collected, there was less awareness of the kind of trenchant analysis offered from the epistemic injustice perspective. By definition, librarians' role is to promote access to content within the existing system. In this context, any African library's attempts to promote literacy is in danger of being seen as supporting linguistic imperialism (Canagarajah and Ben Said 2011). The Rwandan Librarians' views emphasised the way that the "normal" of a Global North research system does not exist in their country. Therefore, the usual premises about how research works also do not hold. At every step, the researcher was hampered compared to their counterparts in the Global North. If we accept that the problematic research context is only partly locally situated (with respect to specificities of the context) but more broadly influenced by the systemic and structural issues explored in the scholarly communications system and cognitive injustices perspectives, then we can start to think of ways in which these issues can be addressed, for example, through open science.

We now turn to the second research question about whether open access and the broader concept of open scholarship have the potential to improve the condition of Rwandan research. While our participants were not uncritical of the scholarly communication system, which is the focus of the reform proposed in open science, they did not see the problem as lying primarily here. Rather, they tended to see the issue through the in-country deficit perspective, which is not deeply touched by the reforms proposed by open science. Open science does little to address the under-investment in research, workloads of scholars or costs they incur. This is apparent if we compare the mapping of issues to the research lifecycle in Table 1, to the representation of open scholarship mapped to the lifecycle as by Grigorov et al. (2016), we can see there are many gaps where open scholarship does not address the fundamental issue in the African context. In this sense, open science does not seem to have immediate value for Rwanda.

Furthermore, current conceptions of open scholarship developed in the Global North fail (not surprisingly perhaps) to challenge the dominance of English language publishing or seek to open up to alternative epistemologies (Hillyer et al. 2017). However, within the epistemic injustices perspective a different model of open scholarship does have some resonance. If open science implies breaking down the barrier between science and citizens, then it does address the key failure that this perspective identifies within African scholarship: the gap between African research modelled on patterns from the global North and its potential publics (Nkoudou 2015). This is not necessarily utopian but to truly work would require many significant shifts. The strands of thinking within open science that give emphasis to democratisation of access and participation would need to come to the fore. In addition, a shift in thinking around the construction of the local research system would be needed. African governments would have to invest more in research and use this to promote research into local issues and local knowledge. Universities would have to give staff more time for research. They would need to give greater status to publication in local journals, in local languages. This would increase local engagement with research by policy makers and citizens. Rather than forcing researchers to operate within the existing scholarly communication system, always working at a relative disadvantage, they would need to commit to a very different model of scholarship. An eagerness in the global north to truly hear different voices in research might be one very positive factor in achieving such change.

In conclusion, our contribution to this debate has been to propose a way of resolving the conflicting discourses on the role of open science in making African (or Global South, more generally) scholarship more visible by illustrating how reframing a dominant in-country deficit perspective through different lenses can offer alternative and more context-specific solutions.

References

Albagli, S.: Open science in question. In Albagli, S., Maciel, M.L., Abdo, A.H., (eds) Open Science, Open Issues, pp. 9–26 (2015). https://www.academia.edu/15431919/Open_Science_Open_Issues

Ahinon, J., Havemann, J.: Open Science in Africa - Challenges, Opportunities and Perspectives. Elephant in the Lab (2018)

Andrews, N., Okpanachi, E.: Trends of epistemic oppression and academic dependency in Africa's development: the need for a new intellectual path. J. Pan Afr. Stud. 5(8), 85 (2012)

Beaudry, C., Mouton, J. (Johann), Prozesky, H. (eds.): The next generation of scientists in Africa. African Minds, Cape Town, South Africa (2018)

Boshoff, N.: Neo-colonialism and research collaboration in Central Africa. Scientometrics 81(2), 413–434 (2009)

Canagarajah, S., Ben Said, S.: Linguistic imperialism. In: Simpson, J. (ed.) The Routledge Handbook of Applied Linguistics. Taylor & Francis (2011)

Chan, L., Okune, A., Sambuli, N.: What is open and collaborative science and what roles could it play in development? In: Albagli, S., Maciel, M.L., Abdo, A.H. (eds) Open Science, Open Issues, pp. 27–57. IBICT, Unirio, Brasilia, Rio de Janeiro (2015)

Chan, L.: Asymmetry and Inequality as a Challenge for Open Access – An Interview with Leslie Chan, (Interview by Joachim Schöpfel). Litwin Books (2018). https://tspace.library.utoronto.ca/handle/1807/87296

Chan, L., Gray, E.: Centering the knowledge peripheries through open access: implications for future research and discourse on knowledge for development. In: Smith, M.L., Reilly, K.M.A. (eds.) Open Development: Networked Innovations in International Development, pp. 197–222 (2013)

Collins, C.S., Rhoads, R.A.: The World Bank, support for universities, and asymmetrical power relations in international development. High. Educ. 59(2), 181–205 (2010)

David, P.A.: The historical origins of "open science": an essay on patronage, reputation and common agency contracting in the scientific revolution. Cap. Soc. 3(2) (2008)

Dlamini, N.N., Snyman, M.: Institutional repositories in Africa: obstacles and challenges. Libr. Rev. 66(6–7) (2017)

Fecher, B., Friesike, S.: Open science: one term, five schools of thought. In: SSRN (2013)

Fonn, S., et al.: Repositioning Africa in global knowledge production. Lancet 392(10153), 1163–1166 (2018)

Grigorov, I., et al.: Research Lifecycle enhanced by an 'Open Science by Default' Workflow, April 2016. https://www.rri-tools.eu/-/research-lifecycle-enhanced-by-an-open-science-by-default-workflow. Accessed 29 Feb 2020

Guerrero-Medina, G., et al.: Supporting diversity in science through social networking. PLoS Biol. 11(12), e1001740 (2013)

Gwynn, S.: How can we strengthen research and knowledge systems in the Global South? Access to research in the Global South: reviewing the evidence 44(1106349), 1–23 (2019). www.inasp.info

Haider, J.: Openness as Tool for Acceleration and Measurement: Reflections on Problem Representations Underpinning Open Access and Open Science. Library Juice Press (2018)

Hecht, F., Hecht, B.K., Sandberg, A.A.: The journal "impact factor": a misnamed, misleading, misused measure. Cancer Genet. Cytogenet. 104(2), 77–81 (1998)

Herb, U., Schöpfel, J. (eds.): Open divide: Critical Studies on Open Access. Library Juice Press (2018)

Hillyer, R., Posada, A., Albornoz, D., Chan, L., Okune, A.: Framing a situated and inclusive open science: emerging lessons from the open and collaborative science in development network. In: Chan, L., Loizides, F. (eds) Expanding Perspectives on Open Science: Communities, Cultures and Diversity in Concepts and Practices, pp. 18–33 (2017)

Levin, N., Leonelli, S., Weckowska, D., Castle, D., Dupré, J.: How do scientists define openness? Exploring the relationship between open science policies and research practice. Bull. Sci. Technol. Soc. 36(2), 128–141 (2016)

LERU: Open Science and its role in universities: a roadmap for cultural change LEaGUE OF EUROPEan RESEaRCH UnIVERSITIES (2018) https://ec.europa.eu/research/openscience/index.cfm

Miles, M.B., Huberman, A.M.: Qualitative Data Analysis (Second). Sage (1994)

Milne, P.: Scholarly communication: crisis, response and future: a review of the literature. Aust. Acad. Res. Libr. **30**(2), 70–88 (1999)

National Academies of Sciences: Open Science by Design: Realizing a Vision for 21st Century Research (2018). https://doi.org/10.17226/25116

Ngongalah, L., Niba, R.N., Wepngong, E.N., Musisi, J.M.: Research challenges in Africa – an exploratory study on the experiences and opinions of African researchers. BioRxiv, 446328 (2018)

Nkoudou, T.H.M.: Stratégies de valorisation des savoirs locaux africains : questions et enjeux liés à l'usage du numérique au Cameroun [Strategies for valuing African local knowledge: issues and challenges related to the use of digital technology in Cameroon]. Ethique Publique **17**(2) (2015). https://journals.openedition.org/ethiquepublique/2343

Nwagwu, W.E.: Open access initiatives in Africa - structure, incentives and disincentives. J. Acad. Libr. **39**(1), 3–10 (2013)

Nyamnjoh, F.B.: 'Potted plants in greenhouses': a critical reflection on the resilience of colonial education in Africa. J. Asian Afr. Stud. **47**(2), 129–154 (2012)

Ondari-Okemwa, E.: Scholarly publishing in sub-Saharan Africa in the twenty-first century: challenges and opportunities. First Monday **12**(10) (2007)

Piron, F., Dibounje Madiba, M.S., Regulus, S.: Justice cognitive libre accès et savoirs locaux. [Cognitive justice, free access and local knowledge] (2016). https://zenodo.org/record/205145/files/Justice-cognitive-libre-accès-et-savoirs-locaux-15écembre2016.pdf?download=1

Rappert, B., Bezuidenhout, L.: Data sharing in low-resourced research environments. Prometheus **34**(3–4), 207–224 (2016)

Raju, R., Adam, A., Powell, C.: Promoting open scholarship in Africa: benefits and best library practices. Libr. Trends **64**(1), 136–160 (2015)

Walker, D., Steinfort, P., Maqsood, T.: Stakeholder voices through rich pictures. Int. J. Manag. Proj. Bus. **7**(3), 342–361 (2014)

Digital Innovation by Displaced Populations: A Critical Realist Study of Rohingya Refugees in Bangladesh

Faheem Hussain[1]([⊠]), P. J. Wall[2] ⓘ, and Richard Heeks[3] ⓘ

[1] Arizona State University, Tempe, USA
faheem.hussain@gmail.com
[2] ADAPT Centre, School of Computer Science and Statistics,
Trinity College Dublin, Dublin, Ireland
wallp2@tcd.ie
[3] Center for Digital Development, University of Manchester, Manchester, UK
richard.heeks@manchester.ac.uk

Abstract. We are living in a time of unprecedented human displacement both within countries and across international borders. The United Nations High Commissioner for Refugees (UNHCR) notes that the number of displaced populations are on the rise, both internationally and within individual countries, with this resulting in a wide range of significant international development challenges. If some of these challenges are to be addressed by technology, an understanding of the manner in which displaced persons access and interact with technology and the conditions necessary for digital innovation in such contexts is vital. This paper adopts a critical realist-based philosophical approach and associated methodology to seek the underlying generative mechanisms that both enable and restrain digital innovation by Rohingya refugees in Bangladesh. The majority of these Rohingyas have severely restricted access to technology as well as practically non-existent access to the Internet. Despite this, innovation in the form of creation and sharing of digital content in mobile phone repair/recharge shops has flourished. This paper provides mechanism-based explanation of this particular form of digital innovation, with a total of three mechanisms being hypothesized as follows: 1) the communications and technological infrastructure built around the mobile phone shops; 2) the motivation and social, cultural, and political belief structures of the Rohingyas themselves; and, 3) the legal and technical infrastructure which applies to the Rohingyas in the refugee camps in Bangladesh.

Keywords: Rohingya · ICT4D · Critical realism · Myanmar · Bangladesh · Refugee

1 Introduction

Wide scale displacement of people is fast becoming one of the most critical challenges for humanity. According to the UNHCR approximately 71 million people were displaced, either locally or internationally, at the end of 2018 [1]. A growing number

© IFIP International Federation for Information Processing 2020
Published by Springer Nature Switzerland AG 2020
J. M. Bass and P. J. Wall (Eds.): ICT4D 2020, IFIP AICT 587, pp. 54–65, 2020.
https://doi.org/10.1007/978-3-030-65828-1_5

of problems created by these crises are also surfacing which are more long-term and developmental in nature instead of being the more traditional, short-term humanitarian crises we have become used to. Some information and communications technology (ICT) enabled preliminary-level development interventions for such displaced groups show promise. However, very little research has been undertaken on this multifaceted topic with the majority of research being confined to a certain geolocation or ethno-identity. Our initial observations show that the majority of these proposed ICT solutions for refugees are significantly context specific and have limited scope to scale up or be used for other challenges. We believe that in order to build a stronger body of scholarship in this domain additional in-depth research examining underlying systems and processes is needed. In addition, a comprehensive understanding of the manner in which displaced people access, interact, and innovate using technology is critically important in order to document, analyze, understand and design possible future iterative and scalable interventions.

1.1 Background of Rohingyas

The Rohingyas are originally from Myanmar and are recognized as one of the most persecuted ethnic groups in the world. Rohingyas have suffered through various atrocities over the past decades including being stripped of their citizenship status in Myanmar due to the discriminatory policies taken by successive governments since that country's independence from the British in 1945. In addition, they have been consistently discriminated against by the army-led administrations in Myanmar with very limited access to education, health, and other basic human rights. All of this, accompanied by ever-increasing levels of hostility and violence towards their community over the past decades, has resulted in a mass exodus of Rohingya from Myanmar. Approximately 400,000 Rohingya refugees were living in Bangladesh before this mass exodus began in 2017, with current estimates putting the Rohingya population in Bangladesh at 1.3 million. The vast majority of these Rohingyas live in refugee camps and have little access to technology or the Internet [2].

1.2 Challenges with ICT and Internet Access for Rohingyas

The government of Myanmar has placed severe restrictions on the use of ICT by Rohingyas. By law Rohingyas are not allowed the use of any ICT with the exception of non-smart or feature phones, and any Rohingyas caught with a smart phone in their possession are subject to severe sanction and punishment [3]. Added to this is the tradition that Rohingya women should not access technology and are likely to be admonished within their own social groupings if they have ownership of any digital devices or phones [4]. To make matters even worse, the ICT infrastructure in Rakhine state in Myanmar where many Rohingya originate is considered to be quite poor.

Bangladesh, the new refuge for the majority of Rohingya refugees, had the potential to offer relatively better ICT access and services. However, this potential was never realized and any Rohingya who wishes to purchase a SIM card in Bangladesh is required to provide official identification and their biometric information to service providers in order to prove legal status in the country. Unfortunately, the vast majority of Rohingyas, especially the ones who arrived in Bangladesh after August 2017, are highly unlikely to have any such legal documents in their possession and this automatically excludes them from obtaining mobile data and voice services legally in Bangladesh. The Government of Bangladesh has tried to address this lack of access to technology and connectivity among Rohingya refugees in a number of ways, but many of these initiatives have been ineffective or unsuccessful. One example is the provision of free telephone booths in different parts of the major refugee camps, but these have been rarely used. These ineffective initiatives, combined with the poor ICT infrastructure in the south-eastern part of Bangladesh where all the Rohingya camps are located, make getting access to any kind of technology or Internet connectivity very challenging indeed.

1.3 Overcoming ICT Challenges and Restrictions

The first outcome of the restriction of mobile phones and Internet usage among Rohingya refugees in Bangladesh was the rapid rise of the illegal SIM market within the various refugee camps. According to our research, the majority of the Rohingyas procured Bangladeshi SIM cards through the black market with the help of a variety of people, mainly ethnic Rohingyas who had previously gained Bangladeshi citizenship. We also found that the refugees consistently paid significantly more than a Bangladeshi citizen for accessing mobile data and other mobile voice related services. In the refugee camps near the border of Myanmar a significant number of refugees carry multiple active SIMs with them which are capable of accessing both Bangladeshi and Myanmar mobile network services. This is because the signal strength of Myanmar's telecom companies is stronger in this particular region of Bangladesh. Hence, such practice became standard in order to ensure constant connectivity between the Rohingya refugee population both within and outside Bangladesh.

By the first quarter of 2018, the overall situation in all the major Rohingya refugee camps had become more stable and organized in terms of access to food, shelter and healthcare. This was when Rohingyas started to more strongly express their multifaceted needs to communicate with others and for accessing various localized information. Around the same period, we witnessed the growth of a support structure for mobile phone repairing and recharging which was in sync with the ever-increasing use of mobile phones by Rohingyas (which was technically illegal). Such supports were primarily provided through numerous small mobile phone repair/recharge shops managed by young Rohingyas and financially supported by local entrepreneurs. This was important for a variety of social and economic reasons as within the refugee camps there are not many opportunities available to young male Rohingyas in the form of education, employment, or entertainment. As a result, these mobile phone shops have become popular hangout places for this particular demographic.

1.4 Services Offered by the Mobile Phone Shops

A typical mobile phone shop offers two to three services as follows: 1) mobile phone repair for both smart and non-smart phones; 2) mobile phone recharging; and 3) the transfer of audio-visual data from a shop's laptop or phone to client's memory card or phone. In addition, we saw the relatively bigger shops sell other products including refurbished mobile phones, memory cards, earphones, mobile chargers, various mobile phone accessories, small and medium sized solar panels, solar lamps, etc. Other services such as photocopying, scanning, printing, laminating, and printing wedding cards were some of the other services provided by the mobile phone shops.

These shops also offer a variety of mobile phone repair services, with the majority of the shopkeepers having had prior technical training and some of them receiving assistance in setting up their services from the host community experts. However, according to almost all the repair personnel and their customers, the level of service provided in the refugee camp areas is very basic and the price range is capped at around BDT 200 (US$2.50).

Due to the lack of electricity in the camp areas, recharging a modern mobile smartphone is a huge challenge. This task is made even more difficult during the monsoon season as the majority of the solar lamps used for domestic purposes become too weak to charge a mobile phone due to the relative lack of sunlight during daytime. Hence, recharging phones is a steady earning source for all the mobile phone shops with each of the shops offering multiple power supply sources including solar panels, car batteries, power banks, and diesel-powered generators. The price for charging a phone is strictly regulated by the shop owners across the camps at approximately US$0.12 for charging any phone completely. In addition, in order to avoid confusions with mobile phone ownership, the shopkeepers came up with their own two-point verification system for verifying ownership of the mobile phones.

1.5 Digital Innovation and an Alternative Internet: Acquisition and Transfer of Audio-Visual Content by Mobile Phone Shops

The third and arguably the most digitally innovative service offered by the mobile repair/recharge shops is audio-visual digital content transfer which we frame as an alternative Internet. As mentioned earlier, due to the restriction on owning mobile phones and accessing the Internet for Rohingyas, there has always been a huge demand for good quality information and entertainment among the refugee communities. It is also worth noting that Rohingyas do not have any official written script based on the newspapers, books, or other literary materials they use. Hence, culturally appropriate audio-visual content among this particular community in their newly adopted host country has become increasingly significant. Despite this, the humanitarian agencies and other NGOs working for the betterment of Rohingyas have mostly prioritized services on physical health, hunger, and shelter related issues over creation and supply of digital news and entertainment content customized for Rohingya consumption. This has led to a dearth of such culturally appropriate services and audio-visual content, which was quickly and organically filled by the mobile phone shops. Each of the shops is usually equipped with at least one laptop and a number of hard drives loaded with a wide variety of audio-visual content. As already mentioned, poor internet connectivity and restricted access to technology means that Rohingyas in Bangladesh are unable to access such content online or in real time. In order to circumvent this lack of access, short audio and video clips on Rohingya related news, reports, and features are being downloaded and saved on the mobile phone shop's laptop and hard drives. This content is then transferred to the customers mobile phone for a small fee.

This highly organized network of digital audio-visual content providers facilitates the supply of up-to-date and relevant content for Rohingyas on a regular basis. This network is mainly comprised of Bangladeshi entrepreneurs who first download the content using high speed Internet which is widely available outside the camp areas in bigger cities like Cox's Bazar and Chittagong. This content is then collated and transferred to mid-sized mobile phone shops on the outskirts of the refugee camps. From there, the mobile phone shop owners from the camps go to these intermediary shops and procure content based on local demand. On average, a 500 GB hard drive filled with downloaded audio-visual entertainment including news and various religious sermons can be sold for approximately US$5. According to our research, the mobile phone shopkeepers' collection frequency of newer content ranges from one to four times per month depending on the level of demand for the content.

2   A Critical Realist Philosophical Approach and Methodology

This section briefly presents the philosophical approach adopted for this research and the associated methodology.

2.1   Field Data Collection Method

We collected field data for this research from various field visits between November 2017 and August 2019. Data was collected at refugee camps within the Kutupalong, Balukhali, Leda, and Teknaf areas of Cox's Bazar district in Bangladesh. During this period, we conducted interviews and focus group discussions with around 200 people including Rohingya refugees, local NGO workers, Government officials, and international humanitarian officials. Furthermore, we conducted around 100 h of participatory observations and contextual inquiries. We faced numerous challenges while collecting the data from the Rohingya refugee camps. With the exception of law-enforcement agency people, no non-Rohingya refugee people were allowed to stay or work in the camp areas after sunset, thus forcing us to leave the camp areas by 4 pm daily. Moreover, as evidenced from our findings, the majority of the areas where we conducted our research did not have any mobile phone service coverage. Such obstacles made our observation and data collection processes significantly more difficult.

2.2   Critical Realism, Mechanism-Based Explanation, and ICT4D

As already mentioned, this research adopts a philosophical approach based on critical realism [5, 6], with the methodology being adapted from Wall et al. [7]. Importantly, the paper answers the call for the increased use of critical realism in ICT4D research as made by Heeks and Wall [8] who suggest that such an approach has many advantages for the field. In addition, this research used the basic principles proposed by Hussain and Brown [9] who utilized a critical realist philosophical approach in collecting in-depth field data and insights from ICT driven grassroots development initiatives in Rwanda and Bangladesh.

A critical realist-based approach is highly relevant to this research as it can enable us to identify the underlying causal mechanisms which both cause and prohibit the digital innovation in the Rohingya refugee camps as described in the proceeding sections of this paper. This has not been done previously and we could find no similar research which carries out a critical realist, mechanism-based exploration of digital innovation in this context. We thus view this as a significant contribution to the ICT4D literature. Moreover, the hope is that this work can create a broader research agenda which seeks mechanism-based explanation in other refugee and internally displaced person (IDP) contexts.

2.3 The Philosophy of Critical Realism

This section will give a brief explanation of critical realism in an attempt to provide some degree of context for this research. Should you wish to delve deeper into this philosophy we refer you to the more extensive works of Bhaskar [5, 6], Archer [10] and Mingers [11]. For those more interested in the application of critical realism to the field of ICT4D we refer you to the recent special edition of the Electronic Journal of Information Systems in Developing Countries (EJISDC) on "Critical Realism and ICT4D Research" as published in 2018 (volume 84, issue 6).

Put simply, critical realism asserts that elements of an independent reality exist through three separate levels of stratification. This stratification is represented as three nested domains as proposed by Bhaskar [5] and represented by Mingers [11] in Fig. 1 below. The research questions posed by this research seek underlying causal mechanisms, but these mechanisms reside in the domain of the Real and we as human beings do not have the ability to perceive them. The Actual domain contains events, and the domain of the Empirical contains the events that we as humans are able to experience.

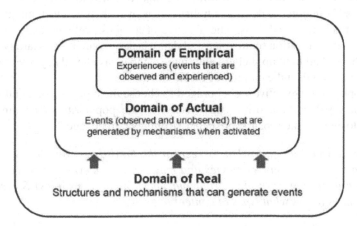

Fig. 1. Three overlapping domains of reality in the critical realist ontology [11]

A variety of technical definitions are available in the literature for these phrases: mechanisms are causal structures that generate observable events [12], and events are specific happenings resulting from causal mechanisms being enacted in some social and physical structure within a particular context [13]. The concept of retroduction is also key to any critical realist-based methodology [5] and requires the researcher to take some unexplained phenomenon and propose hypothetical mechanisms that, if they existed, would generate or cause that which is to be explained [11]. In other words, we as researchers seek causal mechanisms but we can only perceive the events which are in the Empirical domain. Thus, we must retroduce (or hypothesize) the mechanisms that exist in the Real from the events that reside in the Empirical.

Over the past years a variety of methodologies have been developed to achieve this retroductive process. As already mentioned, this paper relies on the methodology as developed by Wall et al. [7] who leverage Margaret Archer's [10] morphogenetic approach. The first step in this methodology is to create a factual case description and a chorological account of events in as much detail as possible. This can be done from interview data, but also from other qualitative methods such as observation and document analysis. From this, the theorization of mechanisms can occur when causal influences in social structures, interactions and relationships have been identified. This is discussed in Sect. 3.2 below.

3 Discussion and Analysis

3.1 Factual Case Study Description and Chronological Account of Events

As mentioned, we conducted a variety of in-depth interviews and focus group discussions between November 2017 and July 2019. This data was then used to create a factual case description and a chorological account of events in as much detail as possible. Some quotes from the data collected are given below in order to provide context for the retroduced mechanisms which follow. The objective was to cover as many diverse shops as possible in order to develop a holistic view of such digital technology centered businesses in adverse conditions. The absence of a robust, reliable and legal mobile network for communication (both voice and data), lack of content and scarcity of power to charge phones and light up shelters within the camp areas played key roles behind the establishment, growth and evolution of these shops.

The shopkeepers are actively encouraged to choose the types of content they would like to populate their hard drives with based on the popularity of certain content. According to one mobile repair shopkeeper (Rohingya, male, age 26);

> "At first we were not sure what to keep in the hard drive. But now we know. We bring new collections (of movies and music video) in every other week from Ukhiya bazaar (a big marketplace right outside the main camp areas). Sometimes, the customers tell us what types of content to bring."

On the demand side, a typical Rohingya customer usually purchases a memory card of 4 or 8 GB which costs between US$2 and US$5 and then transfers the content he chooses onto that memory card. For each such transfer, the customer pays around US$0.50.

In general, the nature of the audio-visual content can be divided into four broad categories: news, entertainment, religious sermons, and education. For many years, Rohingya refugees living in Malaysia, Middle East, Europe, and the USA run news channels based on YouTube and other social media platforms. Rohingya refugees living in the camps access this digital content mainly through memory card transfers. In some cases, when there is mobile network signal available within the refugee camp area Rohingyas share these news clips via WhatsApp, imo, or WeChat with their peers and family members. Similarly, a clear pattern of preferences and popularity emerged when we analyzed the contents on the laptops of the 15 representative mobile phone shops.

When it comes to entertainment, we found that Indian, Pakistani, American, Arabic, Burmese, and Turkish movies, music, and dance videos are in high demand. In many cases, these programs are somewhat unprofessionally dubbed with Rohingya language. Aside from that, Bangladeshi dramas and music videos are also very popular. Religious sermons (of religious scholars belonging to Rohingyas, Bangladesh, etc.) are also very popular. One customer (Rohingya, male, age 32) stated;

"I miss listening to Rohingya Tarana (music). I come to this shop all the time to get new collections of Rohingya Tarana."

Unfortunately, we found content of some of these sermons to be fear mongering, belligerent and filled with false information. On a smaller scale, we found short videos containing educational instructions in the Rohingya language covering issues on the opening of new social media accounts, healthcare, etc. These videos are made by the expat Rohingyas and started getting disseminated via the mobile shops and the Internet.

Besides the demand and supply chain that emerged out of the demand for audio-visual content in camp areas, we observed a strong demand of digital content created inside the camps by the refugees themselves, mostly among the expat Rohingya groups based in South East Asia, Australia, Middle East, and Europe. These contents are also developed and distributed using the same network of mobile phone repair shops, other mid-size shops, and bigger shops with Internet connectivity.

As a whole, the entire network of gatekeepers engaged in collecting, creating, localizing, and distributing audio-visual content for Rohingyas works similarly to the Internet. The mobile repair/recharge shop laptops and hard drives are full of options and the Rohingyas have clear agency to choose, buy, and watch or listen to whatever they would want or need to. For a population persecuted for decades, and for whom the regular internet or mobile network is officially illegal, such options seem like a welcoming change. One user (Rohingya, male, age 24) mentioned;

"We can access the songs and videos we like from this shop and then can watch those with our family. I don't have access to the Internet. But I am using my smart phone and memory card to get what I want from this shop. I am happy."

However, a significant gender imbalance exists with relation to existing services and customers of this alternative network of content and communication in the Rohingya camps. Rohingya women, who are around 55% of the Rohingyas recently arrived in Bangladesh, are not directly benefitting from the mobile repair/recharge shop-based content network. One middle-age Rohingya women (age 39) told us:

"We watch the videos of songs, dramas, and movies our sons share with us. We don't download those or buy such things from others."

This can be partially explained by the attitude of the patriarchy and the religious leadership of Rohingya towards women (especially the younger ones) using mobile phone or the Internet. All the senior and married women respondents in our study believe that it is a "problem" if young, unmarried women get access to mobile phones and the internet. One Rohingya women (age 43) mentioned:

"It's not acceptable for the young women to talk on the mobile phone. There are many crank calls coming for our girls. That is unacceptable."

When we asked different male respondents about their perceptions of women using ICTs or accessing mobile repair/recharge shops, the reactions were almost unanimous. Rohingya males, be they religious or community leaders, young, senior, literate, or illiterate, all agreed on the fact that women should not have a lot of access phones or the internet, and they should not be in any mobile repair/recharge shops. A prominent religious leader (age 50) explained the boundaries or limits of Rohingya women's ICT usage by saying:

"Women can talk over phone, but they should not be allowed to use the phones."

That respondent, along with others during the same conversation further explained that it is okay for the married women to have access to phones in order to ensure food and other relief for their families. However, women should not use it for some other reasons, and most importantly,

"...young and unmarried women should never use mobile phones or the internet."

3.2 Retroduction of Causal Mechanisms

The first step in the methodology as developed by Wall et al. [2] is prepare a factual case study description and a chronological account of events in as much detail as possible. This is then used to empirically identify discrete and separate cycles in the case. From our data we identified three cycles as follows:

1. The "exodus from Myanmar to Bangladesh" cycle (pre-August 2017 to December 2017). This cycle includes the exodus of the Rohingya to Bangladesh because of persecution in Myanmar and takes into account the very poor access to technology and Internet connectivity available to them during that time.
2. The "inception of frugal digital innovation" cycle (January 2018 to mid-2018). This cycle includes the hope for better access to technology and Internet connectivity in Bangladesh, and the ultimate loss of hope when this didn't happen. It also includes the way Rohingyas managed to get access to technology and Internet connectivity and the beginning of the alternative Internet and the mobile phone repair/recharge shops.

3. The "Expansive and increasingly Inclusive Digital Innovation" cycle (mid-2018 to mid-2019). This cycle includes increased access to technology and improved Internet connectivity (because of pressure from UN/NGOs/INGOs to open up mobile and Internet services). Additionally, included is the massive growth in mobile phone repair/recharge shops. As the situation in the refugee camps settled there was also a massive increase in demand for localized content, with this demand being met by the mobile phone repair/recharge shops.

Each of these 3 distinct cycles were then analyzed to produce analytical histories of emergence [10]. Analytical histories of emergence are retroductive, corrigible accounts of sociological transformation over time which are never final because we can always improve on our explanations as more or better data becomes available. These analytical histories of emergence then formed the basis for retroduction. The resulting retroductive process produced a total of three generative mechanisms which are discussed in the following section.

4   Causal Mechanisms Which Explain Digital Innovation Rohingya Refugee Camps

This section briefly presents the three generative mechanisms that were retroduced from the analytical history of emergence, with the first of these mechanisms being discussed in brief. The three mechanisms are as follows:

1. The communications and technological infrastructure built around the mobile phone shops. This mechanism includes what we frame as the alternative Internet where digital audio and video content was downloaded and distributed.
2. The motivation as well as the social, cultural, and political belief structures of the Rohingyas themselves. This includes the attitude towards women having access to technology, the desire to access news and entertainment content of relevance, and the desire to keep in contact with disperse family and other social networks.
3. The legal and technical infrastructure which applied to the Rohingyas in the refugee camps in Bangladesh. Important here were the attempts by the Bangladeshi authorities, under pressure from the UN and other various NGOs and INGOs, to open up mobile and Internet services.

The space restrictions imposed by this paper prohibit a detailed discussion of all three mechanisms, but we do discuss the first of these retroduced mechanisms, i.e. the communications and technological infrastructure built around the mobile phone shops. This mechanism includes all elements of the way the mobile phone shops operate, including the communication structures between the people who downloaded the audio-visual digital content, the mobile phone shop owners and operators, and the final customer who purchases the digital content. An important component of this mechanism is the communication structures that operated within and between the various parts of this supply chain and the way this evolved over time as the Rohingyas were able to access more advanced technology and smartphones. This mechanism also includes elements of

Bangladeshi Government policy to maintain a stable communication network and the legacy technological needs of the Rohingyas themselves.

This mechanism had the important effect of creating an environment where the mobile phone shops could flourish both socially and financially. Another important effect was the creation of a strong and stable social structure where young Rohingya males could gather and socialize. This is important as these young males mostly ran the mobile shops and made up the largest customer demographic. It also gave confidence to those willing to invest their time and money in establishing the shops (mainly Bangladeshi nationals and Rohingyas living in Bangladesh for many years) which was a vital component needed for the long-term viability of the shops themselves.

5 Summary

This research adopts a critical realist philosophical and methodological approach to uncover underlying causal mechanisms which identify why digital innovation occurred in the way that it did in the Rohingya refugee camps in Bangladesh. A total of three causal mechanisms were retroduced, and these mechanisms explain how the interaction of different structural, cultural and agency factors have influence in this particular context. Although we suggest the communications and technological infrastructure built around the mobile phone shops mechanisms is the most important mechanism in this case, it should be noted that all three mechanisms are important and all together go towards explaining why the conditions necessary for digital innovation and the alternative Internet evolved and developed in the way they did. Our belief is that such mechanism-based explanation allows a theoretically informed and empirically rich account of how context and mechanism interact to produce this specific outcome in this specific case.

As a result of this research we add our voices to the recent calls by many scholars for an increased amount of critical realist-based research and mechanism-based explanation [7, 14, 15]. In particular, we call for this approach and methodology to be used for additional research on displaced persons and refugees. The hope is that such mechanism-based explanation will play an important part in promoting a wider research agenda which seeks such mechanism-based explanation in similar cases.

References

1. UN Refugee Agency UNHCR: Figures at a Glance (2019). https://www.unhcr.org/ph/figures-at-a-glance
2. Hussain, F.: Digital Access Isn't a Luxury for Refugees. Slate (2018a). https://slate.com/technology/2018/06/digital-access-isnt-a-luxury-for-refugees-its-a-necessity.html
3. Hussain, F.: Bangladesh Should Legalize SIM Cards for Rohingya Refugees. Freedom House (2018b). https://freedomhouse.org/article/bangladesh-should-legalize-sim-cards-rohingya-refugees
4. Hussain, F.: Network shutdowns in Rohingya camps: how they're damaging the fragile information ecosystem of refugees from Myanmar". Access Now (2019). https://www.accessnow.org/network-shutdowns-in-rohingya-camps-how-theyre-damaging-the-fragile-information-ecosystem-of-refugees-from-myanmar/
5. Bhaskar, R.: A Realist Theory of Science. England, Harvester Press, Hassocks (1975)

6. Bhaskar, R.: The Possibility of Naturalism. Brighton, Harvester (1979)
7. Wall, P.J., Lewis, D., Hederman, L.: Identifying generative mechanisms in a mobile health (mHealth) project in sierra leone: a critical realist framework for retroduction. In: Nielsen, P., Kimaro, H.C. (eds.) ICT4D 2019. IAICT, vol. 552, pp. 39–48. Springer, Cham (2019). https://doi.org/10.1007/978-3-030-19115-3_4
8. Heeks, R., Wall, P.J.: Critical realism and ICT4D research. Electron. J. Inf. Syst. Dev. Ctries. **84**(6) (2018)
9. Hussain, F., Brown, S.: Developing a comparative framework of ICT4D initiatives in the global South: a critical realist approach. Electron. J. Inf. Syst. Dev. Ctries. **84**(6), e12055 (2018)
10. Archer, M.S.: Realist Social Theory: The Morphogenetic Approach. Cambridge University Press, Cambridge (1995)
11. Mingers, J.: Re-establishing the real: critical realism and information systems. Soc. Theory Philos. Inf. Syst. **372**, 406 (2004)
12. Henfridsson, O., Bygstad, B.: The generative mechanisms of digital infrastructure evolution. MIS Q. **37**(3) (2013)
13. Williams, C.K., Karahanna, E.: Causal explanation in the coordinating process: a critical realist case study of federated IT governance structures. MIS Q. **37**(3), 933–964 (2013)
14. Heeks, R., et al.: Critical realism and ICT4D: editorial introduction to the special issue of EJISDC. Electron. J. Inf. Syst. Dev. Ctries., e12050 (2018)
15. Thapa, D., Omland, H.O.: Four steps to identify mechanisms of ICT4D: a critical realism-based methodology. Electron. J. Inf. Syst. Dev. Ctries. **84**(6), e12054 (2018)

A Post-colonial Analysis of Agile Software Development Methods in ICT4D

Scarlet Rahy$^{(\boxtimes)}$ ⓘ, David Kreps ⓘ, Julian M. Bass ⓘ, Tarek Gaber ⓘ, and Abdulhamid Ardo ⓘ

University of Salford, Greater Manchester, UK
S.Rahy@edu.salford.ac.uk
http://www.salford.ac.uk

Abstract. There is evidence that agile approaches to information system development can improve product quality and developer productivity. However, successful adoption of these approaches appears to depend on adaptation to specific contexts. This research contributes to a broader goal to understand what it means to "be agile" in the presence of adaptations to the specific context.

To pursue our research objectives, we have performed 31 semi-structured recorded and transcribed practitioner interviews from three companies in Lebanon. The interview transcripts were analysed using an approach informed by grounded theory.

Agile methods enable learning and improvement through team conversations. Yet, the practitioners in our study shun public self-evaluation, finding it difficult to discuss areas for improvement in public. We also found legacy "top down" management practices that undermine team autonomy and local client companies lack experience of engaging with agile processes. In a more positive vein, we found evidence of rich use of various communications channels to overcome geographical distance.

On the one hand, agile methods represent a "northern" idea being propagated to the Global South. And yet, on the other hand, the agile concept of self-organising teams has the potential to be empowering and emancipatory. Post-colonial theory helps us understand the phenomenon of agile tailoring, where development process ceremonies are adapted to suite a specific local context.

Keywords: Southern theory · Post-colonial theory · Information systems development · Agile methods · Agile method tailoring

1 Introduction

Southern and post-colonial theories seek to look at the world from a non-Euro or US perspective. This leads to either the explicit celebration of indigenous theories, or the critique of euro-centric notions from a Southern perspective. Our aim to is to apply post-colonial theory to a challenge in information systems development in ICT4D in order to investigate what lessons can be learned.

© IFIP International Federation for Information Processing 2020
Published by Springer Nature Switzerland AG 2020
J. M. Bass and P. J. Wall (Eds.): ICT4D 2020, IFIP AICT 587, pp. 66–77, 2020.
https://doi.org/10.1007/978-3-030-65828-1_6

Agile methods are an emerging approach to conducting ICT4D implementations that rely on iterative and incremental project deployment. Agile methods encourage self-organising teams in which developers acquire responsibility for several aspects of development projects normally assigned to project managers.

Our hypothesis, derived from previous research is that "agile methods can enhance software product quality and developer productivity in ICT4D." However, this is only possible when successfully adopted and yet adapted to the specific context. The research questions we have identified for this study, are:

1. What can a critique, using post-colonial perspective, reveal about information system development methods?
2. What challenges do we face in using a post-colonial perspective? And,
3. What can a post-colonial perspective reveal about adaptation to a specific context of information system development methods?

In order to further our research objectives, we have employed an illustrative case study on the adoption of agile software methods in Lebanese small and medium sized companies. We conducted 31 semi-structured, open-ended, recorded and transcribed practitioner interviews, in three companies from four locations in Lebanon. The interview transcripts were analysed using a approach informed by grounded theory.

The rest of the paper is structured as follows. First we present a review of related research in agile software development. Next, we introduce our theoretical perspective based on post-colonial theory. We then discuss our research methods, focusing on research sites, data collection and data analysis. Next, we present our findings from practitioner interviews in Lebanon. We then interpret our findings in a discussion section. Finally we present conclusions, recommendations and references.

2   Agile Methods in Information Systems Development

Agile methods are a family of information system development methods that comprise iterative and incremental approaches [10]. Iterative development methods are cyclic, usually comprised of fixed-length time-boxes, during which a cycle of activities is performed. Incremental development build system functionality in a series of end-to-end functional component.

Agile methods are best described in terms of roles, ceremonies and artefacts. The roles in scrum comprise self-organising teams [16], product owners [1] and scrum masters [21]. Ceremonies are the practices and activities performed by stakeholders when performing agile methods. In scrum, ceremonies include sprint kick-off, daily stand-up meetings [29], customer demonstrations and spring retrospectives. These practices enable the orchestration of the agile software development process. Artefacts are the entities created by stakeholders during the development process (broadly defined) [2].

2.1   Tailoring Agile Methods

Agile software development methods, such as scrum and Extreme Programming (XP), were introduced under the assumption that they could be used in developing any type of project [6]. However, there are many failures in developing software using agile methods [5]. Responding to this problem, the idea of tailoring agile methods emerged where agile methods can be adapted to fit a development context such as culture or organization needs [5].

In the context of software process, software tailoring method is defined as "the adaptation of the method to the aspects, culture, objectives, environment and reality of the organisation adopting it" [5]. Such adaptation is practical as almost all software project development is unique [8]. This means deciding a software development method depends on many factors: technical, organisational or human as well as the project nature. Consequently, it is difficult to find a software development method that is most effectively adopted as it was originally suggested in textbook format [8]. Software organisations could further tailor agile methods in order to fit their country culture, values and strategies [20,23].

To tailor an agile method, there are two main approaches: Method Engineering and Contingency Factors [5]. The Method Engineering approach makes use of meta-method processes to create a new method by using existing method fragments. The new method is developed following all software development activities related to building a software. On the other hand, tailoring software methods using the Contingency Factors approach is handled by selecting multiple existed methods and making them available to the organisation. Thus, during the development process, the method selection is achieved based on factors such as uncertainty level, impact and structure of the project being developed [5].

2.2   Agile Methods in ICT4D

Studies have investigated agile methods adoption in Kenya [15], Ethiopia [23] and Egypt [20]. Whereas, in Kenya where an offshore/onshore collaboration model was employed, in Ethiopia and Egypt, practitioners were adopting agile methods with little prior first hand experience. The stakeholders, in Egypt and Ethiopia, thought there might be some benefit to gained from agile methods because of reports in the grey literature and practitioner community word-of-mouth knowledge transfer.

3   Theoretical Model

There has been a surprising paucity of theory building underlying ICT4D [25]. Dominant research approaches have included interpretative stances [30]. Analysis in cultural studies identified how Europe came to view the rest of the world through the prism of colonialism and empire [24]. Orientalism makes a striking contrast, in terms of attitudes and actions, towards "east" and "west."

More recently, Orientalism has informed a post-colonial branch of critical management theory [14]. The study of imposition of management practices, productivity models and processes has been seen as a form of Americanization [12]. The binary "east/west" dichotomy has splintered into a rich and hybrid set of realities [13].

A colonial lens has been used to understand the relationship between multi-national companies and their subsidiaries [19]. This ethnographic study observed the appropriation of technical knowledge and innovation which flowed from the subsidiary toward the multi-national company's overseas headquarters. Indigenous innovation conducted in an off-shore resource constrained setting has been appropriated into the private ownership of an onshore corporation.

Post-colonial theory has been used to examine the phenomenon of off-shoring in the digital economy [22]. Three main schools of thought can be identified [22]. Firstly, Orientalism [24], which rests on Foucault's [11] discourse analysis, and an appreciation of the asymmetric power relations between post-colonial countries and their former colonial masters. Secondly, a school of thought around the 'subaltern' notion developed most notably by Gayathri Spivak [27,28]. 'Subaltern studies' focus on the 'voiceless' in global society, and the technologies of rule that maintain structures of poverty [26]. Thirdly, a school of thought that argues that the asymmetries are not "one-dimensional and one-sided as suggested by Said [but] inherently complex" [22]. This approach focusses on the complex hybrids that have developed out of the colonial era, producing syncretic mixes of practices from the different contexts of the colonised and the colonisers, and those who have been born and made their own lives and their own compromises in the complex hybrid environments that have resulted [4].

Beyond these three strands, Southern theory is a more recent contribution than post-colonial theory, that focusses on the possibilities of critical thinking taking place in, of, and about the Global South. In this view, those living in the Global South are all too often intellectually subalternised by the universal character of theoretical understandings originating in the Global North [7,9,18]. The rediscovered pre-colonial theoretical traditions of indigenous peoples, alongside newly Global Southern gaze of later descendants of the colonisers, may look back upon the Global North with a critical eye of its own tenor.

This Southern Theory approach, we argue, when considered in tandem with the hybridity of Bhabha, suggests that the complex mixes of pre-colonial tradition, colonial imposition, and post-colonial adaptation, may produce unique customisations of otherwise Globally Northern impositions, and that this process may in fact be requisite both for successful adoption and for effective integration of new technologies and practices in various parts of the world.

4   Research Methods

This research employs a qualitative case study, with a unit of analysis comprise a set of software development practitioners employed in three Lebanese companies.

4.1   Research Sites

There is a paucity of large software development companies in Lebanon. Thus, we chose to sample research sites from small and medium-sized software development companies. Three research sites were chosen from a range of companies that implemented agile methodology in Lebanon. To protect their anonymity, the three sites were labelled LEB1, LEB2, and LEB3. LEB1 is a Lebanese based software development company having three branches in Lebanon. Its main headquarters is in Mount Lebanon and the other two branches are located in North Lebanon and Bekaa Valley. LEB1 provides solutions in areas of insurance, academics, technology, analytics, and banking for clients in Lebanon and abroad. LEB2 is software development company located in Beirut. It is specialized in developing technological solutions and digital transformation for its local and international clients. LEB2 also provides customized software consulting services. LEB3 is a software development company located in Mount Lebanon. LEB3 develops software, applications, and websites for its clients.

4.2   Data Collection

In-depth research interviews were conducted with 31 practitioners. The semi structured interviews were conducted in English and lasted around 40–50 min each. The interviews were recorded and transcribed. The interview respondent job titles and affiliations are available online [3]. The interviews were conducted face-to-face, apart from five which were conducted using Skype due to an outbreak of civil unrest on appointed date. A semi-structured interview guide was used. Open-ended questions were used to seek out indigenous topics from respondents. Probing questions were used to encourage depth in the responses.

All the interview transcripts were analysis using an approach informed by grounded theory. The transcripts were uploaded to the NVIVO (v11) qualitative data analysis tool [17]. The transcript data was first coded. Topics evident in the data, on a sentence-by-sentence basis, were identified. Then the codes, from different interview subjects were compared. This constant comparison technique was used to contrast the code across the respondent population. Memo writing was then used to collect the different perspective on codes from different respondents. Thus, the memos were used to represent higher-level categories identified within the data.

5   Findings

The following section presents the analysis of data collected from our case study. The findings discuss a critique of agile implementation in a post-colonial perspective. The findings reveal four main points: rejection of retrospectives, effective communication between teams, limitation of self-organizing teams by hierarchy, and Complications faced when dealing with Lebanese clients.

5.1 Teams Rejecting Retrospectives

Practitioners find it difficult to self-evaluate their performance in front of the entire team. Practitioners fear public self-evaluation and undermine its effectiveness. Retrospectives are defined as meetings held at the end of each sprint iteration during which, team members reflect on the whole sprint and their performance. Consequently, practitioners indicated that they do not perform retrospectives which is a vital ceremony in agile. S1 explained: "We do not do retrospectives; we don't have formal evaluations." Practitioners fear public self-evaluation may cause loss of their job, hinder any promotions and undermine their position in front of colleagues. For instance, S3 explained: "If I admit my mistake in front of the whole team, I am afraid I might lose my job." Thus, practitioners would rather talk directly to the team manager and try to solve the issue covertly. A2 explained: "The problem is that there is always people who resisted talking because they were afraid that colleagues will undermine them." In addition, practitioners undermine the effectiveness of self-evaluation. Practitioners expressed how they know their responsibilities and the need to complete them. A6 expressed: "I feel everyone is self-aware. Thus, I find it useless to do retrospectives." In addition, there are misconceptions about retrospectives and their purpose. Practitioners lacked a clear understanding of what retrospectives are and their team learning purpose. Practitioners excluded retrospectives from analysing the whole team's effectiveness, celebration of its successes, and acknowledging openings for improvement. Instead of labelling a whole session for team performance evaluation, team leaders tend to encourage team members to perform this evaluation during bi-weekly meetings. V3 explained: "During our bi-weekly meetings we open indirectly the floor to learn from our mistakes. We learn from each other so that we would face the same things." Thus, team leaders would ask evaluation questions without labelling the whole session as a way to encourage members to assess their performance.

5.2 Communication Status

Communication is highly encouraged at the agile implementing software development companies. Diverse communication channels are open for employees. Weekly face-to-face meetings are held specifically for each project and reports are shared with all stakeholders. At the end of the week, the project manager sends a report indicating project progress to all involved teams. V4 highlighted the importance of delivering the message regardless of the technology used: "The target is that they deliver the message not the medium."

Initially, all information was supposed to be communicated through e-mail to all members involved. V3 explained: "Initially everyone was supposed to communicate in a written manner and involve everyone." This was deemed necessary in order to deliver the message and respect the institutional hierarchy. Gradually, practitioners started communicating through messaging platforms and then orally. They were training to communicate everything and involve everyone which lead to a smooth and practical communication in the development projects.

Face-to-face communication is always present among members who are in the same geographical location. When practitioners need to communicate and are present in different geographical locations, they use online video conference platforms. Communication across the diverse geographical location in Lebanon is very smooth. Our definition of geographically co-located teams differs from the conventional definition. Our co-located teams are distributed in the same country but are faced with challenges such as different culture, tradition, and religion which highly affects the person's character in Lebanon. Members do not feel the need to physically visit the different branches instead they will join virtual meetings.

The usage of communication channels depends on the needs and message being delivered. Most practitioners rely on non-written communication; as V8 expressed: "Verbal is the most common way of communicating." Especially if it is a simple update. Instant messaging platforms are also used. V4 explained: "Sometime, I have to send just an informal message so I use WhatsApp." Teams also hold meetings to update all stakeholders and send emails and reports to everyone involved. This communication strategy enables team members to communicate effectively and thoroughly.

5.3 Restrictions of Self-organizing Teams by the Hierarchy

Hierarchy is embedded in the institutional arrangement and individual organization in software development companies. The roles assigned to practitioners, such as project manager and director, reveal that hierarchical structure is entrenched in the institutions. This leads to high levels of bureaucracy which may hinder the development process. V17 claimed: "We find that we are in a bureaucracy box; It consumes a lot of time to get one thing approved."

The hierarchy affects the teams and restricts teams from becoming self-organizing agile teams. Allocation of tasks by managers, time estimations by product owners, and micromanaging of upper management limit the development of self-organizing teams. First, managers and team leaders are responsible to assign the tasks to the team members. V7 explained: "We assign the global tasks for each team and then each team leader will assign the tasks to his/her team." This creates occasional tension between team leaders and project managers from one side, and team members from the other. Team members prefer to choose their tasks. As A7 describes: "I dislike the idea that our leaders allocate the tasks." S6 added: "It would motivation if I chose my open tasks from each sprint."

Second, the time estimation for each project is performed from all the involved departments. The first high level estimation is done by scanning the requirements. Understanding the task consumes time and requires effort prior to implementation. Time estimation is performed by product owner and team leaders which may lead to inaccurate evaluation of the time required for task completion.

Third, dealing with the pressures of the upper management is one of the main challenges faced by employees. Practitioners revealed how the CEO micro-managed the process. A7 explained: "The CEO micro-managed and inter-fered in every single detail." The CEO wanted to know the details of every project in the daily morning meetings. These meeting will last longer than advised and team leaders weren't able to conduct their own stand-up with their team mem-bers. A4 explained: "It was impossible for me to do that again with my team."

5.4   Lebanese Clients vs Western Clients

The mangers expressed the difference in working with different clients. They characterized them into two groups: the Western clients, North America and Western Europe, and Lebanese clients. Managers felt that it is easier to work with the Western clients in comparison to the Lebanese clients. V4 explained how transparency is key when dealing with the Western market: "Working with Western market, is easy. What you have to do is to be transparent and say things as they are. Working with the Lebanese market is much harder."

This is due to several factors pointed out by the mangers. First, the West-ern clients value time and provide a logical estimate for task completion. V2 explained: "In their business culture, they are committed to the set dates. Also, they are very reasonable in discussing the time required to complete each prod-uct." Lebanese clients tend to put unrealistic deadlines for their suppliers. Sec-ond, they are structured, well organized, and cooperative. V3 explained: "They did their due diligence by preparing the requirements. And they work with you in order to have their work done properly and with high quality. You will not find them as clients you'll find them as partners." Third, they have a collab-orative nature and seek to have a successful product. V14 said: "If you have something a bottleneck in certain place and you give the good argument, they will understand and they will help you solve it." Fourth, Western clients are specific about their requirements. V4 explained: "They know exactly what you can do and what they have want. They know their budget and give you the righteous amount for your work."

On the contrary, dealing with Lebanese clients was harder and less efficient. Delays in project time affect the client, as well as the software development company that is keeping resources dedicated for a certain project longer than planned. The coming paragraphs explain several reasons why agile software development companies find difficulty in achieving results with Lebanese clients.

Lebanese clients show low levels of responsiveness to the requests from the software development company. This causes major delays in the due date. A3 explained: "The collection of data was the most difficult part." V3 expressed how clients delay in presenting the required information: "The client will delay in answering back our requirements to get their feedback. So this will lead us not to meet a deadline at a certain point." With clients responding poorly, gathering needed information was a challenging process. A1 explained a case where their client was a university in Lebanon and the project was delayed: "We knew that the educational system is slow by design but we weren't expecting 3 months of delay. Every time we requested data or a specification it would take days and weeks for them to respond." Practitioners indicate how they try to find innovative ways to keep the client engaged and motivate the client to respond promptly. A1 expressed: "We have to sometimes create ways to put pressure like sending emails, calling and texting in the same day."

Managers expressed how certain Lebanese clients stated their initial commitment to the development process, but through the development, the clients' enthusiasm decreased and their commitment became minimal. V2 claimed: "Lebanese client's availability and commitment of staff is not always as promised."

In addition, employees at the clients' premises may show resistance to change and feel threatened by it. V14 explained: "Some employees resist the change because our solutions are seen as a threat. You're taking my work they would say." Lebanese clients are not familiar with the software development industry thus they are threatened by it. So they tend to resist the suggested changes. According to V2: "Some will just try to punch holes in the solution being developed for them."

6   Discussion

In this research we explore the conflicting trade-offs between adoption and tailoring of agile information systems development methods. On the one hand, agile methods originate in the Global North. Hence, agile methods represent a "northern" idea being propagated and adopted in the Global South. On the other hand, self-organising teams are empowering and emancipatory. Agile is about taking power away from managers and putting more responsibility into the hands of self-organising software development teams.

The research around agile tailoring is predicated on the assumption that methods must be adapted to the local context [5]. Conventionally, agile method tailoring tends to focus on factors such as business domain, technology stack and project characteristics (such as project scope or size and disposition of teams).

Our approach here, in contrast with conventional agile method tailoring, has been to address agile tailoring from an ICT4D perspective. So our perspective is not "how should Lebanese software development practices change in order to adopt agile methods" but rather "what adaptations to agile methods are required to achieve success with the approach in developing countries."

RQ1: What can a critique, using post-colonial perspective, reveal about information system development methods?

Our study suggests that agile development needs to expand its corpus of basic frameworks. Agile tailoring should consider the cultural setting in which it is implemented. We suggest, a post-colonial reading of agile information systems development adds important dimensions to our understanding of agile tailoring. While one may argue that the differences between small and medium-sized software companies in the South are more significant than the difference between small software companies in the North and South, we advocate that the difference in agile methods adoption vary, using post-colonial theory, according to Global North and South perspective.

RQ2: What challenges do we face in using a post-colonial perspective?

We found that post-colonial theory, and Southern theory more generally, is a substantial body of research. While the concepts around hybridity in post-colonial theory are helpful, we did not see many previous attempts to apply this to informations system management.

RQ3: What can a post-colonial perspective reveal about adaptation to a specific context of information system development methods?

We found that retrospectives, as described by the agile methodology, were rejected when introduced to practitioners in Lebanon. Culturally, practitioners are not comfortable with public self-evaluation or criticism. Thus, even though retrospective is a major agile ceremony, it is difficult to apply.

We know a lack of end-user involvement is challenging for agile organisations. Practitioners revealed how dealing with Lebanese clients is harder and less efficient than dealing with clients from the USA. Using post-colonial theory, we can say the Lebanese practitioners in our study successfully mimicked agile actions with "Western" clients. But the same mimicry action revealed potential negative impact on the relationship with the Lebanese clients who are not used to such involvement in the developing process.

Hence, we suggest the main contribution to knowledge arising from our research is that post-colonial theory offers new insights into agile method tailoring. Specifically, we propose that conceptions of tailoring needs to look beyond project-specific characteristics and consider wider contexts.

We have enhanced the rigour of this research by collecting a substantial corpus of data and conducting detailed and thorough analysis. However, all interview-based research suffers the drawback that is relies on self-reporting from respondents. We have used triangulation, of different roles and companies, to mitigate this. But we have been able to directly measure the impacts of agile methods on product quality or developer productivity.

7 Conclusions

In this research we have adopted a post-colonial stance, in order to understand the conflicting trade-offs between the adoption and tailoring of agile information system development methods. We concede that on the one hand, agile methods are a "northern" or "Western" innovation being copied and adopted around the world. And yet, on the other hand, agile methods undermine hierarchical management models and offer opportunities for empowerment within software development teams. Agile methods have been shown to have the potential for improved productivity and product quality.

To investigate these conflicting influences, we have undertaken a case study in three software development companies in four locations within Lebanon. Lebanon is emerging as a regional centre for outsourced software development in the middle east and gulf states. We conducted 31 semi-structured, open-ended, recorded and transcribed practitioner interviews.

The practitioners in our study struggled with the public self-evaluation mechanisms that agile method advocate for team learning. Also, we found local business clients were not well-informed about participation in agile projects. On the other hands, we found practitioners adept at using a rich variety of communication methods for overcoming geographical distance.

While agile tailoring is not a new concept, it has predominantly focused on project characteristics in the past. We think the post-colonial perspective presents a new and original framing on the tailoring concept by placing agile methods in a wider "Southern" context.

We are currently investigating adaptation of selected agile ceremonies to better suite the Lebanese context. We will then observe the challenges faced and any benefits achieved.

References

1. Bass, J.M., Haxby, A.: Tailoring product ownership in large-scale agile projects: managing scale, distance, and governance. IEEE Softw. **36**(2), 58–63 (2019)
2. Bass, J.M.: Artefacts and agile method tailoring in large-scale offshore software development programmes. Inf. Softw. Technol. **75**, 1–16 (2016)
3. Bass, J.M.: Agile Software Development in Lebanon, February 2020. https://doi.org/10.17866/rd.salford.11887824.v1
4. Bhabha, H.K.: The Location of Culture, 2nd edn. Routledge Classics, Abington, Oxon (2004)
5. Campanelli, A.S., Parreiras, F.S.: Agile methods tailoring - a systematic literature review. J. Syst. Softw. **110**, 85–100 (2015)
6. de Cesare, S., Patel, C., Iacovelli, N., Merico, A., Lycett, M.: Tailoring software development methodologies in practice: a case study. J. Comput. Inf. Technol. **16**(3), 157–168 (2004)
7. Comaroff, J., Comaroff, J.L.: Theory from the South. Routledge, Abingdon, Oxon (2012)
8. Conboy, K., Fitzgerald, B.: Method and developer characteristics for effective agile method tailoring: a study of XP expert opinion. ACM Trans. Softw. Eng. Methodol. **20**(1), 2:1–2:30 (2010)
9. Connell, R.: Using southern theory: decolonizing social thought in theory, research and application. Plann. Theory **13**(2), 210–223 (2014)
10. Dingsøyr, T., Nerur, S., Balijepally, V., Moe, N.B.: A decade of agile methodologies: towards explaining agile software development. J. Syst. Softw. **85**(6), 1213–1221 (2012)
11. Foucault, M.: Archaeology of Knowledge, 2nd edn. Routledge, London (2002)
12. Frenkel, M., Shenhav, Y.: From Americanization to colonization: the diffusion of productivity models revisited. Organ. Stud. **24**(9), 1537–1561 (2003)
13. Frenkel, M., Shenhav, Y.: From binarism back to hybridity: a postcolonial reading of management and organization studies. Organ. Stud. **27**(6), 855–876 (2006)
14. Goss, J.: Postcolonialism: subverting whose empire? Third World Q. **17**(2), 239–250 (1996)
15. Haxby, A., Lekhi, R.: Building capacity in Kenya's ICT market using cross-border scrum teams. In: Choudrie, J., Islam, M.S., Wahid, F., Bass, J.M., Priyatma, J.E. (eds.) ICT4D 2017. IAICT, vol. 504, pp. 359–366. Springer, Cham (2017). https://doi.org/10.1007/978-3-319-59111-7_30

16. Hoda, R., Noble, J., Marshall, S.: Self-organizing roles on agile software development teams. IEEE Trans. Software Eng. **39**(3), 422–444 (2013)
17. QSR International: NVivo qualitative data analysis software. https://www.qsrinternational.com/nvivo/home
18. Kreps, D., Bass, J.M.: Southern theories in ICT4D. In: Nielsen, P., Kimaro, H.C. (eds.) ICT4D 2019. IAICT, vol. 552, pp. 3–13. Springer, Cham (2019). https://doi.org/10.1007/978-3-030-19115-3_1
19. Mir, R., Mir, A.: From the colony to the corporation: studying knowledge transfer across international boundaries. Group Organ. Manage. **34**(1), 90–113 (2009)
20. Mohallel, A.A., Bass, J.M.: Agile software development practices in Egypt SMEs: a grounded theory investigation. In: Nielsen, P., Kimaro, H.C. (eds.) ICT4D 2019. IAICT, vol. 551, pp. 355–365. Springer, Cham (2019). https://doi.org/10.1007/978-3-030-18400-1_29
21. Noll, J., Razzak, M.A., Bass, J.M., Beecham, S.: A study of the scrum Master's role. In: Felderer, M., Méndez Fernández, D., Turhan, B., Kalinowski, M., Sarro, F., Winkler, D. (eds.) PROFES 2017. LNCS, vol. 10611, pp. 307–323. Springer, Cham (2017). https://doi.org/10.1007/978-3-319-69926-4_22
22. Ravishankar, M.N., Pan, S.L., Myers, M.D.: Information technology offshoring in India: a postcolonial perspective. Eur. J. Inf. Syst. **22**(4), 387–402 (2013)
23. Regassa, Z., Bass, J.M., Midekso, D.: Agile methods in Ethiopia: an empirical study. In: Choudrie, J., Islam, M.S., Wahid, F., Bass, J.M., Priyatma, J.E. (eds.) ICT4D 2017. IAICT, vol. 504, pp. 367–378. Springer, Cham (2017). https://doi.org/10.1007/978-3-319-59111-7_31
24. Said, E.W.: Orientalism. 25th Anniversary Ed with 1995 Afterword Ed Edition, Penguin Books, London (2003)
25. Sein, M.K., Thapa, D., Hatakka, M., Sæbø y.: A holistic perspective on the theoretical foundations for ICT4D research. Inf. Technol. Dev. **25**(1), 7–25 (2019)
26. Masiero, S.: Subaltern studies: advancing critical theory in ICT4D. In: Twenty-Sixth European Conference on Information Systems (ECIS 2018), Portsmouth, UK, vol. 162, pp. 1–13. Association for Information Systems (2018)
27. Spivak, G.C.: Can the subaltern speak? In: Nelson, C., Grossberg, L. (eds.) Marxism and the Interpretation of Culture. University of Illinois Press, Urbana, Reprint Edition, October 1987
28. Spivak, G.C.: A Critique of Postcolonial Reason: Toward a History of the Vanishing Present. Harvard University Press, Cambridge (1999)
29. Stray, V., Sjøberg, D.I.K., Dybå, T.: The daily stand-up meeting: a grounded theory study. J. Syst. Softw. **114**, 101–124 (2016)
30. Walsham, G.: Doing interpretive research. Eur. J. Inf. Syst. **15**(3), 320–330 (2006)

Education and Health

The Adoption of Mobile Health (mHealth) Services by Internally Displaced Persons (IDPs) in Nigeria

Dolapo Bilkis Gbadegesin[(✉)] and Olumide Longe

American University of Nigeria, Yola, Adamawa, Nigeria
dolapo.gbadegesin@aun.edu.ng

Abstract. This study operationalized the unified theory of acceptance and use of technology (UTAUT) to study the attitudes and opinions of internally displaced persons (IDPs) in Malkohi host community Yola, to mHealth if deployed to support their healthcare and health information needs. Findings from the research revealed that the IDPs have a positive behavioral intention towards mHealth technology, which could then lead to its adoption. The study also unveiled new constructs such as "Language" and "No Tariff" which are more vital determinants of the IDPs attitude towards mHealth than the original UTAUT constructs. These newly discovered constructs were added to modify the UTAUT to make it a suitable framework to check attitudes and opinions of IDPs towards mobile health (mHealth).

Keywords: Mobile health · mHealth · UTAUT · Internally displaced persons · IDPs

1 Introduction

Nigeria has a high population of displaced persons living in the country. The major reason for this is the Boko Haram insurgency that has been plaguing the country for almost a decade, with this terrorist group having carried out most of their attacks in the North East region of Nigeria leaving more than 2 million people displaced (Gwadabe et al. 2018). These displaced people seek refuge in IDP camps and host communities, the living conditions of these people having been very well explored in literature and has been stated to be deplorable. The relief items donated and distributed by humanitarian agencies and health care services and information are found to be inadequate, as a result of the overcrowding situation in these camps (Eme et al. 2018). The studies that have been conducted on IDPs in Nigeria have mainly revolved around their living conditions, their plights, physical health conditions, mental health, causes of their migration, educational needs, psychological needs and various other needs (Eme et al. 2018; Gwadabe et al. 2018; Okon 2018; Owoaje et al. 2016). The health problems of these displaced persons in the camps is one of the issues that is stated in almost all the literature reviewed on

© IFIP International Federation for Information Processing 2020
Published by Springer Nature Switzerland AG 2020
J. M. Bass and P. J. Wall (Eds.): ICT4D 2020, IFIP AICT 587, pp. 81–92, 2020.
https://doi.org/10.1007/978-3-030-65828-1_7

IDPs in Nigeria. However, research has not comprehensively covered possible solutions to their lack of adequate healthcare and health information (Owoaje et al. 2016).

Patil (2019) on the role of ICT in the lives of refugees, recommends that we start viewing displacement problem as a development problem rather than just a humanitarian crisis. Thus, technological solutions are being explored in literature for refugees and IDPs to provide sustainable solutions to their plights and to allow them to create self-reliance opportunities. However, this area of research has not gained much popularity in the Nigerian context because the majority of the literature reviewed on refugees and ICT has been carried out in other countries and this has focused on addressing the issues of refugees. Mobile health provides the advantage of the use of mobile phones to provide medical health services to patients in remote areas. Based on the gaps identified from the foregoing, this study aims to explore the attitudes and opinions of IDPs to adopting mHealth technology to support their lack of adequate healthcare and health information. With this in mind, the research asks the following questions:

1. To what extent do IDPs utilize mobile phones?
2. What is the attitude and opinion of IDPs to mobile phones to provide for their health information needs?

The remainder of the paper is structured thus; Sect. 2 explains a brief history of the cause and current situation of IDPs in Nigeria. Section 3 highlights the theoretical foundation adopted for the study. Section 4 explains the research methodology and method of data analysis. Lastly, Sect. 5 explains the empirical evidence and findings, and Sects. 6 and 7 contain the contribution to knowledge and research conclusion.

2 Internally Displaced People in Nigeria

IDPs are people that have been forced to elope from their natural place of habitat or homes but are still within the borders of their country, while refugees are displaced people that have had to run beyond the borders of their county Gwadabe et al. (2018) to seek refuge in other countries. The population of IDPs in Nigeria as at 31st of December 2018 is 2,216,000 as reported by the Internal Displacement Monitoring Centre (IDMC 2018). Nigeria has the worst IDP situation in Africa which has made it become the third in the world after Syria and Columbia (Lenshie and Yenda 2016). Mukhtar et al. (2018) in their study stated that 80% of the IDPs in Nigeria are found in the North-eastern part of Nigeria according to The National Emergency Management Agency (NEMA). This high population of displaced persons in the North East region of Nigeria is as a result of the attacks from the Boko Haram terrorist group that has been ongoing in the country for almost a decade now.

The Boko Haram religious terrorist group started its attack against the Nigeria Government in 2009 in Maiduguri, Borno state (Gwadabe et al. 2018). Borno state is one of the North eastern states in Nigeria, it contains 27 local Government areas and about 20 of these local governments areas are controlled by the Boko Haram terrorist group with the Government controlling the remaining 7 (Sambo 2017). This provides evidence of the reason why Nigeria has such an overwhelming population of IDPs from the year 2009 because the population of people that are displaced due to natural disaster is only about 24%, with the other 12.6% being from the Fulani herdsmen crisis with farmers. The remaining 85% of the total population of IDPs in Nigeria are from the terrorist attacks in the North east (Nwaoga et al. 2017). Adamawa and Yobe state and other North Eastern states also have a high population of IDPs after Borno state with a distribution of 18%, 13% and 63% respectively. IDP camps were created for victims of these terrorist attacks in the local Government areas that are safe from the attacks. Such camps receive donations of relief items from well-meaning Nigerians, the Nigerian Government, International Government and humanitarian agencies (Nwaoga et al. 2017).

2.1 Technological Solutions for Refugees and IDPs

Considering the fact that the world has gone digital over the years, more people (old, young, literate or illiterate) are adopting information and communication technologies. Lewis and Thacker (2016) considers displacement as a continuous trend in the "21st century" and suggests that adequate preparedness should be made to meet the needs of this occurrence. Okon (2018) also suggests that the IDP situation in Nigeria is "recurring and large scale". Much research has been conducted on ways to provide solutions to the issues experienced by IDPs by making recommendations on Government policies to protect their rights, and also suggestion on the role of trained social workers as opposed to just volunteers (Chinwe and Oparaoha 2018). Patil (2019) recommends that the issue of displaced persons should also be seen as a "development problem" rather than just a "humanitarian problem" and also calls for more research to be done on the impact that technology would have on the lives of displaced people. Hence, the need to consider ICT solutions for the problems of displaced persons.

3 Theoretical Foundation

3.1 Unified Theory of Acceptance and Use of Technology (UTAUT)

The UTAUT theory was created through a combination of eight technology acceptance and motivation models which includes the TAM and DOI theories. In the early 2000's technology adoption in organizations became rapid. However, these technologies wouldn't have improved productivity if the users had not accepted the technology. Thus, research on technology acceptance became important and there were various types of theories and models from information systems research, sociology and psychology which researchers were adopting to measure users intentions to use a new systems. Researchers were also faced with the choice to decide among the various number of models, and found they had to pick constructs across the models or pick a "favoured model" which tended to overlook the contributions from other models. This situation prompted Venkatesh et al. (2003) to complete a study that reviewed and synthesized literature on user acceptance models to create a unified view of user acceptance theory. This model is presented in Fig. 1 below.

Gender, age, experience and voluntariness of use are used as moderating variables in the model but are not used in this study. Among the studies that utilize information

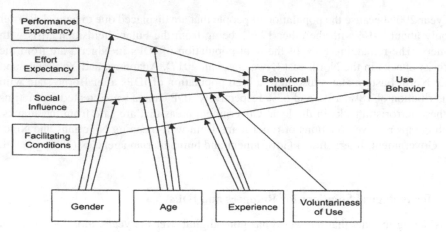

Fig. 1. The UTAUT model (Source: Venkatesh et al. 2003)

technology theories to review the components influencing the adoption of mobile health, the TAM model was utilized more than other models. Perceived usefulness (PU) and perceived ease of use factors (PEOU) in TAM are also very well represented in the UTAUT model as are performance expectancy (PE) and effort expectancy respectively (EE). The performance expectancy, effort expectancy and facilitating conditions from UTAUT are the best in predicting the adoption of mHealth technology as reported in a systematic literature review study on published articles from year 2004–2015 which was designed to discover the factors that influence users adoption of mHealth (Garavand et al. 2017). The UTAUT model is thus a combination of all major technology acceptance theories, and is considered a right fit for the study because it not only consists of constructs that have been tested to be adequate to measure users intentions towards the mHealth technology, but also because it has been reported to have a 70% accuracy rate on testing users intentions compared to other models (Hoque and Sorwar 2017; Garavand et al. 2017; Pheeraphuttharangkoon 2015).

Although the UTAUT model has gained a lot of popularity amongst researchers and its level of reliability is reported as being high, the model poses some limitations. In our study we were able to find out that the constructs of the UTAUT model are not all encompassing, and it required some modification to fit the context of our study. The original constructs of the UTAUT alone wouldn't have yielded a strong positive behavioral intention to adopt the mHealth technology if the new constructs (language and no tariff) were not included in the constructs; i.e. without the new constructs, the results may have shown that the IDPs might not be interested in adopting technology. This is a major limitation because it goes on to insinuate that the UTAUT model would always need modification when it's been used to investigate the intentions of individuals towards technology. In addition, "the original UTAUT model which was focused on large organizations in the business environment has caused an extensive discussion among researchers who contend that the UTAUT constructs alone may not be adequate to clarify user acceptance of new technology in a voluntary setting as its initial purpose of use limits its explanatory power" (Ali et al. 2016).

4 Research Methodology

4.1 Interpretivism

The interpretivist acknowledge that realities exist in the minds of individuals differently. They recognize that notions of "reality" exist in a social setting and that the most suitable method for understanding activities of social actors may not really be through numbers and thorough measurable tests. This view is explained by Roode (2003) who affirms that "the interpretivist scientist perceives that numerous significant issues identified with the improvement, use and execution of information systems personally concern individuals, and acknowledges that the social world exhibits a superior stage to consider these wonders than the simply material universe of technology."

This research has adopted a case study design with a qualitative method which includes observation, focus group discussions and interviews. The data collection process from the IDPs in Malkohi host community started on 9th September and was concluded on 1st October. Having spent some time on the field, we understood to some extent the way of life of the IDPs in that camp. They rely solely on authority in their decision-making process and are mostly united on all other fronts. The data gathering process started off by seeking permission from the host community chairman who is also an IDP, which led on to him being the first interviewee. He felt it was important to include and invite the 9 other elders who have spent the highest number of years in the host community and are very well knowledgeable about the happenings and needs of the community. This led to the focus group discussion that started our data gathering process. Although, the general opinions received from the people was that the response of the chairman and elders was sufficient for them and that he speaks the mind of the people, the researchers still obtained permission to go on with interviewing other participants for research credibility. The 20 other respondents of the interviews included 10 women and 10 men distributed across different age groups.

The participants were all fluent in only the Hausa language, so the data collection process was done with the help of an interpreter who was fluent in both English and Hausa. The interview questions were open-ended questions, with responses to each question interpreted during the discussion and interview process with notes being taken during this process. The community chairman gave an estimate that about one-third of the people in the host community use mobile phones, and they can make calls, receive calls, and also send text messages. A purposeful random sampling method was employed in recruiting other participants that were interested in participating in the study. These included men and women from different age groups that use and own mobile phones. Each interview took about 10–15 min, with a total of 30 participants interviewed. The researcher stopped the process after reaching a level of data saturation; i.e. when no new data was being received (Fusch and Ness 2015).

4.2 Method of Data Analysis

This study adopts a thematic analysis method of data analysis. Transcripts were transcribed manually into a Word document, and the transcribed data was read over and over again to produce a coherent understanding of the data. Notes on the first impression gotten from the data were taken, and the data was run through over again and then used to generate codes from the data. Code generation involves identifying and labelling relevant pieces present in the data, such as opinions, actions, activities, incidents, emotions etc.

The amount of data collected from interviews and focus group discussions was quite large and it was difficult to identify what was relevant to code. However, identifying codes can be done by probably considering a point that appears a couple of times within the data, including points that seemed important to the respondents and points that are new and can be an addition to the study. This also includes preconceived theoretical concepts or points that seem important to the researcher. These codes are then brought together for review to decide which ones are important and relevant to the study, with the codes identified as important then put together in categories or themes. This is done without bias with the codes and themes being strictly defined by the data. At this point the data is beginning to become conceptualized.

When the relevant themes are labelled and the relationships between them have been identified, the process builds the results of the study which provides new information about the world from the perspectives of the participants of the study. The connections between the themes can then be represented diagrammatically to create a thematic map. The results are then described, and this includes detailed descriptions of the themes and the connections between the themes. Also included are some scripts from the respondents which are used to support the results.

5 Empirical Evidence and Findings

This section examines the initial themes generated from the interview codes as derived from the research model. These themes can be seen on Table 1 below and are discussed in greater detail in the following sections.

5.1 Themes Description Based on the Dimensions of Research Model

Performance Expectancy
According to Venkatesh et al. (2003) "Performance expectancy is defined as the degree to which an individual believes that using the system will help him or her to attain gains in job performance". In this case, performance expectancy would refer to the degree to which IDPs believes that mHealth will help improve their current healthcare situation. The majority of the participants of the study believed that if they were provided an alternative to their current health situation, even if it is via a mobile phone, they were willing to accept it. There were also many complaints about the situation of the hospital in the camp. Apart from the host community where the study was conducted, there is another IDP camp very close by and they are also served by the same hospital and one doctor. Some respondents described situations where they have had to stay home throughout their sick days because there was no space for examination or admission in the hospital due to the large number of people seeking treatment at the same time. This

Table 1. Initial themes generated from interview codes

Mobile phone usage	Available healthcare in the host community	Alternative source of health care	Technology as an alternative
Low population of people with mobile phones (about one-third of the population)	1 hospital, 1doctor, Overcrowded	Specialist hospital	Receiving health information via mobile phones will be helpful
Phone calls are more common than text messages/Education barrier	Lack of expertise to treat some cases	Specialist hospital is far	Communication with the doctor for progress and follow up
Inability for some people to afford mobile phones	Lack of adequate drugs to serve the population	Very expensive, very few can afford it	Reduced cost of going to the specialist hospital
I can ask for help when I need to do other things on my phone	Lack of adequate bed spaces for patients	Difficult to return for follow up and check up	Diagnoses and immediate treatment, when the camp hospital is occupied
	Need for more support from the Government	Difficult for Pregnant and breastfeeding mothers to get adequate information	Source of information in emergency situations
			Receiving test results and feedback will be easier and cheaper

is usually common in the rainy seasons when they are more prone to all sorts of diseases, e.g. malaria.

Quite a number of respondents expressed their dissatisfaction about having to go to the specialist hospital for treatment because of the distance, and some of them mentioned they couldn't afford to go there at all and had to rely on whatever services the hospital on the camp provides. There have also been some situations where the doctor in the hospital on site was not equipped to handle some cases that had occurred in the camp and which needed immediate attention.

Effort Expectancy

According to Venkatesh et al. (2003) "Effort expectancy is defined as the degree of ease associated with the use of the system". As mHealth services are dispensed through mobile phones and other wireless devices, the basic phone calls and text messaging services are utilized in some mHealth initiatives. This study involved discovering the capabilities of the IDPs as regards the utilization of mobile phones. Thus, the study purposely chose samples of respondents that utilize mobile phones and would be able to relate to idea of mHealth technology. It should be noted that the population that use mobile phones are less than the population that do not have access to a mobile phone. This is mostly because some of them cannot afford a phone and furthermore some of them cannot use it. The majority of the respondents could however make and receive phone calls with their mobile phones without help, and the younger respondents are able to make calls, receive calls, send, read text messages as well as do other various things on their phones. This is because the younger respondents were more educated than the older respondents. However, the older respondents explained that they receive help from their children to operate the mobile phone when they need to do other things on their phones.

Social Influence

According to Venkatesh et al. (2003) "Social influence is defined as the degree to which an individual perceives that important others believe he or she should use the new system". This was an important factor in the study as the IDPs are people with similar experiences and are able to relate to each other's situation. They are a community of people that have being brought together through crisis and they have had to grow, survive, support, and protect each other on a daily basis. This has enabled them build trust amongst themselves as they always come together as a unit whenever there was a decision to be made about the happenings in the camp. Through this, they also select a representative of their community which is someone they believe has been around for the longest time, is trustworthy and also capable of making good decisions for them whenever the need arises.

Facilitating Conditions

It is suggested that "Facilitating conditions are defined as the degree to which an individual believes that an organizational and technical infrastructure exists to support use of the system" (Venkatesh et al. 2003). mHealth involves the use of mobile phones and mobile phone services, and this services also needs mobile network connectivity. The population of people with mobile phones was relatively low, and the only reliable mobile network is the Globacom network.

Language

This construct was added as a modification to the UTAUT model. This was done in order to check if this would also be a factor that could make a positive influence on the attitudes of the IDPs to the mHealth technology. As already stated, all the respondents in the study were only able to communicate fluently in Hausa language and only a few of the younger respondents declared their ability to understand and speak English. Thus, the general consensus was that they would be more comfortable if they could interact with their healthcare provider in Hausa. The available healthcare provider in the host community also communicates with them in Hausa, so they find it easier to explain their symptoms to him. This construct is considered a strong determining factor to the positive attitude of IDPs towards mHealth technology.

No Tariff

This is a new construct that was discovered during the process of conducting this study.

The Chairman of the camp was the first to raise concerns about this and he was supported by others during the focus group discussion. This then became an addition to the interview questions as everyone raised concerns about having to recharge their phones to utilize the mHealth technology. They complained about their struggle to feed and survive on a daily basis and expressed that it would be difficult to adopt the technology if they had to be recharging their phones all the time to make use of the service.

6 Discussion

The issues of IDPs in Nigeria is a problem which is yet to be provided with a solution. This is not because there has been no effort to find a solution, but because their population around the country continues to grow and has become too complex to manage. In Nigeria, extant studies have investigated the issues experienced by IDPs in the IDP camps. The solutions recommended in most these studies have been geared towards Government policies, but barely any study has been geared towards technological solutions for their plights. This is the research path followed by this work, with the study based on the quest to discover IDPs mobile phone use and their attitudes and opinions towards adopting mHealth technology. Healthcare is vital to society and this happens to be one of the major needs of the IDPs. This was established in extant literature and also confirmed during the course of this study. Many technology innovations have failed in the past as a result of the refusal of the users to adopt the technology, which is why technology acceptance theories were created in the social sciences to investigate users' intentions towards a particular technology. This study adopted the UTAUT model to analyze the attitudes and opinions of IDPs in the Malkohi host community, to mHealth technology, with the model being modified to fit the empirical situation. The findings from the study based on the theoretical foundation are discussed in the following sections.

Performance Expectancy
The healthcare situation in the Malkohi host community was found to be inadequate and the IDPs were interested in an alternative solution. The kidnappings and other life-threatening crisis that had occurred in the past to volunteers in the camp were explained to be a major reason why healthcare providers are scared to stay in the host community. Hence, they have had to make do with just one doctor that has been there since the invention of the camp, who is an indigene of the community, conversant with the environment, and is comfortable staying back to provide his services to the IDPs. However, the services provided are inadequate, the respondents of the study discussed some of their present situation which they think having access to a healthcare provider even if it is via a mobile phone will help solve these problems. Therefore, performance expectancy is a construct that would strongly influence the IDPs intentions to adopt mHealth technology.

Effort Expectancy
This a strong determinant of user's intentions to adopt a technology, if the effort needed to use a new technology is greater than what is existing users are most likely to reject the technology. Here, mHealth services can be provided through the basic phone calls and text messages. As mentioned, the IDPs have the ability to make and receive phone

calls and also to send and read text messages. Some of the respondents that stated that their mobile phone use ability is limited to making and receiving phone calls, and they also mentioned that they get help from their educated children to read and send text messages. This construct has a strong positive influence on the IDPs intentions to adopt the mHealth technology.

Social Influence
The circumstances in which the IDPs find themselves have made them dependent on each other. However, it has also built the trust which they have amongst themselves. Social influence is a construct that will have a strong positive influence on their intentions to adopt the technology. They believe that if other members of the community can use the technology they will also use it, with the chairman of the community being the most influential factor.

Facilitating Condition
A technology solution cannot be effective without existing infrastructures that will enable smooth operation of the technology. An example is the availability of network and mobile phones required to enable the mHealth technology. The findings from the study showed that Globacom network is the only reliable mobile network that is available in the host community, and this is a hindrance to the smooth operation of the mHealth technology. Also, as many of the IDPs cannot afford mobile phones the number of people that use mobile phones in the community is relatively few.

Language
This construct was introduced into the study due to the geographic location of the study site. The study confirmed that IDPs in the Malkohi host community mostly communicated through the Hausa language, with only a few of the younger participants of the study able to communicate using the English language. Despite this they were still of the opinion that they would be more comfortable if the healthcare providers could communicate in Hausa language. This was also found to be one of the strongest determinants that could positively influence the IDPs intentions to adopt the health technology.

No Tariff
This construct is the second strongest determinant of IDPs positive attitude towards the mHealth technology. They believe that the Government should provide support that makes such services free to them. This includes introducing mHealth services that require charges which are likely be rejected by the IDPs. This is because the IDPs are people that have been affected a crisis which has seized their means of livelihood. Although they attempt to survive in the new environment in which they find themselves, they are still living in deplorable conditions where the poverty rate is high. Thus, any technology that requires extra expenses would most likely not be used.

6.1 Additional Model Modification

The already modified UTUAT model was further extended/modified based on findings from the research by adding a "No Tariff" construct. This is because this construct was considered to be vital to the positive behavioral intention of the IDPs to accepting mHealth. Also, the opinions from the participants about the host community chairman being a very important influencing factor on whether or not any new technology would be accepted. Thus, leadership was added to the model as a moderating factor affecting the construct social influence (Fig. 2).

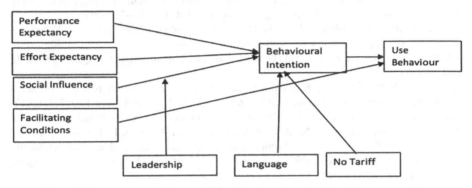

Fig. 2. Finding-based modified UTAUT model

6.2 Contribution to Theory and Practice

Our modified and extended UTAUT model can be applied in other studies that involve IDPs and technology acceptance. It has also contributed to the dearth of knowledge on technology solutions for IDPs in Nigeria, a research area that is gaining much prominence in other parts of the world. The study can also be a source of reference to the Government and non-governmental organizations (NGOs) on alternative ways to provide supports to address the issues of IDPs in Nigeria.

7 Discussion

As previously mentioned, the problem of refugees and IDPs should be seen as a devel-opment issue and not just a humanitarian issue. This is why technological solutions are being recommended for the needs of the IDPs in this case. This study aimed to make recommendations of technology solutions for IDPs by exploring their mobile phone use and their attitudes and opinions towards mHealth technology. Adopting the previously described research approach, findings shows that IDPs have a positive behavioral inten-tion towards the mHealth technology. The findings also revealed new constructs which became a modification to the original UTAUT model and are considered to be the more vital constructs to determine the successful adoption of mHealth by IDPs.

References

Ali, T., Mazen, E.-M., Maged, A., Alan, S.: Extending the UTAUT model to understand the customers' acceptance and use of internet banking in Lebanon: a structural equation modeling approach. Inf. Technol. People **29**(4), 830–849 (2016). https://doi.org/10.1108/ITP-02-2014-0034

Chinwe, N.R., Oparaoha, N.U.: The role of social workers in ameliorating the plight of internally displaced persons (IDPs) in Nigeria. Niger. J. Soc. Psychol. **1**(1), 63–75 (2018)

Eme, O.I., Azuakor, P.O., Mba, C.C.: Boko Haram and Population Displacement in Nigeria: A Case for Psychological Input, pp. 77–98 (2018)

Fusch, P.I., Ness, L.R.: Are we there yet? Data saturation in qualitative research. Qual. Rep. **20**(9), 1408–1416 (2015)

Garavand, A., Samadbeik, M., Kafashi, M., Abhari, S.: Acceptance of health information technologies, acceptance of mobile health: a review article. J. Biomed. Phys. Eng. **7**(4) (2017)

Gwadabe, M., Salleh, M.A., Ahmad, A.A., Jamil, S.: Forced displacement and the plight of internally displaced persons in Northeast Nigeria. Hum. Soc. Sci. Res. **1**(1), 46–52 (2018)

Hoque, R., Sorwar, G.: Understanding factors influencing the adoption of mHealth by the elderly: an extension of the UTAUT model. Int. J. Med. Inform. **101**, 75–84 (2017). https://doi.org/10.1016/j.ijmedinf.2017.02.002

Lenshie, N.E., Yenda, H.B.: The international journal of humanities & social studies Boko Haram insurgency, internally displaced persons and humanitarian response in Northeast Nigeria. Int. J. Hum. Soc. Stud. **4**(8) (2016)

Nwaoga, C.T., Okoli, A.B., Uroko, F.C.: Self-acclaimed Religious terrorism, Refugee crisis, and the Plight of Internally Displaced Persons in Nigeria. J. Soc. Sci. **8**(3), 189–195 (2017). https://doi.org/10.5901/mjss.2017.v8n3p189

Okon, E.O.: Poverty in Nigeria: a social protection framework for the most vulnerable groups of internally displaced persons. Am. Int. J. Soc. Sci. Res. **2**(1), 66–80 (2018)

Owoaje, E.T., Uchendu, O.C., Ajayi, T.O., Cadmus, E.O.: A review of the health problems of the internally displaced persons in Africa, 161–171 (2016). https://doi.org/10.4103/1117-1936.196242

Patil, A.: The role of ICTs in refugee lives, 7–12 (2019). https://doi.org/10.1145/3287098.3287144

Pheeraphuttharangkoon, S.: The Adoption, Use and Diffusion of Smartphones among Adults over Fifty in the UK. University of Hertfordshire (2015)

Sambo, A.S.: Internal displaced persons and their information needs (2017)

Venkatesh, V., Morris, M.G., Davis, G.B., Davis, F.D.: User acceptance of information technology: toward a unified view. MIS Q. **27**(3), 425–478 (2003). https://doi.org/10.1016/j.inoche.2016.03.015

Embracing uMunthu: How Informal Caregivers in Malawi Use ICTs

Efpraxia D. Zamani[(✉)] and Laura Sbaffi

Information School, The University of Sheffield, Regent Court,
211 Portobello, Sheffield S1 4DP, UK
{e.zamani,l.sbaffi}@sheffield.ac.uk

Abstract. This paper explores the way informal caregivers in Malawi use different types of ICTs for the purposes of caring for their loved ones, supporting each other and building a community under adverse circumstances. We collected empirical material in the Mangochi district during a field study through a focus group and a workshop with informal caregivers and NGOs. For the purposes of our analysis, we draw from the uMunthu philosophy of Malawi in order to explore and understand the contextual conditions and the local phenomena. Our findings show that, the communal character of ICTs and their shareability often allows informal caregivers to come together as a community and overcome the scarcity of ICT resources through sharing, which is in line with the uMunthu principles. Quite often, though, sharing can lead to unintended consequences. The paper contributes to the ICT4D literature by theorising around the concept of sharing and shareability of ICTs; in doing so, we join our voices to the growing discussion on the use of southern theories and paradigms.

Keywords: Informal caregivers · Malawi · uMunthu · ICTs · Thematic analysis · Shareability

1 Introduction

Informal caregivers are people without formal training or education in healthcare, who have taken up caring responsibilities for one or more family members [1]. In African countries, where extended families are the norm and kinship is considered one's "safety net", informal caregivers face the challenge of day-to-day care by default [2]. Yet, African philosophy does not consider this as a challenge but rather as a way of being. Specific to the Malawian context where this study is situated, the uMunthu philosophy entails that the essence of being revolves around responsibility towards the community, whereby caring, empathy [3] and sharing are core to one's identity [4]. This does not mean that caring for a family member comes with no challenges. In such resource-constraint settings, it rather means that there are additional caveats, such as being the sole provider for the household.

To address this challenge, existing literature has emphasised the role of ICTs. Some studies have focused on how ICTs can support health-related outcomes in developing

© IFIP International Federation for Information Processing 2020
Published by Springer Nature Switzerland AG 2020
J. M. Bass and P. J. Wall (Eds.): ICT4D 2020, IFIP AICT 587, pp. 93–101, 2020.
https://doi.org/10.1007/978-3-030-65828-1_8

countries [e.g., 5, 6], whereas others discussed how ICTs promote social connectedness, and empowerment [e.g., 7]. Others, however, have focused on the detrimental effects of ICTs, such as economic inequalities [e.g., 8]. However, studies that look directly into ICTs and informal caregivers themselves within a developing country context are lacking.

The aim of this study is to fill this knowledge gap by looking into the way informal caregivers use ICTs. We explore how and what ICTs are used by informal caregivers in Malawi. Our empirical material derives from a field study in the town of Namwera, in the Mangochi district of Malawi. The analysis of the collated material uncovered two important, and to an extent interrelated, themes. ICTs are primarily shared rather than owned. Through sharing, informal caregivers manage to support each other in line with their uMunthu philosophy of being. However, sharing ICTs often leads to unintended consequences.

Therefore, the research question driving this study is: in what ways are ICTs affecting the daily life of informal caregivers in rural Malawi?

In what follows, we present a brief overview of the literature on ICTs and informal caregivers and then present a discussion on the uMunthu philosophy. We then present our methodology and our findings. We conclude the paper with a discussion on the implications of our study.

2   Informal Caregivers and ICTs in Developing Countries

A major area where we see multiple ICT-based interventions is that of healthcare, possibly because healthcare is burdened with multiple inequities, adversely impacting the poorest of society [9].

There is a wealth of studies focusing on how ICTs can facilitate health-related outcomes in developing countries. For example, Holeman and Barrett have examined the implementation and the redesign of technology for the support of healthcare workers in Kenya who work in the cold storage of vaccines [10]. Similarly, Mbelwa et al. have looked into the factors that drive healthcare workers to adopt mobile health applications, with the aim to increase the collection and transmission of remote data, thereby improving healthcare services [11]. Another stream of ICT4D research focuses on the use of ICTs by the patient, with the aim to either self-manage their condition and/or to become empowered, socially embedded and financially included. For example, mobile phones, even simple ones, can be gateways of information. In India, mobile phones are used to disseminate information on health programmes and healthy practices [9]. Other studies show that mobile phones can help not only reduce maternal morbidity and mortality rates, but also support pregnant women in identifying and using entrepreneurial opportunities [7, 12].

Yet, there is a lack of ICT4D studies that place the informal caregiver at their core. Generally, studies at the nexus of ICTs and informal caregivers design and develop ICT-based solutions within and for western paradigms [e.g., 13]; as such, findings and solutions are not typically transferable within the Global South, where the contextual conditions are strikingly different. On the other hand, assuming that the informal caregiver is treated as co-producer of sustainable healthcare ICT solutions [14] and that ICTs can indeed be beneficial, even in their simplest form [15], it is critical to first understand the local ways of knowing and being. This not only provides the researcher with sensitivity regarding the local context, but also with a way to appreciate what informal caregivers value for themselves and their communities.

3 The uMunthu Philosophy

'Umuntu ngumuntu ngabantu' captures the essence of uMunthu[1]. Its English translation is "[a] person is a person through persons" [16], which emphasises the importance of kinship, whereby interrelationships among individuals define behaviours and regulate communities [17]. Ultimately, this means that the fate of an individual and that of the community are inescapably linked [16]. The uMunthu philosophy prioritises empathy, caring, and understanding, where the contributions of all individuals are equally valued and cherished, and where reciprocity and responsibility towards the community and others are of distinct importance [3]. In other words, duty outranks privileges, and sharing is seen as testament to their social interconnectedness [18]. As such, sharing and "neighbourly assistance" is part and parcel of the African identity [4].

The core values of uMunthu are: respect for all human beings and their dignity and life; and "sharedness, obedience, humility, solidarity, caring, hospitality, interdependence and communalism" [17]. Several of these values seem counterintuitive to the Western ones, and we note that for African countries, collectivism and communal embeddedness are the mainstream [16]. Due to this focus on collectivism, uMunthu has been criticised for imposing compliance over individualism [3]. However, this is a misconstrued criticism, as uMunthu promotes personal development, personal interests and preferences as well as individuality, without promoting individualism, as long as individuals remain aware of their interdependence to others, and their community [3].

4 The Context of the Study

Malawi is among the least developed countries according to the ODA list. Its population is approximately 18.6 million and, in 2018, there were 1 million people living with HIV/AIDS, with 38,000 people newly infected with the disease [19]. Informal caregivers of HIV/AIDS patients in the Mangochi district have formed support groups at community level, and meet on a regular basis (biweekly, monthly, bimonthly etc.). The purpose of these groups is to support one another and learn from each other how to care for their loved ones along the lines of nutrition, cooking, bathing tips, first aid etc. The carers bring food and other resources (such as oil) and cook together, share stories and experiences. While not all support groups are equally effective, those that are have managed to substitute the formal healthcare provision that is severely lacking.

4.1 Data Collection

In order to gather in-depth knowledge on informal caregivers' unmet needs and use of ICTs, this study adopted a qualitative research design involving a) a focus group with

---

[1] The term also appears as Umuntu and Umunthu.

primary informal carers of people living with HIV/AIDS and b) a workshop with relevant stakeholders in the field of HIV/AIDS, both of which took place in June 2019.

For the focus group, we adopted convenience sampling. The participants were recruited through one of the community-based support groups for informal caregivers. The focus group consisted of 10 informal caregivers, nine females and one male. The gender discrepancy is a reflection of the current caring situation in the country, which, traditionally, still requires women to cover nurturing roles. Upon their arrival, the participants were briefed about the scope of the study by a Chichewa-speaking (a local Malawian language) Research Assistant functioning as translator and we obtained verbal informal consent. We wanted to get insights into the experiences of the caregivers as lived and felt. As such, we wanted participants to feel free to contribute and express themselves or feeling pressured in anyway by the presence of individuals who could potentially influence and exert power over them (e.g. Community Chiefs).

The workshop was organised separately from the focus group. The participants to the workshop, 11 in total, were representatives of key stakeholder groups including academia, NGOs and local communities. The objective of the workshop aimed at understanding the structures and mechanisms that underpin the healthcare system in Malawi, and exploring the existing and foreseen government initiatives at local and central levels. In addition, we wanted to gauge a higher level understanding with regards to how ICTs are actively used today in Malawi and how they can support informal caregivers in the future in caring for their loved ones.

Both the focus group and the workshop were audio recorded; the questions were first asked in English and the Research Assistant translated them into Chichewa. Responses by individual participants were then translated back into English.

In addition, we collected empirical material through archival research into published reports with regards to ICT-driven initiatives and projects undertaken by the government in Malawi in recent years. We also collected material via informal discussions with informal caregivers and their extended families during visits to their villages and households. This helped us contextualise some of the information offered by our participants, cross-validate our interpretations with regards to findings, and gain an intimate understanding of their everyday life.

4.2 Data Analysis

We coded the empirical material using the NVivo package, and we started by using a broad coding scheme, as themes begun emerging from our preliminary reading of the transcripts. In our study, three main themes emerged: sharing and shareability, supporting each other and giving back to the community, and unintended consequences. For each of these themes, we coded our material in a data-driven and theory-driven way, drawing both from our empirical data and from the relevant literature, as proposed for thematic analysis studies [20].

There was a continuous comparison between our coding, the interpretations of our findings and the literature. Newly identified themes formed new codes, and secondary material from our archival research, and our observations helped us corroborate evidence from the focus group and the workshop, further enabling triangulation.

5 Findings and Discussion

In this section, we begin with what ICTs informal caregivers share and how they use them. We move on to highlight how informal caregivers have managed to support each other under adverse circumstances, and how they have arrived at a point to be able to give back to their community. Finally, we discuss the unintended consequences of their sharing practices, as documented during our field study.

5.1 Sharing and Shareability of ICTs

Sharing of resources, however scant, is considered the norm in the community. This includes ICTs as well, such as mobile phones and radio receivers, as well as other technologies, like solar panels, which are quite popular in the villages.

It is very common to have a radio receiver within the household, and once the chores of the day are done, the caregiver usually spends some time with their loved ones to discuss the events of the day. In addition, there are several radio listening clubs, whereby people from the communities come together, catching up with the news, or more specifically, in the case of informal caregivers, to receive radio-transmitted health advisory messages: *"Here in Malawi, we have radio listening clubs where people come together around one radio receiver. [...] people who were diabetic would sit down just to listen to health education materials and all that"*.

With regards to mobile phones, ownership is not very common. Among our participants, only half of them had a mobile phone, and only one had a smartphone. If a phone is owned, this is usually shared with the rest of the household. However, in many cases, there are households without any communication means. This poses a significant challenge for informal caregivers, especially in times of a crisis, i.e., when the patient needs immediate help which the caregiver cannot provide. In such a case, *"[they] borrow from those that have the phones"* or *"just send boys or someone to go to those houses that have got phones."* This allows them to call the closest health centre and get some immediate advice, or call the district hospital and possibly arrange to have their family member transported there.

Informal caregivers are able to enact sharing practices because the available ICTs exhibit a degree of shareability. In their striking majority, mobile phones are used with pay-as-you-go schemes. This suggests that caregivers can buy credit from one of the many operators, top up somebody else's phone and use it for their own purposes: *"The others [those without a mobile phone], what they do is if there is some emergency, when they have some money, they buy airtime and put it in somebody's phone and they speak while the owner is there. They say what they want and then after that they are done, they give back the phone. They can just have some money and put in some units."* Alternatively, they can reimburse the owner for the airtime they have spent.

Smartphones are uncommon. However, when they are available, their enhanced capabilities allow for different ways of sharing: *"This year our political campaigns used social media quite a lot. Messages went through WhatsApp (...) even some people in the village were asking me some questions and I was able to play some clips on my phone."* In other words, while people cannot make direct use of the smartphone, they can still access informational resources through third parties, and, from there, diffuse the information within their community, hence resembling the principles of the radio listening clubs.

5.2 Supporting Each Other and Giving Back

The caregivers support each other on different levels. They encourage each other against the challenges of everyday life and of caring for their family members (*"We also go to that support group once a month where we also do counselling and encourage each other."*). They further share their caring and life experiences, best practices and what they have learned by caring for their family members, through doctors' and or healthcare workers' visits. They do so during the support groups meetings. Similar support groups exists for children who have been found positive to HIV/AIDS, where they can play with each other, learn skills and tips for caring for themselves and easing the burden on their mothers (*"And there we have two groups, we have adults therapy and we have got children therapy of which we normally discuss how to take the drugs at what time and advise what to eat and what not to eat."*).

At the same time, the support groups serve a purpose in helping the caregivers to improve their own well-being, as well as initiate small scale entrepreneurial activities, such as preparing, cooking and selling samosas in the market: *"It's like we teach each other cooking methods like how to prepare and bake samosa, doughnuts so that we don't rely on begging for support from our relatives and friends. We can open up small scale businesses and make some income."* Such advice is of critical importance for the caregivers, because in their vast majority they are the sole household provider, and often have needs that extend beyond the disease: *"I am taking care of a child and in the past we didn't worry about school materials and needs but now the child has started school and I don't have the money to buy school books, uniforms and other materials".*

The support groups are crowdsourced, which poses several challenges. For one, it means that when the caregivers have no resources, i.e., no ingredients for cooking, baking, or no fertiliser for gardening and farming, the support group cannot function as well, which denotes in many cases a financial dependency. Each caregiver brings whatever they have available. However, when they do not have anything, they revert to less resource-intensive activities, like talking. Ultimately, by pooling their knowledge and experiences, they have managed to build a crucial capacity of best practices around caring and caregiving through meetings and interactions over the last few years.

At the same time however, the capacity they have built through the support groups, and as a result of their sense of responsibility for their community, they use it to give back to the community. They provide counselling themselves to others, who go for their first diagnosis and who find themselves in the same position (*"Actually now we are the ones who are doing counselling in our communities to those who used to discriminate us. We are the ones who encourage people in the community to go for HIV testing."*). However, whereas most of the counselling services and advice provided by the formal healthcare structures in the area are directed towards the patient, our participants indicated that they themselves follow a different direction. They specifically start with the person who will be acting as the caregiver of the patient, or as they call them, the guardian: *"So for us we start with the guardian, guiding her that it is not the end of the world. She then in turn will encourage the patient not to think this as the end."*

5.3   Unintended Consequences of Sharing ICTs

Sharing mobile phones with others comes with a price as it highlights and exacerbates the economic inequalities within the community [8], as well as raise privacy issues [21]. When caregivers have to make a call using somebody else's phone, it means they have to sacrifice their privacy, as the owner of the phone will be present during the call. These phone calls are, in many cases, directed to immediate or extended family, living abroad, or, to emergency healthcare services: *"[When we want to talk to relatives abroad or in an emergency] we just use the phone. And there is no privacy at all since the owner is there with you listening"*.

When it comes to calls to family members, it is often the case that informal caregivers receive support from their siblings who live in the city or abroad (*"Whenever she is facing some challenges she has got some brothers working in South Africa."*, *"I have brothers who send money to help take care of mom"*). They may wish to inform their families regarding the condition of the patient or ask for financial support. When the call concerns the healthcare services, by definition the call will concern healthcare-related matters, which are generally seen as private. As such, placing a call under these circumstances can be quite detrimental or stressful for the caregiver.

As mentioned earlier, another way caregivers go about sharing others' mobile phones is by buying top up credit or reimbursing the owner for how much time they have used the phone. In these cases, what was shared with us is that what this arrangement means for the caregivers is that most often there is leftover credit, which the caregiver cannot use as it remains in the account of the mobile owner; as such the owner benefits at the caregiver's expenses: *"When they have some money, they buy airtime and put it in somebody's phone and they speak while the owner is there. (...) They can just have some money and put in some units. Then the owner benefits from the left over units."* For some people, these leftovers may be the difference between feeding their dependents or not.

5.4   Embracing uMunthu

We have witnessed a number of ways in which informal caregivers experience and enact the uMunthu values in their everyday life. As part of the uMunthu philosophy of living and being, we have observed that for our participants, caregiving is not seen as a burden, as opposed to the Global North [22]. Instead, for Malawians, it is a way of life (*"We just think it is part of our life."*, *"The problem is in my house so what else can you do."*). In addition, sharing their experiences, as part of the support group and sharing their scant resources, is their only way of living. This attitude and openness to sharing are in line with the Malawian epistemology of uMunthu, whereby, what gives human life meaning is living as part of a community, where sharing is the organising logic of such community; it is only then that a person actually achieves their personhood [23].

While sharing can lead to unintended consequences, as shown earlier, we posit that, because the uMunthu values are so ingrained into the very fabric of everyday life, responsibility and caring for their dependents take precedence for the caregivers, who are, therefore, willing to sacrifice other things, such as their privacy (*"We make sure the patient is well and comfortable and then we can go and do what we can so that when we come back home we have something to eat with the patient."*). uMunthu can be observed also in the informal caregivers' commitment to their community, their support group and others in a similar role to theirs, as they become their supporters through counselling.

Most crucially, as a result of their community-centric view that stems out of the Malawian uMunthu way of life, the caregivers are willing to share best practices and resources, as members of these support groups. Also, sharing with each other and through the support groups is seen as a fundamental emotional anchor.

6 Conclusions

Sharing and collectivism are critical factors for the wellbeing of caregivers in Malawi, which is in contrast to what we have come to know in the Global North. The sharing practices are discussed through the lens of the uMunthu principles. Although it is clear that ICTs are facilitating information exchange and support, there is still little evidence that Malawian's lives are significantly affected for the better. Future ICT4D studies might want to explore how this sub-Saharan humanistic approach can be channelled to promote and support better quality of life through the use of accessible and shareable technologies grounded in the Sustainable Development Goals.

Our study comes with some limitations. The participants of our focus group come primarily from one of the support groups, which comparatively is the most efficient one across the district. As such, our findings do pertain to those who are most committed and engaged with the community. We only focused on mobile phones, as these were the most prevalent in the area; different forms of ICTs could had possibly provided us with different findings. Finally, the theoretical link we identified among the emerging themes was that of the uMunthu philosophy, and we did not consider alternative explanations. However, we consider this to be a compelling enough theory, which manages to provide a holistic lens while having been brewed within the local context, and therefore being sensitive of the local dynamics and characteristics.

References

1. Horrell, B., Stephens, C., Breheny, M.: Capability to care: supporting the health of informal caregivers for older people. Health Psychol. **34**, 339–348 (2015)
2. Moore, A.R., Henry, D.: Experiences of older informal caregivers to people with HIV/AIDS in Lome. Togo. Ageing Int. **30**, 147–166 (2005)
3. Kayira, J.: (Re)creating spaces for uMunthu: postcolonial theory and environmental education in southern Africa. Environ. Educ. Res. **21**, 106–128 (2015)
4. Bidwell, N.: Ubuntu in the network: humanness in social capital in rural Africa. Interactions **17**, 68 (2010)
5. Oyeyemi, S.O., Wynn, R.: Giving cell phones to pregnant women and improving services may increase primary health facility utilization: a case–control study of a Nigerian project. Reprod Health **11**, 8 (2014)
6. Watkins, S.C., Robinson, A., Dalious, M.: Evaluation of the Information and Communications Technology for Maternal, Newborn and Child Health Project Known locally as "Chipatala Cha Pa Foni" (Health Center by Phone). Invest in Knowledge Initiative (IKI), Village Reach, Balaka District, Malawi (2013)

7. Dasuki, S.I., Zamani, E.D.: Assessing mobile phone use by pregnant women in Nigeria: a capability perspective. Electron. J. Inf. Syst. Dev. Ctries. **85** (2019). https://doi.org/10.1002/isd2.12092
8. Ya'u, Y.Z.: The new imperialism & Africa in the global electronic village. Rev. Afr. Polit. Econ. **31**, 11–29 (2004)
9. Ismail, A., Karusala, N., Kumar, N.: Bridging disconnected knowledges for community health. Proc. ACM Hum. Comput. Interact. **2**, 1–27 (2018)
10. Holeman, I., Barrett, M.: Insights from an ICT4D Initiative in Kenya's immunization program: designing for the emergence of sociomaterial practices. JAIS **18**, 900–930 (2017)
11. Mbelwa, J.T., Kimaro, H.C., Mussa, B.: Acceptability and use of mobile health applications in health information systems: a case of eIDSR and DHIS2 touch mobile applications in Tanzania. In: Nielsen, P., Kimaro, H.C. (eds.) ICT4D 2019. IAICT, vol. 551, pp. 579–592. Springer, Cham (2019). https://doi.org/10.1007/978-3-030-18400-1_48
12. Nyemba-Mudenda, M., Chigona, W.: mHealth outcomes for pregnant mothers in Malawi: a capability perspective. Inf. Technol. Development. **24**, 245–278 (2018)
13. Renyi, M., Teuteberg, F., Kunze, C.: ICT-based support for the collaboration of formal and informal caregivers – a user-centered design study. In: Abramowicz, W., Paschke, A. (eds.) BIS 2018. LNBIP, vol. 320, pp. 400–411. Springer, Cham (2018). https://doi.org/10.1007/978-3-319-93931-5_29
14. Badr, N.G., Sorrentino, M., De Marco, M.: Health information technology and caregiver interaction: building healthy ecosystems. In: Satzger, G., Patrício, L., Zaki, M., Kühl, N., Hottum, P. (eds.) IESS 2018. LNBIP, vol. 331, pp. 316–329. Springer, Cham (2018). https://doi.org/10.1007/978-3-030-00713-3_24
15. Lorca-Cabrera, J., Grau, C., Martí-Arques, R., Raigal-Aran, L., Falcó-Pegueroles, A., Albacar-Riobóo, N.: Effectiveness of health web-based and mobile app-based interventions designed to improve informal caregiver's well-being and quality of life: a systematic review. Int. J. Med. Inform. **134**, 104003 (2020)
16. Bandawe, C.R.: Psychology brewed in an African pot: indigenous philosophies and the quest for relevance. High. Educ. Policy **18**, 289–300 (2005). https://doi.org/10.1057/palgrave.hep.8300091
17. van Dyk, G.A.J., Matoane, M.: Ubuntu-oriented therapy: prospects for counseling families affected with HIV/AIDS in sub-Saharan Africa. J. Psychol. Afr. **20**, 327–334 (2010)
18. Boykin, A.W., Jagers, R.J., Ellison, C.M., Albury, A.: Communalism: conceptualization and measurement of an Afrocultural social orientation. J. Black Stud. **27**, 409–418 (1997)
19. UNAIDS: Malawi. https://www.unaids.org/en/regionscountries/countries/malawi. Accessed 25 Feb 2020
20. Fereday, J., Muir-Cochrane, E.: Demonstrating Rigor using thematic analysis: a hybrid approach of inductive and deductive coding and theme development. Int. J. Qual. Methods **5**, 80–92 (2006)
21. Avgerou, C.: Information systems in developing countries: a critical research review. J. Inf. Technol. **23**, 133–146 (2008)
22. Berglund, E., Lytsy, P., Westerling, R.: Health and wellbeing in informal caregivers and non-caregivers: a comparative cross-sectional study of the Swedish general population. Health Qual Life Outcomes **13**, 109 (2015)
23. Sindima, H.: Bondedness, Moyo and UMunthu as the elements of aChewa spirituality: organizing logic and principle of life. Ultim. R. Mean. **14**, 5–20 (1991)

Constraining and Enabling Factors in the Use of ICT in Rural Schools in Nepal

Dhiraj Thapa$^{(\boxtimes)}$ ⓘ, Dai Griffiths ⓘ, and Ann L. Kolodziejski ⓘ

University of Bolton, Deane Road, Bolton BL3 5AB, UK
dt3eps@bolton.ac.uk, dthapa@email.com

Abstract. The OLE-Nepal project has deployed over 6,500 XO laptops in schools in Nepal, pre-installed with materials designed to support the national curriculum. This has raised hopes that technology can transform the quality of education available in remote regions. In order to investigate if and how the technology can have this impact, a case study was carried out which gathered detailed data on the use of the computers in three schools in contrasting remote rural areas of Nepal. The principal data collection methods were interviews, focus groups, classroom observations, and questionnaires. The results show that the effectiveness of technology in transforming schools is strongly dependent on local conditions and practices. This paper identifies constraining and enabling factors which can be identified in the case study data: infrastructure, classroom management, gender, and teacher motivation and training.

Keywords: Nepal · Remote · Rural · Education · Computers · XO · One-laptop-per-child · ICT · OLE-Nepal

1 The Motivation for This Study

In early 2000, as a medical representative for a drug company, the first author travelled to different parts of rural Nepal. On visits to remote communities, he observed several challenges faced by small public schools in rural villages, isolated by land and lack of transport. Textbooks were limited and often delivered with long delays. Informal classroom observations and several conversations with the teachers and the locals in the village, showed that, in the absence of appropriate teaching material, not much teaching and learning was taking place, with little motivation for teachers to teach or learners to learn. A decade later, on revisiting some of the remote villages, it was intriguing to witness that some schools from the same community were now using computers in their classrooms. Although distant and isolated from the city, it was a surprise to watch children using visual content and learning to read with digital devices, just like the children did in the metropolitan cities. Computers and communications infrastructure seemed to be reconstructing the practice of education in many of these schools.

The teachers from some schools commented that since the deployment of the technology in schools, student enrolment had improved, and the dropout rate had dropped

© IFIP International Federation for Information Processing 2020
Published by Springer Nature Switzerland AG 2020
J. M. Bass and P. J. Wall (Eds.): ICT4D 2020, IFIP AICT 587, pp. 102–113, 2020.
https://doi.org/10.1007/978-3-030-65828-1_9

considerably. The teachers explained that the Non-Governmental Organisation (NGO) Open Learning Exchange-Nepal (OLE-Nepal) had significantly contributed to providing access to computers and resources. OLE-Nepal has worked on this in collaboration with the Department of Education, and with the One Laptop Per Child (OLPC) initiative. These impressions, and the perceived potential of technology for remote schools, led the first author to explore further to understand if this was a situation for all schools located in other regions of diverse backgrounds.

2 Literature Review

ICT initiatives in education in the developing world are well studied and documented in the literature, see for example the literature review in (UNESCO 2016; Toro and Joshi 2012). Within this body of literature, the OLPC program has received its share of attention, for example (Nugroho and Lonsdale 2010). However, the research which has been carried out has two limitations. Firstly, little work has been done with remote schools, presumably because they are too difficult to access. In the view of the authors, these schools are the most interesting to investigate, because they provide an opportunity to contrast the introduction of ICT in schools with a previous complete absence of technology, and because the effect ICT in negating distance should be at its strongest in geographically remote schools. Secondly, the focus in previous work has been primarily on evaluating the effectiveness of the technology or applications, or on documenting the attitudes and perceptions of learners and teachers regarding ICT. It is still unclear what happens in classrooms when computers are introduced into remote schools, and there is little evidence to explain why some rural schools perform better in examinations than other schools in different geographical location using the same technology. This study seeks to fill these gaps in knowledge, by examining how social factors, geographic situation, school, and pedagogic approaches all combine to enable or constrain the success of the OLE-Nepal programme in remote schools.

In undertaking this research, we take a realist position, informed by the insights of Pawson and Tilley (Clarke et al. 1998). In practice, this means that our explanations are formulated in terms of causal mechanisms, which act within specified contexts to produce an outcome. In doing this, we seek evidence from as many sources as possible to confirm or discount the existence of proposed causal mechanisms, following the use of multi-methodology proposed by, for example in Mingers and White (2010). In our study, this has involved the combination of questionnaires, the analysis of documents, interviews, and observations.

3 The Research Context

In Nepal, private school learners perform better in examinations than public school learners, and the contrast is even higher with rural public schools (Shrestha 2016). To improve the quality of public schools, the Government of Nepal developed the ICT in Education Master Plan 2013–2017. The plan foresaw the use of ICT in education at all levels to improve classroom delivery, increase access to learning materials and ensure quality primary education for all. One of the initiatives identified as contributing to achieving these goals was OLPC (Munyantore and Mbalire 2017). OLE-Nepal explored the contribution which ICT could make to improving the education sector in Nepal, mainly targeting public schools in rural regions Thapa and Sein (2016)[1]. A collaboration resolved problems for both organisations, and OLE-Nepal launched the OLPC programme in 2008, to provide rural schools with access to XO laptops with pre-loaded software (Nugroho and Lonsdale 2010).

OLE-Nepal convinced the Department of Education (DOE) of the Government of Nepal to work with them to develop digital learning content. Subject specialists, translators and technical experts were provided to review and prepare educational materials and created interactive educational software together with a team of OLE-Nepal (Thapa and Sein 2016). The result was E-Paath activities, which is closely aligned with the national curriculum for years 1 to 8 in English, Maths, Science and Nepali. All the digital contents from OLE-Nepal are freely available online (OLE-Nepal 2020).

According to the OLE-Nepal official website, the program has been running in more than 200 schools in 54 districts across Nepal and has reached over thirty-five thousand learners using over 6,500 OLPC laptops (OLE-Nepal 2020). OLE provides digital libraries known as E-Pustakalaya, where thousands of e-books and videos are available through its server to schools in the remote areas (OLE-Nepal 2020).

4 Methodology

4.1 Adoption of a Case Study Approach

This study explores the consequences of technological intervention in rural schools in Nepal. This could be done by surveying all the rural schools in Nepal and comparing their reported experiences. The results would provide some insight but would have two principal drawbacks. Firstly, the data would not be reliable if schools presented themselves as 'good' users of the technology. Secondly, the educational context for the use of ICT in education is complex and varied, and explanations for the way that the technology is used, and the consequences of that use, are dependent on the experiences of individual schools, classes and individuals. To understand these processes, a rich data set is necessary. As Yin (2013) describes, a case study offers an in-depth, multi-sided approach used in case studies that can shed light on aspects of human thinking and behaviour that it would be unethical or impractical to study in other ways. Consequently, a case study was used to observe and document the use of technologies in selected schools, identifying patterns of use and the factors which enabled or constrained the effectiveness of the use of computers.

4.2 Identification of the Case Study

Schools were selected entirely at random from a list provided by OLE-Nepal. The schools considered were actively participating in the OLE-Nepal programme and willing to participate in the research. However, this selection was constrained in three ways. Firstly, all selected schools had been involved in the programme for at least two years. Secondly,

---

[1] Thapa is no relation to the present author.

one school was selected from each geographical area to facilitate comparison between regions. Thirdly, A spectrum of technological experience was explored to assess if variations in experience of learning via technology had an impact on the attitudes and practise of learners and teachers. Of the three schools selected for the study 'Annapurna' had been using the XO laptop for over two years, 'Everest' had been using them for more than four years, and 'Makalu' school had been using for over six years. Everest School is located in the mountain region; Annapurna School is located in the hilly area, while Makalu School is located in the plains. The schools' identities are anonymised.

4.3 The Role of the Researcher

In order to ease tensions and allow participants to express their views openly, the first author spent at least 2–3 days in each village community, rather than the minimum time needed to collect data. He engaged with learners in activities such as sports and engaged with locals in tea shops, with talks about their communities, their culture, and their everyday lives. Such interactions, as indicated by Wertsch (1993), led to understanding the social meaning and cultural values that are closely interrelated with the participants' understandings.

As Hellawell (2011) argues, a researcher may have comparative data about research sites, but be unable to interpret this because the environment in which those sites are situated is insufficiently understood. The first author was born and brought up in a similar community in Nepal and has been a teacher in a rural school for around three years. He may, therefore, be considered an insider. Although he visited these schools before conducting the research, he was unknown to the respondents in this study and, in this sense, he was an outsider. Unluer (2012) believes that, depending on the circumstances, a qualitative researcher may have different roles, such as a friend, acquaintance, or researcher and that these different roles need to be explained. During the data collection, the researcher was treated as a community member, welcomed to the school and asked for an evaluation of the teaching activities in the classroom. Nevertheless, this appeal was politely refused to maintain the unbiased position of the researcher as an observer. In this case, shifting between insider and outsider characters required management and reflection.

4.4 Data Collection

As Norman (2011) affirms, "obtaining socially and contextually meaningful information in a natural setting is critical". Accordingly, the primary data collection methods used were qualitative interviews and focus groups, asking open-ended questions to teachers, parents, principal and learners about the overall experience of learning with the computer in the classrooms. However, Tashakkori and Creswell (2007) points out that the inclusion of data from documentation and questionnaires allows for investigation from many perspectives. Consequently, quantitative data were collected from student questionnaires, and documentation of annual examination results for selected learners before and after the introduction of OLE-Nepal activities.

Data was gathered in two periods—Phase One in 2017 and Phase Two in 2018. Phase one study was carried out in two schools, as described in Table 1. Phase one showed that there was a variation in the performance of the schools in standardised examinations in the two regions. Similarly, questionnaires and interviews uncovered differences in the use of computers by boys and girls and differences in teachers' interest in computers. It became clear that questionnaires and teacher interviews alone would not be sufficient to clarify the use of computers in the classroom. Furthermore, interviews with parents and headteachers, as well as classroom observations, were required. There was also a decision to add a third school in another area.

Table 1. Phase one data collection

School (Pseudonyms)	Interview		Questionnaires	Observations
	Teachers	Headteachers	Students	Classrooms
Annapurna	2		33	2
Makalu	2		32	2
Total	4		65	4

Phase two data collection was conducted a year later in August 2018, again with Annapurna and Makalu schools, and with the addition of Everest school, as shown in Table 2. Interviews with teachers ranged from 20 to 50 min and mainly discussed the ways that the computers were used in classrooms. The interviews with parents focused on their perception of technology and the importance of schools in rural villages. Focus groups with learners discussed learners' attitudes, opinions and reflections on learning with the technology. The classroom observations lasted 30 to 45 min and documented pedagogic practices with computers and the interactions of learners and teachers during classroom lessons. An observation checklist was used, and field notes were taken on teaching and learning atmosphere, classroom infrastructure, teaching and learning activities, and behaviour of the teacher and learners. Also, classroom facilities and the arrangement of the furniture were recorded.

Table 2. Phase two data collection

School (Pseudonyms)	Interview			Focus group	Observation
	Teachers	Headteachers	Parents	Students	Classrooms
Annapurna	3	1	5	3	3
Everest	3	1	5	3	3
Makalu	3	1	5	3	3
Total	9	3	15	9	9

All interviews and focus group discussions were conducted in Nepali, transcribed, and analysed in Nepali to maintain the accurate response messages. All details regarding respondents and their schools were immediately anonymised after compilation and data were stored in a safe location.

4.5 Data Analysis

The data collected in each phase was compiled, transcribed and analysed at the end of that phase. The qualitative data were coded and categorised using Nvivo 11, while the questionnaire data from phase one was analysed using a spreadsheet. Sixty-five questionnaires were distributed, with a response rate of 100% because they were completed in the classroom. Six themes have been generated concerning the use of computers in classrooms and students' perceptions of digital learning, which are merged into four areas in the findings below. Quantitative data from the learners' records from the schools were anonymised and stored in the spreadsheet, giving an overview of each learner's performance for the last few years.

5 Findings

The findings not only focused on the patterns of usage of technology in rural schools but also the teachers' and learners' experience of working with computers in different geographical settings, and on teachers understanding of the equipment and the teaching methods that could be used with it. Equally important is the insight gained into how similar schools with a different background in a different geographical region using the same technology and following a related curriculum can vary in the outcome of the learner. The study proposes that the differences in the performance of learners and the patterns of usage can be associated with four aspects, as we now discuss.

5.1 Infrastructure

All schools had allocated a computer room, referred to as a laboratory. Annapurna and Everest had XO laptops. However, OLE-Nepal has experienced problems in obtaining adequate XO laptops, the E-Paath software has also been integrated on desktop PCs, and this is the case in Makalu. In observations, the learners appeared comfortable with the devices, which they operated without much difficulty, and were able to follow the teacher's instructions quite easily. Not all the computers were in working order, as shown in Table 3 below.

Table 3. Number of equipment in case study schools

School	Year received	XO laptops received	Desktop PCs received	Functional	Out of order
Annapurna	March 2015	40	0	32	8
Everest	June 2014	35	0	31	4
Makalu	August 2011	0	20	18	2

All the schools were initially equipped with electrical supply, batteries and a backup power supply inverter, internet connection, routers and network servers. Table 3 above shows the number of devices in each school and the number of devices that were functioning during the observation class. Schools are responsible for maintaining this infrastructure, but the data gathered showed that some schools were unable to fulfil this commitment and had a number of slow or non-functional laptops, as shown in Table 3.

Partly as a result of this, in all schools, some learners had to share their devices, making it difficult for them to follow instructions. It is interesting to note that PCs were more reliable. Non-functioning and slow-performing devices had implications for the effectiveness of classes, as the lesson did not start until all the laptops lessons were on the screen and ready. In almost all schools, one or two computers were sluggish. Although the allocated laboratory class is 45 min, one particular lesson in Makalu lasted for only 25 min, because of technical issues. It also was clear that if the number of learners in the laboratory was higher than the number of computers, then problems surfaced in time management and focus on tasks. The Everest school backup power supply was out of order, so in power cuts, the learners would have to miss the laboratory class. Despite the original provision of an internet connection, none of the participating schools had functioning internet access due to financial constraints, so computers ran pre-loaded applications and resources. Teachers and learners were, therefore, unable to upgrade their devices, which reduce the value of computers as a tool to look for new resources and position teachers and learners as consumers of resources.

Interviews with headteacher and teachers, and observations at the schools, reveal that remote location, a poor local economy, the budget constraints of schools and the lack of interest from school administrators are contributing causes of infrastructure problems, and particularly of the lack of internet access. The importance of school management providing internet access, so teachers can update their knowledge of technology and improve their teaching skills, has long been recognised as a critical factor in the success of IT in classrooms and was emphasised some years ago by Yuen et al. (2003). Similarly, Tezci (2009) showed that limited access to the internet impacted on teachers' use of ICT in instructional activities.

In summary, the schools have difficulty maintaining their infrastructure. The schools do not have replacement computers, and even minor malfunctions with an individual computer can have an impact on learning effectiveness for the entire class. The lack of internet connectivity means that materials cannot be updated and that teachers cannot develop their skills, and open web learning is not possible. Thus, it is not possible to make a generalised statement on the effectiveness of XO computers, or of OLE-Nepal, but only in terms of how they fit into the infrastructure available in a specific context. In the present case study, the infrastructure available in the schools is a significant constraint on the educational effectiveness of the computers, and on the patterns of use which are observed.

5.2 Classroom Management

Classroom management is strongly linked to the role of the teacher and to the way the teacher handles the daily issues that may arise in the classroom (Vairamidou and Stravakou 2019). Laboratory observations have shown that classroom management is a crucial factor in the organisation effective classroom environment, and we now discuss the key aspects.

Classroom Scale and Furniture Layout
Laboratory observations showed that schools with adequate classroom furniture that is arranged appropriately have enabled more productive use of computers. The laboratories in participating schools tended to be smaller than other classrooms in the same school, showing that schools were not willing to reduce traditional class provision to maximise the effectiveness of computers. In Annapurna, the laboratory furniture was set up as a regular classroom, per row of six benches and tables, with three lines. Learners would pick up laptops from the docking station and take them to their desk. The teachers used eye contact to confirm understanding and to check that the learners were on task. However, the case was different in Everest and Makalu, desk and benches were positioned in such a way that some of the learners were facing the teacher or the whiteboard and others were facing the wall. Both schools had a two long rectangular table in the middle of the room, placing their devices on the desk with benches on both sides of the long table for eight learners to use. These long tables in the middle seemed to cause a significant challenge for teachers walking around and guiding learners when necessary. Makalu had desktop computers arranged against the three corners of the wall to utilise maximum space. Everest had a similar set up of the desk and benches against the wall where learners carried their laptop from the docking station to the desk. The pupils facing the teacher and the board were in eye contact with the teacher but, the ones facing the wall had opportunities for inactivity and concealed activities.

In contrast to the sitting arrangements at Makalu and Everest, the classroom layout at Annapurna's allowed teachers to have more eye contact with learners and move around the classroom more swiftly, making it easy for teachers to get to the students' tables. This may be partly due to the fact that the room used for the laboratory in Annapurna was wider than the other two schools. Nonetheless, observations suggested that unnecessary and unused furniture could have been eliminated from the room, providing more space in Everest and Makalu schools.

ICT and Learners' Behaviour
Teachers recognised that technology offers a way to manage a large number of learners in a crowded laboratory by keeping learners occupied with audio and visual lessons. They also said that digital devices made learning materials more accessible to learners than traditional books. This is consistent with the notes in the laboratory observations diary. Still, it should be noted that teachers could not provide comments about which learners were using the computers productively, which suggests that the use of computers constrained their teaching activities. In particular, in Makalu and Everest, the teachers were not able to establish eye contact or gain access to the learners' desk to check whether the learners were working on lessons or engaged with other activities. Teachers also mentioned that if they assigned an unplanned computer activity to their class, then monitoring learners was an extra burden. The majority of teachers at all schools confirmed that digital devices enabled them to engage the learners, particularly when they had a large number of learners. Still, it prevented them from evaluating each student's activities individually. Teachers were asked whether the computers had relieved them of

certain of their academic management responsibilities, such as checking for activities or assessing individual progress. They reported that computers enabled learners to revisit and validate their learning, using self-assessment activities included at the end of the lessons of E-Paath. This supported teachers in carrying out the assessment, as they could keep a record of the learners' performance. Observations in the classroom showed that when there were more learners than devices, the class was distracted, and the learners were unable to focus on their assignment. It is not clear to what extent this issue could have been mitigated by improved practice in the control of classroom behaviour.

To summarise, the teachers recognise the potential of computers for learner engagement and classroom dynamics. However, comparison between schools shows that computers are not resources which can simply be added to existing classroom activities. They represent an active intervention into classroom management, and the classroom layout and teaching methods need to be designed accordingly. Differences in these aspects may explain much of the difference in performance between schools, because if the classroom teacher is unable to manage the class, then planned learning would not take place, regardless of advances in technological resources.

5.3 Gender

All the participating schools were public and co-educational. The questionnaire and focus group results showed that in all the schools the boys were more interested in computers than the girls. However, the questionnaires and focus group discussions also showed that girls have lower attendance at school. From the first author's personal experience, and teacher interviews from Annapurna and Everest schools, in most rural communities menstruating girls are considered impure untouchables. Moreover, school observations showed that toilet facilities are inadequate in all the participating schools. The data from teachers and parents confirmed that because of the condition of the toilets, even girls who do not come from families who hold this belief tend not to go to school when they are menstruating. It is reasonable to propose that this irregular attendance contributes to the lower achievement of girls in examinations. Data from parents shows that girls are encouraged to do housework at homes such as cooking, cleaning, farming and washing clothes, and as a result, they arrive late for schools or miss school. During the focus group discussion, two girls from Everest school reflected on their low attendance:

I wake up early in the morning at five o'clock. I have to milk the cows, feed them and start cooking food for the whole family. By the time we all eat and finish I hear the school bell. I always try to be on time, but I only manage it once or twice a week.
Both my parents are labour workers in the fields. When one of my parents is not well, they ask me to miss school and nurse them. I do not like to stay at home and miss my lessons. But I have no choice. Sometimes I wish they would ask my brother instead.

To summarise, while boys make more use of computers than girls, and achieve better academic results, it cannot be assumed that this is because of the innate gender characteristics. The girls may be interested in learning but cannot spend as much time at school. As a result, they are less familiar with computers and achieve less expertise.

5.4 Teacher Motivation and Training

The level of professional commitment shown by teachers varied considerably between the case study schools. In the first author's experience, many of his former colleagues in rural schools in Nepal joined the profession because they needed a job and saw teaching as an employment opportunity. Such teachers tend to see the activities of education as a list of tasks to be completed. The introduction of computers means the addition of new and unknown tasks, which are unlikely to be welcome. On the other hand, the teachers from Annapurna school were very committed to the purpose of the school in transforming the lives of their learners, to the point that they have contributed a part of their small salary to employ additional teachers to meet the needs of the children. In this context, any initiative which has the potential to improve outcomes will be welcome, including the introduction of computers.

In the interviews, all three principals confirmed that some teachers were motivated by teaching with computers in the beginning, but when the performance of the laptop deteriorated, they started to feel that running the computers took time from the classes and that it would be more effective to teach from a book. Nevertheless, the school has scheduled classes with computers that they have to carry out. This can lead teachers to have a negative perception of lessons with computers.

Out of the thirteen teachers interviewed, ten of the teachers confirmed that the training provided by NGOs was useful, but not sufficient. For example, Bishnu a teacher from Everest said

After the NGO installed XO laptops in our schools, we had a week training on how to operate the computer. The training included presentations, interactions, hands-on activities, and practice teaching to prepare to conduct classes with computers. The training was conducted many years ago; we need regular exercise so we can update our knowledge

The training needs to be refreshed and updated, especially in the absence of the internet. The NGOs have to deal with hundreds of schools, and they are in no way able to track and support them all, and Rabi Karmacharya, the founder of OLE-Nepal, admitted that the support provided to teachers was limited (Wodon 2015). Consequently, there is a gap between the expectations of schools and teachers and the capacity of NGOs. This also applies to the maintenance of computers.

In summary, the success of the use of OLPC computers depends on the existing motivation of teachers to focus on the outcomes for learners, rather than on their own tasks. Teachers' belief in the capacity of the computers to achieve these outcomes can be eroded by inadequate training and maintenance.

6 Concluding Remarks and Future Work

This case study has documented the way in which OLPC XO computers and PC's are used in schools in rural Nepal. It has made use of this data to identify the factors which enable and constrain the success of the OLE-Nepal programme, which have been discussed under the categories of classroom management, infrastructure, gender issues and teacher motivation and training.

The findings show that the effectiveness of educational IT projects in general, and the OLE-Nepal programme in particular, depend on the way in which they interact with the local context in schools. Any progress in the use of technology must focus on detailed planning for the use of computers, process improvements and the development of infrastructure at the national, regional and village level. Much of this work will not be possible without the assignment of resources and decision-making capacity to the appropriate level.

We note that the XO laptops in the OLE-Nepal programme are primarily used as a means to deliver teaching materials. This is indeed a valuable capability for remote schools that cannot receive sufficient printed teaching materials. The lack of internet makes the schools entirely dependent on these pre-loaded materials. However, this fits poorly with the vision of XO as "A project developed and distributed with a low-cost machine for children with an intention for the children to learn without or despite their teacher and schools" (Warschauer and Ames 2010, p. 34). At this most general level, we again see how the ambitions and design of systems are transformed by the local context in which they are deployed.

In future work, the results presented here will be contrasted with data examination results and school performance, and patterns of use of the technology in the classroom will be identified. The results will also be contrasted with a school which no longer participates in the XO project and a school which has never used laptops.

References

Baker-Sennett, J., Rogoff, B., Bell, N., Wertsch, J.V.: Voices of the mind: a sociocultural approach to mediated action. Am. J. Psychol. **105** (1992). https://doi.org/10.2307/1423207

Becker, L., Denicolo, P.: Teach. High. Educ. (2013). https://doi.org/10.4135/9781526435996

Clarke, A., Pawson, R., Tilley, N.: Realistic evaluation. Br. J. Sociol. **49**(2), 331 (1998). https://doi.org/10.2307/591330

Mingers, J., White, L.: A review of the recent contribution of systems thinking to operational research and management science. Eur. J. Oper. Res. **207**(3), 1147–1161 (2010). https://doi.org/10.1016/j.ejor.2009.12.019

Munyantore, J., Mbalire, M.: The role of one laptop per child project in academic performance in primary schools. Int. J. Manag. Appl. Sci. **3**(6), 41–45 (2017)

Norman, D.K., Lincoln, Y.S.: The SAGE Handbook of Qualitative Research, Thousand Oaks, California (2011)

Nugroho, D., Lonsdale, M.: Evaluation of OLPC programs globally: a literature review (2010)

OLE-Nepal (2020). http://www.olenepal.org/. Accessed 27 May 2020

Shrestha, S.: Exploring mobile learning opportunities and challenges in Nepal: the potential of open-source platforms. University of West London (2016)

Tashakkori, A., Creswell, J.W.: Editorial: the new era of mixed methods. J. Mix. Methods Res. **1**, 3–7 (2007). https://doi.org/10.1177/2345678906293042

Tezci, E.: Teachers' effect on ICT use in education: the Turkey sample. Procedia Soc. Behav. Sci. **1**(1), 1285–1294 (2009). https://doi.org/10.1016/j.sbspro.2009.01.228

Thapa, D., Sein, M.K.: Information ecology as a holistic lens to understand ICTD initiatives. In: Proceedings of the Eighth International Conference on Information and Communication Technologies and Development - ICTD 2016, pp. 1–4, September 2016. https://doi.org/10.1145/2909609.2909610

Toro, U., Joshi, M.: ICT in higher education: review of literature from the period 2004–2011. Int. J. Innov. Manag. Technol. **3**(1), 20–23 (2012). http://www.ijimt.org/papers/190-M633.pdf

UNESCO: Developing and Implementing Competency-based ICT Training for Teachers, vol. 1 (2016). https://doi.org/10.2217/1745509X.4.6.579

Unluer, S.: Being an insider researcher while conducting case study research. Qual. Rep. **17**(58), 1–14 (2012). http://www.nova.edu/ssss/QR/QR17/unluer.pdf

Vairamidou, A., Stravakou, P.: Classroom management in primary and secondary education literature review. J. Educ. Hum. Dev. **8**(2) (2019). https://doi.org/10.15640/jehd.v8n2a7

Warschauer, M., Ames, M.: Can one laptop per child save the world's poor? J. Int. Aff. **64**(1), 33–51 (2010)

Wodon, Q.: Technology in Nepal's classrooms: using impact evaluation as a learning device (2015). World Bank Blogs website. https://blogs.worldbank.org/education/technology-nepal-s-classrooms-using-impact-evaluation-learning-device. Accessed 5 Feb 2020

Yin, R.K.: Applications of case study research. Appl. Soc. Res. Methods Ser. **34**, 173. (2013). https://doi.org/10.1097/FCH.0b013e31822dda9e

Yuen, A.H.K., Law, N., Wong, K.C.: ICT implementation and school leadership: case studies of ICT integration in teaching and learning. J. Educ. Adm. **41**(2), 158–170 (2003). https://doi.org/10.1108/09578230310464666

Educational Technology as a Positioning Tool in Rural Bangladesh

Taslima Ivy[✉]

Manchester Institute of Education, University of Manchester, Manchester, UK
Taslima.ivy@postgrad.manchester.ac.uk

Abstract. In this paper, I argue that educational technology can become a symbolic tool for teachers' social positioning as much as a pedagogical tool for the classroom. Drawing on Holland et al.'s (1998) concepts of cultural artefact, semiotic mediation, and positional identity, I explore the experiences of PowerPoint use of one rural teacher in Bangladesh. Through her story, I shed light on the processes through which PowerPoint was becoming a positioning tool and how, at the same time, a shift in her positional identity was emerging.

Keywords: Educational technology · Positioning · Figured worlds

1 Introduction

The discussion in educational technology centres predominantly around how practical, pedagogical, psychological, or even philosophical factors shape or underpin teachers' use of technology in the classroom [25, p. 89]. The focuses in these areas have forwarded our understandings in practical ways and therefore, will continue to be of central importance in the field. However, it has been argued that most of these studies do not take appropriate account of the 'wider social relations' or competing voices shaping technology use in education [22, 24]. There have been calls to study teachers' use of technology as situated within a wider context and from a sociological point of view [26, 27].

In line with Selwyn's [25–27] call for more sociological studies in educational technology, an emergent line of research has shown that educational technology develops not strictly based on material properties but is shaped by social, cultural and political structures as well [4, 20, 21, 26, 27]. In most research in educational technology, the sociocultural structures and social relations have been found to be resilient or non-developing. Educational Technology has been claimed to be shaped to the context- either reinforcing existing practices, relationships, and structures or being rejected altogether [2, 18, 25]. At the same time, educational technology use has been shown to shape the context, not particularly by changing the structures, cultures and social relations but by producing or exacerbating existing power relations, social control, and inequality [3, 8, 17]. The day to day on ground experiences and social processes which contribute to such shaping is still relatively unexplored.

© IFIP International Federation for Information Processing 2020
Published by Springer Nature Switzerland AG 2020
J. M. Bass and P. J. Wall (Eds.): ICT4D 2020, IFIP AICT 587, pp. 114–125, 2020.
https://doi.org/10.1007/978-3-030-65828-1_10

At the micro level educational technology has been shown to be shaped by teachers' identity trajectories, past experiences and digital dispositions [6, 13, 22, 30]. How technologies might shape teacher identities has received less attention. The possibility of whether and how technology might produce a new technological identity for teachers is still unexplored.

This paper draws on Holland et al.'s theory [14] to study the day to day social processes through which educational technology and the social were shaping each other. It additionally sheds light on how, at the same time, a positional identity was emerging through these social processes.

2 Context

The government of Bangladesh aimed for 'digital' reform in primary and secondary classrooms by initiating a project titled 'multimedia classroom and 'teacher-led digital content development programme' in 2010. The project was overseen by a division of the Prime Minister's office titled a2i (Access to information). The project aimed to bring about changes through technology to the traditional educational culture characterised by "one-way transfer of information from teacher to student" and 'limited opportunities of classroom interaction" [31]. a2i believes that multimedia technology by visualising 'hard to grasp concepts' could be an agent in promoting more participation, interaction, enjoyment and interest in classrooms and thus promote a culture of student-centred pedagogy [1]. The choice of software to train teachers on visualisation and consequently to use in classrooms was the PowerPoint. This choice firstly was based on cost. Within the budget a2i had, it was not possible to set up fully-fledged computer labs, but it was possible to set up a multimedia classroom consisting of one laptop and one projector in every school.

a2i also aimed to connect all 900000 primary and secondary teachers across the country through an online portal called shikkhok batayon. The teachers are expected to contribute and collaborate in shikkhok batayon, which acts as a platform for peer collaboration and a repository for digital content [1]. Through these initiatives, a2i aimed to create and promote a new vision of being a teacher, with a new label 'multimedia teacher'. To generate motivation among teachers to become a 'multimedia teacher', the government implemented a 'gamification' strategy which included recognition by featuring a 'best multimedia teacher' every week on the portal for quality digital content, rewarding best multimedia teachers through promotions, national awards and leadership positions. At first, a2i implemented the multimedia learning project in an attempt to enable urban teachers to help rural teachers. However, very quickly, it turned out to be the rural teachers who began to show the most enthusiasm in contributing to the portal and becoming 'multimedia' teachers. According to a2i, 90% of the PowerPoints on the portal were created by multimedia teachers [1]. This intrigued me, and through my PhD I aimed to explore how and why educational technology use was emerging the way it was in rural Bangladesh.

3 Methods

3.1 Data Collection

This paper presents part of my findings from my PhD study. For data collection, I used multimodal artefact production and Golpo/adda (Bengali genre of informal discussion) as primary methods. Multimodal artefact production in this research was a method where participants captured their experiences of technology use in a mode/medium of their choice. The advantage of using participant-generated data lies in the fact that aspects of identity and experiences can be observed and learned about which might never have been imagined by the researcher [19, p. 33]. Moreover, multimodal artefact production creates a space for participants in research and might help participants to express their realities in their way.

In this paper, I focus on the story of one of the participants in my PhD research, Aparajita (Pseudonym chosen by the participant). When I started my PhD, I had contacted a2i for permission to conduct research with rural multimedia teachers. The programme director arranged for the research to take place in rural Hatia. During an initial 15-day fieldwork on the island, I discussed the concept of informed consent with teachers and discussed the participant information sheets. A total of 6 teachers agreed to participate in my PhD research. I requested participants to send me artefacts every two weeks in response to two prompts: what does multimedia mean to you? And what are your significant experiences of the week? The artefact production period continued from October 2017 to May, 2018. Aparajita had sent in different combinations of artefacts each two weeks. At the end of the data collection period Aparajita's artefacts included 6 audio clips, 3 video clips, 28 diary entries, 54 images with captions, 5 links, 19 screenshots, 3 poems and 8 PowerPoints.

Besides multimodal artefact production, I conducted two golpo sessions with Aparajita. A golpo is a distinctive Bengali form of discussion which communicates equal relations, friendliness and emotional connection. I used this contextually meaningful way to engage with Aparajita instead of interviews to communicate at a deeper level and position myself more as an equal. The first golpo session was face to face (50 min) to know about her story of becoming a multimedia teacher, to understand how she developed over time since 2012, future intentions, feelings and opinions as well as build rapport. At the end of data production, we engaged in a second golpo session (45 min) in which we discussed in-depth the themes that I constructed from the data. For instance, with regard to positioning we discussed if, how and why this feeling of position had developed from 2012 and her current views on this aspect.

The goal of this qualitative study is to provide a rich, contextualized understanding of how the meaning of educational technology was emerging through analysing Aparajita's experiences over time. Aparajita's story of positioning via educational technology is representative of all 6 participants who took part in my PhD research. However, how generalisable this finding is of other multimedia teachers in context remains subject to further research.

3.2 Analysis

I did a thematic analysis of Aparajita's artefacts and interviews to understand how technology and social were influencing each other and how technology related identity was emerging. I followed the steps from Braun and Clarke [5] for thematic analysis. The first step was reading and re-reading the data to allow underlying meanings and concepts to evolve before coding. I also transcribed the data in this phase. I transcribed in Bengali to keep the meaning intact and avoid losing connotations in the process of translation. In the second step, I coded the data (in Bengali) inductively with a focus on how technology and the social were interacting with each other and how identities were emerging. In the third step, I deductively coded the data in light of Holland et al.'s [14] theory, particularly drawing on their conceptualisation of cultural artefact, positioning and identity. The final step involved sorting and combining codes into potential themes. I also tried to understand the relationships between different themes and subthemes. The story of Aparajita that I constructed below is a result of the interaction between my structured prompts, golpo sessions, Aparajita's artefacts and my interpretation of these based on Holland et al.'s [4] theory.

4 Conceptual Framework: Figured Worlds

Holland et al. [14] illuminate the continuous, iterative, connected and bi-directional development process of the cultural artefact, identity and lived worlds that happen through participation in everyday and local activities rather than approaching the artefact, the person and the lived worlds as final, finished products. Holland et al. [14] argue for examining the heuristic development of the artefact over time to understand better how artefacts, people and lived worlds become what they are. Holland and Valsiner [15, p. 254] cite the example of a study on the use of Marijuana which showed how novice smokers not only learned techniques for ingesting the drugs from others but more significantly, learned the meaning and purpose of ingesting Marijuana from others over time. The 'smoker's high' sensation that expert smokers felt were not felt initially by the novice smokers, they were 'trained and encouraged' by other expert smokers to do so. In other words, motivation, meaning and purpose for using the drug was socially shaped over time rather than being a result only of the artefact's (cigarette's) physical effects.

Following Vygotsky, Holland et al. [14, p. 225] argue that cultural artefacts are 'not only part of the context but are part of the content of 'inner life' in a modified way." People encounter and learn cultural artefacts socially, through interaction with others. Over time these become symbols to be incorporated in the mental processes. When the individual takes these artefacts to be 'meaningful for herself' they become potential mediating devices for 'organising knowledge. By 'making meaningful', Holland et al. [14, p. 6] mean using it for one's purpose, i.e. using the artefact for guiding problem-solving, shaping feelings, remembering goals, reminding oneself about their identities, in short to effect, guide and evaluate own actions and thoughts. For example, the cigarette over time became a symbol of pleasure and could be used to control one's mood. While individuals use the devices to manage their behaviour, the device itself starts to evoke related thoughts and emotions and thus influences the person. While the artefact is social in that it originates in the social world, it then becomes equally individual as it starts to constitute the thought, emotion and behaviour of the person by whom it is being reproduced [14, p. 225]. In this way, cultural artefacts can act as a mediational link between culture and cognition. [23, p. 193]. This is called semiotic mediation.

Through semiotic mediation, people might develop identities related to cultural arte-facts. Identification is the shift that occurs when people appropriate the cultural artefacts to guide actions and emotions [9, p. 251]. For instance, Deirdre et al. [9, p. 251] cite the example of how the cultural artefact white coat was internalised by doctors through semiotic mediation to develop self-understanding and motivation. Putting on the white coat made students feel like a doctor which in turn allowed 'self-direction' to act like a doctor. Holland et al. [14] discuss two aspects of such identities, i.e. figured identities and positional identities. For this paper, I will discuss the concept of positioning and positional identity. According to Deirdre et al. [9, p. 251], positional identity refers to:

> A person's apprehension of their social position in the lived world. We claim position and we position others every day through social interaction…positional identity is about inclusion and exclusion, entitlement, silencing, distance and affil-iation. As novices enter a Figured World they gain a sense of their position within it,…. Day to day positioning in cultural worlds is therefore another mediator of identity.

Positional identity develops through positioning acts which are acts indicating power, status privilege, distance affiliation, entitlement and how these are negotiated. It is about how experiences of inclusion, exclusion, recognition, humiliation shape our sense of position and how we view ourselves [9, p. 251].

Holland and Lave [16, p. 8] also highlight the importance of paying attention to the inner struggles in the process of mediation. Other social voices might be in conflict with the use of the artefact as a symbolic tool. Close attention to participants' inner debates might highlight these social tensions. For instance, a group of environmentalists interviewed by Holland and Lave [16, p. 8] were found to be developing in relation to the artefact of waste. At the beginning they had little knowledge about their waste production. By participating in the group over time they learned ways of weighing and producing less waste. They met weekly and discussed how they felt bad about high amounts of waste produced by Americans. In this way they developed new meanings and 'emotional evaluations' regarding the waste produced by themselves and others. They were forming as environmentalists in local practice through semiotic mediation of the cultural artefact of 'waste.' However, they were also found to be struggling over whether they were too extreme. The activists sometimes fell back on terms such as 'granola head' or 'treehugger' that were used by their parents and friends to communicate disdain. This sheds light on the broader social tensions around environmental activism in America.

5   Findings

5.1   PowerPoint as a Tool for Social Validation

Aparajita was one of the earliest adopters of multimedia technology in the island of Hatia. Despite infrastructural challenges such as only a couple of hours of electricity per day, Aparajita was a regular user of technology and had received quite a few awards for her contributions as a multimedia teacher. In our first golpo session Aparajita started her story with how she became a primary teacher:

> "I wanted to become a teacher but never a primary school teacher. I always wanted to be a college teacher. I had a dream to be a college teacher…My father died and I could not go for higher studies outside the island. Because, you know, I am the eldest daughter of the family, all responsibilities fell on me. I graduated from a local degree college here. Then because of family pressure I appeared in an interview for the primary teacher post. I got the job"

This quote exemplifies her previous sense of position in the social hierarchy. The primary teacher position is usually considered the lowest in the hierarchy of teachers in Bangladesh. In the following sections, I will provide examples from my data regarding how, through social interactions, PowerPoint use was becoming a symbol of social position. I will also describe how technology use seemed to be shaping social relations (from Aparajita's point of view) and shifting Aparajita's sense of position.

Social Appreciation
One of the ways Aparajita experienced a different positioning than before was through social validation. In most of Aparajita's audio clips and a few places in the golpo, she talked about how PowerPoint use led to different forms of social validation from different social groups. She received higher appreciation from students, colleagues, and higher-level officials. A typical example of how students were positioning Aparajita as more appreciated than before was as follows:

> "When I do a multimedia class, I cannot keep other classes out of the multimedia room. The whole school gathers in my class. Everyone keeps saying, "Do it for us, we want to see this too! Oh, the happiness that I see in them after the multimedia class! After doing a multimedia class what happens is, they do not want to do a 'normal' class" (golpo, October 2017)

In context, the relation between teachers and students is usually that of power and deference. PowerPoint mediated classrooms brought in "fun and enjoyment through animations, videos, and songs" (golpo, October 2017). Technology use seemed to add a new dimension to the student-teacher relation, that of appreciation and interest. Not only students, Aparajita's diary entries regularly mentioned experiences of being appreciated by teachers across the country in the portal. For instance, diary entry, 13th December 2017: "Other teachers' appreciative comments are giving me the inspiration to work even more" Or "It is because the unity within us and inspirations from my colleagues that I have come so far (diary entry, 20th March 2018). Whereas previously colleagues rarely commented on each other's work, a different relation seemed to be developing based on appreciation and inspiration. She also mentioned a few times how she received attention and appreciation from higher officials whom she expected never to notice a 'primary teacher' and 'villager' like her:

"In the digital mela we were supposed to present our PowerPoints. The programme director was concerned about me-"she has come from Hatia, can she do it?' Another official said let's give her a chance. In my PowerPoint, there was a poem connected to the topic to create emotions in children. Sir called me after the presentation-where did you get the poem from, was it from google? I said no sir, I wrote it myself. He was astonished, he called everyone and started to say, listen she wrote this herself. He was so happy-he started to say this is the kind of teacher we need-we need creative people like you, from then on, he has always inspired me to go forward. It is precisely this valuing and this recognition- this valuation is the reason I want to work more and more" (2nd golpo, May 2018)

Aparajita narrated many similar experiences which demonstrated instances of possible changing relations: from deference to recognition. She was being positioned and defined based on her capabilities. She was becoming someone to be appreciated instead of her identity as a villager or primary school teacher. Use of PowerPoint in this way seemed to mediated ground relations with higher-level officials, colleagues and students in the educational system.

Inclusion and Exclusion

Another way Aparajita's sense of social position might have been developing was through experiences of access to specific spaces related to technology use. According to Holland et al. [14, p. 134], spaces can act as vehicles of positioning by including/excluding people or signifying greater and lesser access. Holland et al. [14, p. 134] term this inclusionary/exclusionary work which is 'simply done by including or excluding certain people from sites.'

Quite a few of the images Aparajita sent me as significant experience showed her along with other multimedia teachers attending government organised educational fairs like shikkha upkoron mela (educational artefact fair), unnoyon mela (development fair), specialised training, workshops, special conferences, and retreats. These were arranged by the government to showcase educational and developmental achievements in local communities. Aparajita, along with other multimedia teachers, were the ones chosen to represent education in these spaces. Primary teachers not interested in technology use had no access to these.

Not only spaces but also various awards, and leadership positions created by the government for multimedia teachers might have also been acting as an inclusion/exclusion device. Aparajita received the best teacher award in 2013. She received the award for teachers' portal popularization in 2017. These gave Aparajita a sense of honour and recognition. One of the typical examples of this was when, she recounted her feeling in the following way after receiving the award for teachers' portal popularization: "I am overwhelmed with this respect, this achievement. My heart is like a kaleidoscope sky with a thousand colours of happiness" (5th December 2017). Teachers not interested in using technology did not have an alternative recognition system for valuing their work. Multimedia teachers hence had a kind of privileged access, consequently producing additional value compared to other school teachers.

Stories of Mouth

The recognition and acknowledgement seemed to produce a ripple effect in Aparajita's island and the teacher community through stories of mouth. All of the participants, local government officials, her family members, her headteacher whom I met during my fieldwork mentioned Aparajita as a person of respect. In my research, all of the participants mentioned a few times, how Aparajita was a person of respect and inspiration in the community. For instance, one of the participants, Henna commented on how trainers were always mentioning Aparajita to them, "She was very famous, her name was on everyone's mouth, like a woman from Hatia island has done such a great job, so creative. This kind of turned into an inspiration for me." Another participant Jeba commented on how Aparajita was a renowned name in the teachers' community: "When the multimedia classes first started, I first heard that our Aparajita had received training on this and she has achieved fame across the country." In this way, experiences of appreciation, inclusion/exclusion and recognition seemed to be giving rise to modified relations and new positioning experiences for Aparajita.

5.2   Internalising the PowerPoint as a Positioning Tool

Through these positioning experiences over time, recognition and appreciation seemed to become one of the preferred purposes of PowerPoint use. Aparajita equated being a multimedia teacher more with special awards, recognitions and privileged access than use in the classroom. For instance, in response to the prompt significant experiences of being a multimedia teacher, she sent a video titled 'my most memorable moments'. The video featured her experiences of being appreciated and recognised through various awards, workshops, and training. There was no mention of pedagogical use in the classroom.

The following quote also shows how she perceived the PowerPoint as a tool for achieving social appreciation. When I asked how she used to develop her PowerPoints, she replied:

"I felt as if I was in a kind of trans, I was mesmerized. I always used to think, I am doing something in one way in the slides-but how can I make it better? There was a thirst for more and more appreciation- there was a yearning for more good comments from everyone. I wanted everyone to appreciate my work. This thirst of appreciation, of recognition, kept me working without stopping"

I found more examples like this throughout her diary entries and audio clips. For instance, "I have uploaded content in batayon today. Teachers' encouraging comments will generate more inspiration for me to work" (audio clip, 15th February 2018). Identification happens when people appropriate a cultural artefact to guide emotions and actions. We can see that Aparajita had appropriated the socially developed meaning (of validation) to guide her actions and emotions (achieve validation) regarding the PowerPoint. Whereas previously she felt undervalued as a teacher now she had developed a sense of valued position: "I am being able to work even within such a busy life only because I am being recognised and valued (diary entry 18th October 2017). Uploading the PowerPoints seemed to help her enter a new world, experience a new social positioning and become a new 'I'. This sense of becoming a different 'I' can also be seen in her comments: "I can't even imagine. I started working with multimedia without understanding anything. Now look where I have arrived! I can't imagine… I am uploading content, downloading content, making members on batayon." In other words, Aparajita seemed to have developed a new positional identity in relation to technology use.

5.3 Conflicts and Tensions

However, using PowerPoint was not only a source of social validation and new relations but also a source of social conflict. Aparajita, in the first golpo session mentioned how she was limited in her scope due to being an assistant teacher:

> "My headteacher doesn't see value in technology. If I ever become a headteacher I have a dream to change my whole school, all of the classes into multimedia classrooms. This is one of my dreams…because assistant teachers like me have a lot of limitations. They can't do a lot of things even if they wish. That's why as an assistant I can't do a lot of things. But maybe if I become a headteacher, maybe 10 years from now, I have a dream to make my school a model multimedia school"

The quote illustrates different experiences of positioning in her world as a multimedia teacher. She cannot use the PowerPoint all the time as the headteacher sees it as 'detrimental to education'. Due to the existing social structure and hierarchy, she silenced herself rather than protesting and expressing her belief in technology use. Thus, the hierarchy was reproduced within the boundaries of the school. However, she showed some resistance to this positioning by imagining her future practice where she, as a headteacher will use multimedia as extensively as she wants. She also showed resistance by continuing to produce PowerPoints in the e-portal.

Another tension was emerging with non-ICT using teachers. Aparajita mentioned how the non-ICT 'group' were spreading rumours about multimedia classrooms:

> "I think the reason for this is professional jealousy. They are trying to spread that multimedia is harming the education of children. They are only highlighting any possible disadvantages. They are not talking about the advantages. Guardians misunderstand us multimedia teachers. The headteacher is not very positive after this" (Diary entry, November 2017)

Here she is positioned as detrimental to education and resists this positioning by arguing how this is not the case. She is giving more weight to technology. In another place, Aparajita showed resistance by positioning herself as separate from non-ICT using teachers and casting them as 'ancient':

> "I have two types of colleagues. Ancient (traditional) and progressive. When I started to work, then a number of these people, who had aged a bit, close to retirement, they used to disturb me. They used to say no, what are these? Why are you doing these? We don't need these. These destroy classes, harm children. They had influenced the headteacher a lot. Younger teachers did not create problems for us."

This quote also serves to exemplify the conflict with the cultural notion of good education. Technology use clashed with the existing definition of a good teacher and education based on teaching the textbook and teaching to the examination. The restricted definition of good education constructed multimedia teachers as detrimental and positioned them as harmful in context. Aparajita drew attention to the problem of introducing anything new let alone technology, "No one wants to accept anything new, they just say, eh! What is this? Why do we need this?"

6   Discussion and Conclusions

The examples from my data above show how the PowerPoint was being used for social purposes, i.e. negotiation and renegotiation of positioning. Previous research has concentrated predominantly on the 'product' or outcomes of the social shaping of educational technology (as discussed in the introduction). The brief account above shows some examples of the 'processes' through which educational technologies might emerge. Through day to day processes of appreciation, recognition, exclusion/inclusion, stories of mouth, distancing and imagining, technology use was emerging as a social tool in teachers' world.

Material practices of creating and using the PowerPoint became intertwined with Aparajita's subjective understanding of who she was through a process of semiotic mediation. The government had created the subject position of a multimedia teacher along with possibilities of rewards. However, material practices like making and using the PowerPoint led to day to day social experiences of respect, appreciation, recognition in the community. Over time, Aparajita attached these emotional meanings to the PowerPoint and started using the PowerPoint for achieving these purposes. The experiences also created a shift in Aparajita's sense of position. Therefore, the change Aparajita underwent was much more than a change in behaviour; it was a change in positional identity. Moreover, Aparajita's previous understanding of herself as an undervalued primary teacher and villager might also have been a reason why she experienced use of the PowerPoint as social validation. Other teachers who do not feel undervalued might not develop the same emotions and consequently, a positional sense of self in relation to the PowerPoint. The results of this research also imply like Selwyn [29] that engagement with technology can create a sense of separation between technology and non-technology users. The superordination of the multimedia teacher and subordination of other teachers went on through positioning processes. It was a medium through which multimedia teachers could conceptualise themselves as validated and respected. Technology itself did not exclude any group of teachers; it was the validation, recognition, spaces and circulating stories that acted as a vehicle for such inclusion and exclusion. This understanding adds to the gap in educational technology research by shedding light on how educational technology becomes part of conceptualizing the self [12].

By adopting a developmental view of both individual and social, in contrast to previous studies, I have shown how social-relational changes might have started to emerge in incremental steps. Relations with students, colleagues and higher-level officials were being perceived as of a changed nature by Aparajita. Technology implementation also led to reproducing the hierarchical relationships among the assistant teachers and head-teacher within school boundaries. Aparajita did not accept the position offered by the headteacher but showed resistance through activities like continuing to make Power-Points for the portal. Also, by imagining a future world where she would be able to use technology according to her wishes. This points towards the importance of alternative material and imaginary spaces for resisting contradictions and developing agency. Besides being a matter of power dynamics or hierarchy, social resistance to technology in schools was reflective of tension with larger structures like the pedagogical culture. For years the education system in Bangladesh was textbook-based and examination driven. Any departure from the textbook or any content not related to the examination was perceived as detrimental. In this way, clashes with wider structures like hierarchy and pedagogy were playing out in local conflicts through processes of positioning, discursive resistance like imagining, distancing and material resistance like practicing in alternative spaces. From the realm of material practice, PowerPoint use entered the realm of subjective and social practice to form, signal, and maintain position. This paper aimed to present one teacher's perceptions and experiences of educational technology in depth. Future research could aim to understand the points of view of all other relevant social groups, i.e. students, higher officials, headteachers, non-technology using teachers and more multimedia teachers to understand further how educational technology might have emerged as a positioning tool in rural Bangladesh.

References

1. Access to Information (a2i) Programme: The Teachers' Portal as a Tool for Teachers' Professional Development in Bangladesh. Special Feature on 3rd Anniversary of Multimedia Classroom. Prime Minister's Office, Dhaka (June, 2015)
2. Agalianos, A., Whitty, G., Noss, R.: The social shaping of Logo. Soc. Stud. Sci. 36(2), 241–267 (2006)
3. Bernstein, S.: OER and the value of openness: implications for the knowledge economy. Global. Soc. Educ. 13(4), 471–486 (2015)
4. Beckman, K., Apps, T., Bennett, S., Lockyer, L.: Conceptualising technology practice in education using Bourdieu's sociology. Learn. Media and Technol. 43(2), 197–210 (2018)
5. Braun, V., Clarke, V.: Using thematic analysis in psychology. Qual. Res. Psychol. 3(2), 77–101 (2006)
6. Burnett, C.: Pre-service teachers' digital literacy practices: exploring contingency in identity and digital literacy in and out of educational contexts. Lang. Educ. 25(5), 433–449 (2011)
7. Clegg, S., Hudson, A., Steel, J.: The emperor's new clothes: globalisation and e-learning in higher education. Br. J. Sociol. Educ. 24(1), 39–53 (2003). https://doi.org/10.1080/014256 90301914
8. Collin, S., Brotcorne, P.: Capturing digital (in)equity in teaching and learning: a sociocritical approach. Int. J. Inf. Learn. Technol. 36(2), 169–180 (2019)
9. Deirdre, B., Solomon, Y., Bergin, C., Horgan, M., Dornan, T.: Possibility and agency in Figured Worlds: becoming a 'good doctor'. Med. Educ. 3(2017), 248–257 (2017)
10. Guilherme, A.: AI and education: the importance of teacher and student relations. AI Soc. 34(1), 47–54 (2017). https://doi.org/10.1007/s00146-017-0693-8
11. Grieshaber, S.: Beyond a battery hen model? A computer laboratory, micropolitics and educational change. Br. J. Sociol. Educ. 31(4), 431–447 (2010). https://doi.org/10.1080/01425692. 2010.484920
12. Goos, M.: A sociocultural analysis of the development of pre-service and beginning teachers' pedagogical identities as users of technology. J. Math. Teacher Educ. 8(1), 35–59 (2005)

13. Henderson, M., Bradey, S.: Shaping online teaching practices: the influence of professional and academic identities. Campus-Wide Inf. Syst. **25**(2), 85–92 (2008)
14. Holland, D.C., Lachicotte Jr., W., Skinner, D., Cain, C.: Identity and Agency in Cultural Worlds. Harvard University Press, Cambridge (2001)
15. Holland, D.C., Valsiner, J.: Cognition, symbols, and Vygotsky's developmental psychology. Ethos **16**(3), 247–272 (1988)
16. Holland, D., Lave, J.: History in Person: Enduring Struggles, Contentious Practice, Intimate Identities. SAR Press (2001)
17. Johnson, D.: Technological change and professional control in the professoriate. Sci. Technol. Human Values **38**, 126–149 (2013)
18. Karasavvidis, I.: Activity Theory as a conceptual framework for understanding teacher approaches to Information and Communication Technologies. Comput. Educ. **53**(2), 436–444 (2009)
19. Mannay, D.: Visual, Narrative and Creative Research Methods: Application, Reflection and Ethics. Routledge, New York (2015)
20. Oliver, M.: Learning technology: theorising the tools we study. Br. J. Edu. Technol. **44**(1), 31–43 (2013)
21. Oliver, M.: What is Technology. In: Rushby, N. (ed.) The Wiley Handbook of Learning Technology, vol. 1, pp. 35–57. Wiley (2016)
22. Phillips, M.: Processes of practice and identity shaping teachers' TPACK enactment in a community of practice. Edu. Inf. Technol. **22**(4), 1771–1796 (2016). https://doi.org/10.1007/s10639-016-9512-y
23. Robinson, C.: Figured world of history learning in a social studies methods classroom. Urban Rev. **39**(2), 191–216 (2007)
24. Rosenberg, J.M., Koehler, M.J.: Context and technological pedagogical content knowledge (TPACK): a systematic review. J. Res. Technol. Educ. **47**(3), 186–210 (2015)
25. Selwyn, N.: The use of computer technology in university teaching and learning: a critical perspective. J. Comput. Assist. Learn. **23**(2), 83–94 (2007). https://doi.org/10.1111/j.1365-2729.2006.00204.x
26. Selwyn, N.: Making sense of young people, education and digital technology: the role of sociological theory. Oxford Rev. Educ. **38**(1), 81–96 (2012)
27. Selwyn, N., Facer, K.: The sociology of education and digital technology: past, present and future. Oxford Rev. Educ. **40**(4), 482–496 (2014)
28. Selwyn, N.: Technology and education—why it's crucial to be critical. In: Bulfin, S., Johnson, N., Bigum, C. (eds.) Critical Perspectives on Technology and Education 2015, pp. 245–255. Palgrave Macmillan, New York (2015)
29. Selwyn, N., Nemorin, S., Johnson, N.: High-tech, hard work: an investigation of teachers' work in the digital age. Learn. Media Technol. **42**(4), 390–405 (2017)
30. Tour, E.: Digital mindsets: teachers' technology use in personal life and teaching. Lang. Learn. Technol. **19**(3), 124–139 (2015)
31. UNDP (United Nations Development Programme). Bangladesh School Classrooms Get High-Tech Makeover [Video File]. https://youtu.be/FCMkM1LrSGk. Accessed 10 Feb 2011

Inclusion and Participation

ICT-Based Participation in Support of Palestinian Refugees' Sustainable Livelihoods: A Local Authority Perspective

Osama Aradeh$^{(\boxtimes)}$ ⓘ, Jean-Paul Van Belle$^{(\boxtimes)}$ ⓘ, and Adheesh Budree$^{(\boxtimes)}$ ⓘ

University of Cape Town, Rondebosch, Cape Town 7700, South Africa
ardosa001@myuct.ac.za,
{jean-paul.vanbelle,adheesh.budree}@uct.ac.za

Abstract. This study investigates how e-participation could improve the livelihoods of marginalized and disadvantaged groups, in particular, refugees in the Gaza Strip in Palestine. They constantly faced problems of basic services of water supply, electricity, housing and infrastructure in their daily lives. This study was conducted from the perspective of municipalities which are local authorities which providing services and responsible to address these issues. This study used a qualitative research method by means of in-depth interviews. Thirteen interviewees from four municipalities in the Gaza Strip participated in the study and were given open-ended questions to express their views about the phenomenon. Thematic analysis was adopted to analyze the interview transcripts. Two theme clusters were uncovered: consequences of e-participation as increasing information and raising awareness among refugees, saving time, and long-term direct relationships with their stakeholders, and livelihood outcomes which include poverty alleviation and unemployment reduction as well as increased well-being. There are challenges that persist in e-participation implementation in the Gaza Strip including ICT infrastructure and the culture of the society. However, the findings of this study reveal evidence of the benefits of e-participation implementation and how livelihood outcomes have influence in refugee contexts.

Keywords: E-participation · ICT-based participation · Sustainable livelihoods · Livelihoods outcomes · Refugees · Palestine · The Gaza Strip

1 Introduction

The importance of Information and Communication Technologies (ICTs) has been emphasized in refugee studies, for example, in the role of ICTs in the integration of refugees [1] and the facilitation of social inclusion of newly resettled refugees [2]. One form of ICT usage, e-participation, "technology-facilitated citizen participation in (democratic) deliberation and decision-making" [3: 408], enables the transformation and extension of participation in consultative processes and societal democracy and embodies democratic values [4].

© IFIP International Federation for Information Processing 2020
Published by Springer Nature Switzerland AG 2020
J. M. Bass and P. J. Wall (Eds.): ICT4D 2020, IFIP AICT 587, pp. 129–141, 2020.
https://doi.org/10.1007/978-3-030-65828-1_11

However, while there has been an increasing interest in e-participation, research to date has focused on government-citizen interaction [5] and engaging citizens in government decision-making [6]. As yet, there is limited research on e-participation in refugee contexts and its impact on the sustainability of their livelihoods. E-participation has the potential to connect refugee voices to the relevant stakeholders; establish mutual trust and long-term relationships between refugees and service providing institutions to enhance access to services and enhance overall livelihood improvement [7]. E-participation can be useful in the thus far under-researched context of refugees such as those living in the Gaza Strip in the Middle East.

Palestinian refugees in the Gaza Strip constitute every person whose normal place of residence was Palestine from 1 June 1946–15 May 1948, and who lost both home and means of livelihood as a result of the 1948 Arab-Israeli conflict [8]. Since the 1948 the United Nations Relief and Works Agency (UNRWA) has provided humanitarian relief, access to services and employment for Palestinian refugees pending the regional political settlement to release the economic blockade on Gaza [9]. The UNRWA, in collaboration with other donor agencies, have been engaging in the development of sustainable livelihood strategies in the delivery of essential health, social and educational services, employment and vocational training [10].

The Palestinian ICT sector is recognized by both the Palestinian private sector and the Palestinian Authority as an important sector for economic viability and growth [11]. Palestinian telecommunications companies provide internet services via digital subscriber line, fiber optics and microwave communication through neighboring countries such as Israel, Jordan and Egypt [12]. Despite the conditions and restrictions are imposed by the Israeli authorities [11, 13], the ICT sector in the Gaza Strip progressed in early 2018 with the launch of telecommunications providers of the 3G services to the population of the Gaza Strip [14]. Given this and the fact that, according to the census of [15], 75.5% of households in the Gaza Strip in Palestine have smartphones, the infrastructure for e-participation is available.

The overarching purpose of this study is to explore the influence of e-participation on the sustainability of livelihoods among Palestinian refugees in the Gaza Strip. The study further purposes to investigate the relationship between e-participation and livelihood outcomes. Finally, the study aims to provide insights into the forms of e-participation that are present in the context of refugees.

Therefore, this study asks the following main research questions: *What are the results of e-participation based on the use of e-channels and activities between refugees and local authorities* and *How does e-participation influence sustainable livelihoods of refugees in the Gaza Strip?*

Section two of this paper highlights the use of ICT in the refugee context and links key theoretical concepts of e-participation to sustainable livelihoods. The conceptual model used in this study, which is based on the theories of e-participation and sustainable livelihoods, is outlined, followed by a methodology section that justifies an interpretive paradigm and a qualitative approach to understanding the interplay between context and e-participation. The findings are then revealed and explained.

2 Background

2.1 ICTs in Context of Refugee Studies

The importance of ICTs has been emphasized in refugee studies; for example, the role of ICTs in the integration of refugees, the facilitation of social inclusion on newly resettled refugees (allowing refugees to connect effectively in communities and areas that have become fragmented during their movement), and ICTs use is seen as beneficial to vulnerable groups, such as refugees, as they can more easily communicate with society and stakeholders [14, 16, 17].

ICT-based participation has earned considerable attention from different disciplines, such as contributions from political science, management, economics, psychology and technology-oriented studies, which are key to the role of transnational communication for and research on refugees [16]. Thus, the interest of charitable and humanitarian organizations in ICT initiatives has increased and could serve as a potential solution for refugees where ICT-based communications, such as smartphones, provide a convenient means of accessing information related to humanitarian assistance, food, water, and other social services [18].

With increasing access to social media in all its forms, ICT-based participation is expanding worldwide across several channels to meet community needs and enhance collaboration between communities and governments as they aim to achieve better and greater participation of society [19]. In this vein, governments around the world have made significant investments to utilize the potential of ICTs for participation to inform and to consult with public stakeholders [6]. The definition of ICT-based participation is considered in the follow.

2.2 E-participation

The concept of e-participation revolves around the promotion of community participation and open participatory governance through ICT. E-participation aims at improving access to information and public services, empowering individuals and benefiting their communities [20]. There is growing evidence pointing to the noticeable and rapid expansion of e-participation as a tool to enhance community engagement and interaction with local authorities [20]. Furthermore, the use of ICTs in public participation is termed e-participation [18]. Public participation acts as an interaction channel between the community and the government to formulate better decisions that have a positive influence on the lives of refugees [21, 22]. Thus, public participation can be considered the basic building block underlying e-participation [6].

The improved use of ICT in Palestine is a key component of national infrastructure to improve living standards, especially when used to facilitate public services [11]. The Gaza Strip faces challenges in the infrastructure of the water and sanitation sector, electricity, roads and the exacerbation of environmental problems [23]. Refugees and the population generally, depend heavily on local authorities such as municipalities for improvements [24]. To this end, this study seeks to investigate a form of ICT, which is e-participation between refugees and municipalities.

2.3 Sustainable Livelihoods, Use of ICTs and E-participation

The term "livelihood not only refers to people, their capabilities and means of living but also to the ownership and articulation of information that is vital for the effective utilization of the assets people use to obtain a living" [25: 209] and to "maintain and sustain their life" [21: 7]. ICTs play a crucial role in social and economic development as well as in ensuring sustainable livelihoods [22]. Furthermore, ICTs have a meaningful influence on sustainable livelihoods, which include natural, social, human, physical and financial capitals [26]. ICTs can also promote the delivery of strategies between the poor for their livelihoods [27] when institutions involved in promoting sustainable livelihoods are using ICTs to collect and disseminate information to the community [26]. In addition, public participation has become a central concept contributing to an increase in well-being [17]. Increased well-being is considered an important outcome of livelihoods [28].

ICTs used for sustainable livelihood is popular in the refugee context and many studies have focused on how ICT use is leverage either for providing information or through interactive mobile app to improve lives of refugees [1]. Studies on ICT use as a form of e-participation is lacking though in the refugee context. However, e-participation phenomenon is bound to exist in the context if refugees are interacting with authorities through the ICT channel to sustain their livelihood. To this end, this study, relying on the conceptual model in Table 1, seeks to explore the influence of e-participation consequence on refugee livelihoods outcomes.

Table 1. Proposed conceptual model for the study

ICT-BASED PARTICIPATION CONSEQUENCES	*LIVELIHOOD OUTCOMES BASED ON E-PARTICIPATION*
• *Increase Information and Raising Awareness* • *Save Time and Money* • *Long-Term Direct Relationships*	• *Reducing Poverty* • *Increased Well-Being.*

2.4 Conceptual Model for the Study

Adopting on Sustainable Livelihoods Approach as used by [28]. However, while [28] underscored the analytical and functional role of ICTs as information technology, this study focused on e-participation consequences and livelihood outcomes conceptualized as an influence in refugee livelihoods. Table 1 shows the conceptual model for the study.

3 Research Methodology

The purpose of this research is to study the phenomenon of ICT-based participation and its impact on the livelihoods of refugees in the context of the Gaza Strip, Palestine. The interpretive paradigm was to investigate this phenomenon. In the interpretive paradigm, a researcher makes understands and interpretation transcribed documents, data and notes collected throughout the investigation [29]. Face to face interviews were done with representatives of local authorities and the data were analyzed using thematic analysis. The researcher encountered difficulties to obtain permission from service providers in the Gaza strip due to restricted access. However, the researcher managed to obtain approval to conduct interviews from some municipalities which are also mandated to providing community services. The qualitative approach is usually used to look at the creation of meaning or interpretations in particular contexts because they investigate phenomena from multiple aspects [30]. Furthermore, this methodology is convenient when the objective of the study is to investigate a phenomenon in a specific context, that has not or only marginally been addressed in other studies [31].

Written approvals were obtained from those municipalities and interviews were conducted between February and May 2019. Participants were informed that participation is voluntary, and they could withdraw at any time. The consent to recording the interview was obtained from the participants, except two interviewees who refused to record and simply answered the questions. Flexible and open-ended questions were asked to provide participants with the opportunity to give open and in-depth answers about the phenomenon of e-participation effects on the sustainable livelihoods of refugees in the Gaza Strip, Palestine. The interviews lasted between 30 to 40 min for each participant. Preliminary observations were written on each answer for initial analysis. When participants' answers were vague, subsequent questions were asked for more information. Thematic analysis was conducted to analyze the qualitative data [32]. The interviews were conducted individually and separately. During the individual in-depth interviews, their verbal and non-verbal information was registered on the phenomenon of "e-participation and its influence on the livelihoods of refugees in the Gaza Strip".

4   Study Sample

This study was conducted where more than sixty-five percent (65%) of the population lives as refugees in the Gaza Strip [33]. Thirteen interviews were conducted in four main municipalities in the Gaza Strip: *Rafah, Khan-Younis, Nuseirat and Jabalia.* The interviewees include three mayors, four public services and relations department officials, two community activities department official, two social media supervisors, and two members who work in ICT and e-service in their municipalities as shown in Table 2. Although the author noted that some women are working in the administrative field in the four municipalities (place of study), the approvals granted for interviews were for men only. The interviewees were between 26 and 50 years of age, ranging from 5 years to more than 15 years of experience* (Table 2). The qualifications of the participants are at least a bachelor's degree.

Table 2. Participants' demographic information

Positions	Mayor of municipality			Public services and relations				Social media supervisors		Community activities		ICT and e-service	
ID	P1	P7	P13	P2	P3	P8	P12	P5	P10	P9	P11	P4	P6
Age	>45	36–45	36–45	26–35	26–35	36–45	>45	26–35	36–45	26–35	>45	26–35	26–35
Exp*.	>15	>15	>15	10–15	10–15	10–15	>15	10–15	10–15	1–5	>15	1–5	1–5

5 Findings and Discussion

Thematic analysis is conducted to analyze the qualitative data [32]. The thematic analysis was used for all interviews to attempt to understand and evaluate study data. A pre-defined set of themes were derived from the conceptual model. The transcripts were read several times. Extract of the transcripts that matched the pre-defined themes were grouped in the respective themes. Data analysis followed a deductive approach. Two main themes were categorized. The analysis section illustrates and discusses the follow themes: e-participation consequences and livelihood outcomes based on e-participation.

5.1 ICT-Based Participation Consequences

In this main theme, *ICT-based Participation Consequences*, three outputs of the coherent interaction between refugees and service providers were described based on the existing e-participation implementation strategies.

Increasing Information and Raising Awareness. The data showed that interviewees focused on the role of e-participation channels to increase information and raise awareness among refugees relating to their well-being and basic needs. Participant **P12** said, *"e-participation is a very effective means to refute the rumours, raise awareness among people..."*. That was confirmed by participant **P9**, *"the municipality's specialized media team prepares awareness-raising short videos through social media platforms..."*. Whereas participants **P8** and **P11** emphasised that e-means of participation play a big role in transferring information -quickly among the local community.

Despite the negative view of many community members, including refugees, that the municipality is only for the collection of information, municipalities are trying, through e-participation tools and activities, to change this concept in society as much as possible, as asserted by participant **P13**. However, there is a different view from participant **P12**, who stated, *"providing basic information to the community members for increasing information and raising awareness is vague, because it does not make sense to publish unnecessary information..."*

Consequences of E-channels Use and E-activities of Communication and Interaction Between Refugees and Service Providers from Municipalities. The interviewees agreed on the positive role of these channels in sharing information and improving the quality of decisions within the municipality. This supports what [16] argued. Institutions and organizations involved in livelihoods also use ICTs to collect and disseminate information to the community [27].

Saving Time and Money. Through the analysed data of this sub-theme, it can be noted that e-channels have greatly helped people to minimize the transportation costs and efforts of visiting the services providers' offices, particularly the disadvantaged, elderly and disabled. Participant **P10** confirmed that *"citizens and refugees can communicate with the municipality through e-platforms and direct contact that save the transportation cost..."*. This finding is equally supported by participants **P3** and **P7**. A further indication of *"saving cost"* agreed upon by participants **P4, P12** and **P13** is that some municipalities exempt the refugees from paying fees of some services if they use the intended electronic channels to communicate.

A majority of interviewees pointed to the importance of ICT-based participation in "Saving Time and Money" for all parties, whether providers such as municipalities, or beneficiaries such as refugees. Accordingly, this is in line with [34], who stated that the use of ICT-based tools such as mobile phones in livelihood activities reduces the frequency of movements and thus saves time and money [34]. However, participants **P4** and **P9** declared that the additional costs resulting from the use of e-participation channels, such as the cost of the Internet and electronic devices, cannot be ignored [35].

Long-Term Direct Relationships. The sub-theme of a long-term direct relationship was analysed as a result of the implementation of e-participation among refugees and decision-makers of the municipalities. The interpreted data of this study shows the role of e-participation channels in eliminating the functional pyramid of most transactions within the municipality and enabling the public to reach the decision-maker. Participant **P3** confirmed that he had "e-participation channels reinforce open-door policy and provides people with opportunities to communicate and interact with the mayor and decision-makers directly…". Participant **P8** agreed that *"e-participation helped to create a direct relationship and remove the barriers between the decision-makers in the municipalities, and members of the community …"*. Participants **P1, P2, P4, P5, P6, P9** and **P13** agreed with this argument.

However, access to the decision-makers and head of the municipality through e-participation channels does not completely rule out of institutional procedures, as Participant **P12** mentioned. He adds, *"the municipality has certain regulations and procedures that cannot be ignored even in the presence of direct relations between refugees and decision-makers within the municipality…."*.

Despite the weakness and interruption of the Internet in the Gaza Strip, as confirmed by participants **P4, P7** and **P9**, it can be argued that e-participation processes have contributed significantly to the formation of long-term direct relationships between refugees and decision-makers within municipalities. That is in line with [7].

Therefore, the first research question *What are e-participation effects as to the results of using ICTs-based tools and activities?* has successfully been addressed.

5.2 Livelihood Outcomes Sustained by E-participation

In this study, two main livelihood outcomes were highlighted: Reducing Poverty and Increased Well-Being [22].

Reducing Poverty. Poverty is a global issue [36] that cannot be solved solely by a municipality or limited interventions. However, data of this study show that e-participation channels support refugees measurably in unemployment reduction by the advertisement and circulation of job vacancies via e-channels. The municipalities are eager to utilize the unemployed by mobilizing them in implementing projects that serve the province by offering job creation opportunities and possibilities for a specific period. The Participant **P13** mentions, *"when the municipality decided to start the project "Paving Al-Fallujah Road" we announced through our e-platforms and social media requested need of manpower for that project"*. Participant **P13** added, *"we have already received a lot of applications through a link (Google Form) was created by the* *municipality to be able to fill it...".* This kind of advertisement was implemented by other municipalities interviewed, as Participants **P1, P7, P8** and **P12** declared.

Participant **P12** states, *"that e-participation channels have somehow contributed to the reduction of poverty. For instance, by interacting electronically with some refugees to identify their needs and trying to assist them by employing them in the municipal projects or exempting them from the fees of some e-services at times...".* Thus, it can be said that e-channels contribute to the reduction of poverty and unemployment amongst refugees. This is consistent with [36] and [37]. In contrast, Participants **P3** and **P11** assume that e-participation channels do not lead to poverty alleviation because of the deteriorating economy in the Gaza Strip, in support of [38].

The interviewees who supported the poverty-reduction view believe that this has been achieved due to several factors: advertising and circulation job vacancies of the municipalities' projects via e-channels, minimizing transportation costs to visit municipal offices and headquarters, as well as a municipal exemption on service and bills through online platforms as mentioned by participants **P4, P12** and **P13**. This is in line with [36].

Increased Well-Being. Increased refugee well-being was also among the livelihood outcomes [2] in this study. Through a number of evidences cited by interviewees, we can say that increasing refugee well-being can be achieved through electronic refugee petitions related to, for example, healthcare, safety, cleanliness and road repair. One of the most popular evidence of e-Petitioning is when Rafah governance residents appealed to the local and international communities in order to establish a hospital under the hashtag *#Rafah_needs_hospital* and *#rafahneedshospital*, since about 65% of the population in Rafah are refugees [33]. This was confirmed by Participants **P12** and **P13**. One of the interviewees mentioned another example of the role of electronic channels in enabling people with disabilities to appeal to the municipality to provide services and facilities. Participant **P7** said, *"... the municipality, after the appeals through social media platforms, repaired a road leading to the house of a wounded man who lost his leg during the recent war on the Gaza Strip....".* Participant **P7** further stated, *".... a street in the refugee camp was very terrible, and drivers urge through social media platforms to repair the road. We have formed a committee to study this case, and it was addressed indeed...".* Based on many examples cited by the interviewees, the most famous was the appeals of Rafah residents, 84% of whom are refugees [33], through social media platforms, specifically Facebook and Twitter,, in order to build a hospital serving Rafah city. Participants **P12** and **P13** pointed out that the Kuwaiti government has responded to these appeals, which began in 2014. The participants confirmed that the Kuwaiti Government will begin work on this project soon. The interviewees also added that Rafah municipality is following up this subject closely. It can be argued that e-participation channels can help increase and improve the well-being of refugees. This is in line with [2]. Information, communication and knowledge, facilitated by ICTs, are important in the ability of individuals to formulate appropriate strategies for sustainable livelihoods [27]. In addition, the use of ICTs positively affects people livelihoods [39]. ICTs are a crucial element of positive change in terms of people's livelihoods, involving principles, assets, policies, and institutions [27].

Thus, the second question of this study: How livelihood outcomes are influenced by e-participation implementation? was answered.

5.3 The Challenges of E-participation Implementation

The implementation of e-participation faces many challenges, especially in developing countries [40]. In the context of refugees in the Gaza Strip as determined through interviews, some challenges were identified. These include the culture of society [40] where some individuals, especially the elderly, are not convinced of the benefits of these electronic channels. Furthermore, frequent power outages in the Gaza Strip [38] and the lack of access to internet services for a segment of refugees due to their high cost or infrastructure [41] are further deterrents.

Among the obstacles mentioned by the interviewees and related to the implementation of e-participation, the prime obstacle is the dominant culture of society in accepting change. Therefore, it was necessary to motivate members of Palestinian society, including refugees, and urge them to use the available e-channels to communicate with municipalities. Participant **P7** said: "... *the adoption of the motivation principle will help to achieve the desired results and accelerate the process of change in the mainstream culture...*".

6 Conclusion

The present study offers a more comprehensive insight from the municipality's perspective for e-participation consequences and its influence on sustainable livelihoods of refugees in the Gaza Strip, Palestine. The municipalities are the main local authorities responsible for providing basic services such as water, electricity, infrastructure and social services to refugees. These services represent the basic needs of refugees' livelihoods. Municipalities are always faced with funding issues and should work in collaboration with refugees to better understand their needs, which will help to improve their planning for providing services with limited funding. E-participation which is a form of ICT usage reflects the interplay between the context and ICT usage and therefore reflects the interaction between the municipalities and refugees for clearer insights.

The findings of this study show that there are positive attitudes expressed by the respondents with the e-participation implementation that would be rendered feasible in the context of refugees. The authors acknowledge that there are also many possible and fewer actual negative effects of e-participation. However, the authors believe the benefits far outweigh the negative effects and focus on the paper is on how e-participation, given the lack of other currently available public participation channels, can benefit marginalized communities.

Two key themes were analyzed: e-participation consequences and livelihood outcomes. The former includes "increasing information and raising awareness", "saving time and money" and "long-term direct relationship". These themes did not produce a strong agreement, although there were positive trends of interviewees in all of these themes. Similarly, there were positive attitudes relating to the themes of e-participation-based livelihood outcomes, which are: "reducing poverty" and "increased well-being".

Given the positive orientations of the respondents in the discussed themes, e-participation has been found to be feasible in the context of sustainable livelihoods of refugees. This study, therefore, provides a basis for future work to provide a more coherent view of the phenomenon of e-participation and its implications within the context of sustainable livelihoods in developing countries, in contrast to the more traditional focus on the political context of e-participation in developed countries.

This study presented explanatory insight into ICT-based participation and its adoption in the context of poor, marginalized and disadvantaged groups using the aforementioned conceptual framework. Future research could look at refugees in other settlements. Future research could also enhance the conceptual model proposed in this study by formulating additional coherent propositions that present high-level guidance to researchers and practitioners working in similar contexts. Finally, the perspective of other actors, as services providers, providing services to refugees could be investigated.

References

1. Bisimwa, K.B., Johnstona, K.A.: Impact of mobile phones on integration: the case of refugees in South Africa. J. Commun. Inform. **4**(9), 1–12 (2013)
2. Andrade, A.D., Doolin, B.: Information and communication technology and the social inclusion of refugees. MIS Q. **2**(40), 405–416 (2016)
3. Sanford, C., Rose, J.: Characterizing e-participation. Int. J. Inf. Manage. **6**(27), 406–421 (2007)
4. Cantijoch, M., Cutts, D., Gibson, R.: Internet Use and Political Engagement: The Role of E-Campaigning as a Pathway to Online Political Participation. Center for the Study of Demogracy, p. 32 (2013)
5. Meneses, M.E., et al.: Overcoming citizen mistrust and enhancing democratic practices: results from the e-participation platform México Participa. Inf. Technol. Int. Dev. **13**, 138–154 (2017)
6. Panopoulou, E., Tambouris, E., Tarabanis, K.: e-Participation initiatives: how is Europe progressing. Eur. J. ePractice **7**, 15–26 (2009)
7. Rexhepi, A., Filiposka, S., Trajkovik, V.: Youth e-participation as a pillar of sustainable societies. J. Clean. Prod. **174**, 114–122 (2018)
8. UNRWA: Where We Work (2016). https://www.unrwa.org/where-we-work/gaza-strip. Accessed 07 Oct 2018
9. ICAI: DFID's Support for Palestine Refugees through UNRWA. Independent Commission for Aid Impact (2013). https://icai.independent.gov.uk/wp-content/uploads/ICAI-UNRWA-report-FINAL-110913.pdf
10. Mcloughlin, C.: Sustainable livelihoods for refugees in protracted crises. K4D Helpdesk Report. Institute of Development Studies, Brighton, UK (2017). https://opendocs.ids.ac.uk/opendocs/handle/20.500.12413/13108
11. Corps, M.: Palestinian ICT Sector 2.0: Technology sector development report and recommendations relevant to regional and global market opportunities. Solutions for Development Consulting (2013)
12. PITA: ICT sector profile, Palestinian Information Technology Association of Companies (2019). http://home.pita.ps/wp/ict-sector-profile. Accessed 11 Aug 2019
13. Abushanab, O.: The role social media in recruitment process: case study companies in ICT sector in gaza strip. In: The Islamic University–Gaza (2016)

14. PCBS: Palestinian Central Bureau of Statistics (PCBS) and the Ministry of Communications and Information Technology issue a joint press release on the eve of the International Day for Telecommunication and Information. Palestinian Central Bureau of Statistics (2018). http://www.pcbs.gov.ps/post.aspx?lang=en&ItemID=3141

15. PCBS: Household Survey on Information and Communications Technology, 2019 Main Findings Report. Palestinian Central Bureau of Statistics (2019). http://www.pcbs.gov.ps/Downloads/book2510.pdf

16. Wirtz, B.W., Daiser, P., Binkowska, B.: E-participation: a strategic framework. Int. J. Public Adm. 1(41), 1–12 (2016)

17. Pivskur, B.a.D., Ramon, J.M.J., Ketelaar, M., Smeets, R.J., Norton,, M., Beurskens, A.J.: Participation and social participation: are they distinct concepts? Clin. Rehabil. 3(28), 211–220 (2014)

18. He, G., Boas, I., Mol, A.P.J., Lu, Y.: E-participation for environmental sustainability in transitional urban China. Sustain. Sci. 12(2), 187–202 (2016). https://doi.org/10.1007/s11625-016-0403-3

19. Davison, R.M., Martinsons, M.G.: Context is king! Considering particularism in research design and reporting. J. Inf. Technol. 3(31), 241–249 (2016)

20. United Nations: Citizen Engagement (2020). https://publicadministration.un.org/en/eparticipation. Accessed 29 Apr 2020

21. De Vriese, M.: Refugee Livelihoods: A Review of the Evidence. UNHCR (2006). https://www.unhcr.org/4423fe5d2.pdf

22. Shirima, C., Sanga, C.: Assessment of contribution of ICT for Sustainable Livelihoods in Kilosa District. In: Information Technology Integration for Socio-Economic Development, pp. 260–283 (2016)

23. Alastal, A.I., Salha, R.A., El-Hallaq,, M.A.: The reality of gaza strip cities towards the smart city's concept. A case study: Khan Younis City. Curr. Urban Stud. 1(7), 143–155 (2019)

24. Ali, M.A.: Integrity, transparency and accountability in the work of local communities in the Gaza Strip. AMAN. Transparency Palestine (2012). https://www.aman-palestine.org/cached_uploads/download/migrated-files/itemfiles/af9962d23bdaf24e39417dc5457d6475.pdf

25. Baah-Ennumh, T., Forson, J.A.: The impact of artisanal small-scale mining on sustainable livelihoods: a case study of mining communities in the Tarkwa-Nsuaem municipality of Ghana. World J. Entrepr. Manage. Sustain. Dev. 3(13), 204–222 (2017)

26. Zaremohzzabieh, Z., Samah, B., Omar, S., Bolong, J., Shaffril, H.: A systematic review of qualitative research on the role of ICTs in sustainable livelihood. Soc. Sci. 6(9), 386–401 (2014)

27. Makoza, F., Chigona, W.: Interaction patterns and ICT use to support the livelihoods of microenterprises. Int. J. ICT Res. Dev. Afr. (IJICTRDA) 1(4), 20–40 (2014)

28. Duncombe, R.: Using the livelihoods framework to analyze ICT applications for poverty reduction through microenterprise. Inf. Technol. Int. Dev. 3(3), 81–100 (2006)

29. Creswel, J.W.: Research Design: Qualitative, Quantitative, and Mixed Methods Approaches, 4th edn. SAGE, Thousand Oaks (2009)

30. Neuman, L.W.: Social Research Methods, 6th edn. Pearson Education, London (2007)

31. Denzin, N.K., Lincoln, Y.S.: The Sage Handbook of Qualitative Research, 4th edn. SAGE, Thousand Oaks (2011)

32. Braun, V., Clarke, V.: Using thematic analysis in psychology. Qual. Res. Psychol. 2(3), 77–101 (2006)

33. PCBS: Estimated Population in the Palestinian Territory Mid-Year by Governorate, 1997–2016. Palestinian Central Bureau of Statistics (2017). http://www.pcbs.gov.ps/Portals/_Rainbow/Documents/gover_e.htm

34. Samuel, J., Shah, N., Hadingham, W.: Mobile communications in South Africa, Tanzania and Egypt: results from community and business surveys. Vodafone Policy Paper Ser. **3**(2), 44–52 (2005)
35. Burchert, S., et al.: User-centered app adaptation of a low-intensity e-mental health intervention for syrian refugees. Front. Psychiatry **9**, 663 (2019)
36. Adera, E.O., Waema, T.M., May, J.: ICT pathways to poverty reduction: Empirical evidence from East and Southern Africa. IDRC/CRDI (2014)
37. Lapeyre, F., Al Husseini, J.J., Bocco, R., Brunner, M., Zureik, E.: The Living Conditions of the Palestine Refugees Registered with UNRWA in Jordan, Lebanon, the Syrian Arab Republic, the Gaza Strip and the West Bank (2011)
38. Kurz, A., Dekel, U., Berti, B.: The crisis of the Gaza Strip: a way out. Institute for National Security Studies, Tel Aviv, and EcoPeace Middle East, Amman, Bethlehem, Tel Aviv (2018)
39. Soriano, C.R.R.: Exploring the ICT and rural poverty reduction link: community telecenters and rural livelihoods in Wu'an, China. Electron. J. Inf. Syst. Dev. Ctries. **1**(32), 1–15 (2007)
40. Sari, A.M., Hidayanto, A.N., Purwandari, B., Budi, N.F.A., Kosandi, M.: Challenges and issues of e-participation implementation: a case study of e-complaint Indonesia. In: 2018 Third International Conference on Informatics and Computing (ICIC), pp 1–6. IEEE (2018)
41. Miah, S.J., Gammack, J., Greenfield, G.: An infrastructure for implementing e-participation services in developing countries. In: 2009 3rd IEEE International Conference on Digital Ecosystems and Technologies, Istanbul, pp 407–411. IEEE (2009)

Appraising WhatsApp in the Indian Context: Understanding the Rural Sentiment

Anushruti Vagrani[1], Saroj Bijarnia[1], P. Vigneswara Ilavarasan[1], and Silvia Masiero[2(✉)]

[1] Indian Institute of Technology, Delhi, India
[2] University of Oslo, Oslo, Norway
silvima@ifi.uio.no

Abstract. Web-based instant messaging applications are predominant as means of Internet usage in rural settings. This becomes particularly interesting in the Indian rural context where applications like WhatsApp are accepted and used extensively, while the Internet is still rather an alien concept for a large part of the population. While adoption of these applications is motivated by ease of access, ease of use, and other facilitating conditions, to better understand the collective acceptance, the role of social influence needs to be contextualized for the rural areas in point. To this end, we use the analytical lens of social capital to understand and elaborate on the rural sentiment around the usage of WhatsApp. We triangulate a thematic analysis of qualitative details from an ethnographic study with the sentiment analysis of selected parts of interviews conducted during the study. This mixed-method study throws light on how social constructs in rural households play a role in defining technological usability and habits, as well as individual-level perceptions and sentiments. Our study, which illustrates the usefulness of mixed methods in ICT4D, has implications for various stakeholders to understand the usage patterns and perception of digital platforms in rural contexts.

Keywords: Digital platforms · WhatsApp · Social capital · Sentiment analysis · Rural India

1 Introduction

With more than half a billion people using the Internet in India in 2019 (IMRB 2019), the growth of Internet adoption in the country sees rural adoption acquiring increasing importance. This significant increase in Internet penetration has led governments to deliver various services in online mode and also to invest in building digital platforms such that inclusion is achieved (Mir et al. 2019a, b). However, it is well understood that the types and frequency of the usage, impact, and also the pattern of consumption of online services are significantly different in urban and rural areas owing to the different socioeconomic profiles of urban and rural internet users (Venkatesh and Sykes 2013; Kenny and Kenny 2011; Galloway 2007). ICT4D research has attempted to understand

J. M. Bass and P. J. Wall (Eds.): ICT4D 2020, IFIP AICT 587, pp. 142–156, 2020.
https://doi.org/10.1007/978-3-030-65828-1_12

these differences through theoretical means including the Sustainable Livelihoods Approach (Scott et al. 2005), the choice framework (Kleine 2010), and social network theory (Venkatesh and Sykes 2013) among others. However, studies with a focus on the social aspect around ICT adoption and impact in rural areas are still relatively scarce, with few examples constituting exceptions (Selouani and Hamam 2007; Thapa 2012).

With rural people spending more time online, it becomes more interesting to understand how their offline social structure plays a role in online interactions and how these interactions affect their social structure. In any social structure, these interactions depend on personal, material, and social factors. Understanding these factors demand more micro-level, in-depth studies. In rural areas of India, with an increasing number of smartphones and other mobile devices, and with increasing levels of Internet penetration, the study of how social structures are reflected in online interactions and vice versa, presents an interesting case; on which limited ICT4D research has been conducted so far.

WhatsApp is a Web-based instant messaging application that makes it for a large part of global Internet usage, with more than 200 million active users in India before 2018 (Statista Report 2017). A large part of online interactions takes place through WhatsApp across many communities including those in rural India (Sánchez-Moya and Cruz-Moya 2015; Digital Empowerment Foundation 2018). Research shows that WhatsApp has gained popularity due to reasons including the design features that allow 'emergent users' (Devanuj and Joshi 2013) like those in developing countries to overcome the barriers towards technology usage (Balkrishan et al. 2016). In this study, we focus on understanding types of usages that WhatsApp is serving in rural areas and explore the sentiments related to these usages. We ask the following research questions:

1. What are the rural sentiments related to various usages of WhatsApp?
2. How does social capital play a role in the generation and development of these sentiments?

To answer our questions, we triangulate a thematic analysis of data collected from an ethnographic study of rural Rajasthan (North India) with sentiment analysis of selected parts of interviews conducted during the study. Our data reveals that offline social relations in the rural social environment are reflected in the patterns of usage of WhatsApp and the sentiments associated with them. One-to-one or group interactions on WhatsApp leverage upon *bridging, bonding,* and *linking* social capital (Putnam 2000; Woolcock 2001) in ways that we discuss below. Social capital theory helps to understand the interconnected links between personal, material, and social factors in a rural setting. Based on the results of our analysis, the links we establish in the discussion help in understanding the appraisal of instant messaging platforms in the context of the rural sector in developing countries.

This paper is structured as follows. Section 2 contextualizes sentiment in the information systems' space, justifying the choice of social capital as a theoretical lens for the study. Section 3 explains the research flow, followed by our research method. In Sect. 4 we analyze our data, and in Sect. 5 we discuss the implications and conclusions from the study.

2   Literature Review and Theoretical Framework

Moving from the classical to the neo-classical theory of capital introduces value to the masses in the form of Human Capital, Cultural Capital, and also, Social Capital (Lin 2017). While human capital is a form of investment in human factors (e.g. skill, knowledge, experience), that provides profit or benefit to an individual; social capital derives its value based on the collective interactions of a group, in turn providing benefits to the society and its members.

Social capital is a term used in many different ways in various fields of research. The central idea means that all the various associations of a person or a group work as assets to them. Bourdieu was one of the antecedents to discuss social capital while defining it as "the aggregate of the actual or potential resources that are linked to possession of a durable network of more or less institutionalized relationships of mutual acquaintance and recognition" (Bourdieu 1986). Later Coleman focuses on its functions (Coleman 1988) and Putnam discusses two different forms of social capital called bridging and bonding social capital. While bridging social capital is inclusive and is often related to weak ties between individuals, bonding social capital is exclusive and represents strong ties in close relationships with family, friends or neighbors (Putnam 2000, 2002).

The initial approach in terms of social capital for online interactions was the same applied for media in general; that of time displacement. It suggested that the time spent online comes most likely from an earlier offline activity which was social (Nie et al. 2002). Later on, it was argued that unlike traditional media, the internet is an interactive space having sociability *within* (Williams 2006; DiMaggio et al. 2001). Several of the studies focus on understanding how various factors from the real-life affect the online social behavior while using online social network sites and applications including WhatsApp. These studies establish the role played by experience (Leong et al. 2018) and psychological factors including social support (Aharony and Gazit 2016; Gazit and Aharony 2018). Aharony also studies the kind of social capital that WhatsApp interactions generate (Aharony 2015). In this study, we focus on the sentiments around WhatsApp usage and explore the role that social capital plays.

2.1   Sentiment Analysis

Opinions expressed by people are subjective expressions of their sentiments (Liu 2010). With the growing trend of people expressing their opinion on various web platforms, numerous techniques have been developed that enable analysts to process these in text form and dig out meaningful information using linguistics and natural language processing (Liu et al. 2012). Content analysis and sentiment analysis represent types of such techniques that have been used extensively in information systems research (cf. Rathore et al. 2017; Bijarnia et al. 2020). A number of these studies are based on the analysis of a large amount of data from social media such as Twitter and Facebook. The data analysis is used to get insights on various business and prediction aspects including market research e.g. product co-creation (Rambocas and Pacheco 2018; Rathore et al. 2016; Chamlertwat et al. 2012), customer engagement (Bijarnia et al. 2019), financial market study e.g. stock prediction (Mittal and Goel 2012), election prediction (Singh et al. 2012) among others. Recent mixed-method studies have used these techniques on text data from other sources like reports and qualitative interview transcripts (Parmar et al. 2018; Güven et al. 2014). In this work, we use content analysis including sentiment analysis on interview transcripts and triangulate it with thematic analysis.

3 Method

The research flow of this mixed-method study is shown in Fig. 1 below. Subsequently, the research methodology is explained in detail. An ethnographic study was conducted by the lead researcher in a rural Gram Panchayat (village area) in Rajasthan, a state of north India, to explore the interplay between broadband and various socio-economic and cultural factors in an Indian rural setup. The researcher spent around eight months during the year 2018 in the core village and the adjacent town while collecting data through in-depth interviews, observations during interviews, and informal interactions. The interviews were audio-recorded, transcribed, and coded with multiple rounds of thematic analysis with the help of NVIVO12. During the process of coding, the usage of the messaging application WhatsApp emerged as one of the prominent elements. The recurrent presence of this topic in the discussions led our focus in the direction of examining rural sentiment around WhatsApp specifically.

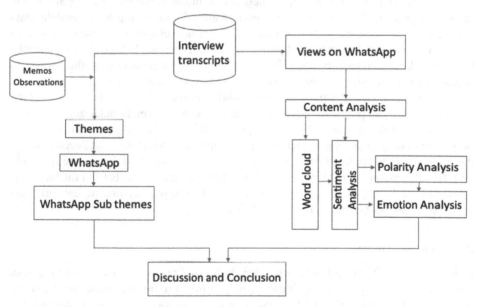

Fig. 1. Flow of research

Thematic analysis and content analysis are two common approaches used for an in-depth understanding of a phenomenon. For an overall detailed understanding of the same phenomenon, these approaches can complement each other quite well. Thus, we parallelly conducted a content analysis of the text from the transcripts. While a word cloud (Fig. 2) indicated major concepts emerging in interviews, a sentiment analysis

(Fig. 3) in the form of polarity analysis helped in understanding whether emotions were positive or negative. A detailed Emotion analysis then provides a detailed score of eight different kinds of emotions. We see the results from these parallel analysis processes together and then discuss the implications. The process is described in Fig. 1.

3.1 Demographic Description

Baral is located in the Ajmer district of Rajasthan State in India, 70 km from the district headquarter. With around 500 households at the core of this rural area, the population is a good mixture of two religions and various castes. As a common practice, men in households work in the mills on temporary or permanent jobs, while females take care of agriculture and livestock. Literacy is said to be close to a hundred percent in Ajmer district, however, the level of education varies by a large magnitude. The majority of the elderly population has two to ten years of school education. Younger adults, 20–35 years old ones, have mostly completed school education at the least. Occupation choices involve the job of a painter, carpenter, confectioner, tailor, construction worker, property dealer, general store owner, mobile and electronics store owner, and teacher among others. In the other part of the Gram Panchayat, which is attached to the town, teachers, banking professionals, charted accountants, doctors, electronic, automobile, cloth, and other merchandise shop owners are included in the list of occupations. On income standards, the majority of the population falls under the lower middle class and below that. On average, every two out of ten households were such that one or more members contained a keypad phone, but no smartphone. In households where the household head is relatively younger, within the range of 20–40 years, the household heads mostly own a smartphone. In other cases, the young adult male/s in the household most frequently own a smartphone. Female adults in the household in the majority of the cases own a keypad phone for their use. Younger and newlywed females and those who are about to get married are often an exception to this case. Some girls who are earning or are continuing higher studies have their smartphones. WhatsApp has become one of the most common applications used in recent years. Before 2016 there were relatively very few WhatsApp users there in the village. For this study extracts from the interview transcripts of 34 respondents who talked about WhatsApp usage in different forms are used. Respondents belong to age 15 to 60 years.

3.2 Content Analysis

Content analysis (Harwood and Garry 2003) is used to find out the hidden meaning from large text data. This type of analysis uses principles from text mining and natural language processing (Kayser and Blind 2017). We have used two content analysis techniques i.e. Word cloud (Heimerl et al. 2014) and sentiment analysis (Pang and Lee 2008). Word cloud is a set of words that are most frequent in the text data. Using NVIVO12, we created a word cloud with the selected text consisting of the responses of the qualitative interviews regarding WhatsApp. In Sentiment analysis, we try to identify how sentiments are expressed in a text. For the sentiment analysis, we perform polarity analysis and Emotion analysis. Polarity analysis suggests whether the sentiments expressed in the text are overall negative or positive, while in Emotion analysis the text is evaluated in terms of emotions including anger, anticipation, disgust, fear, joy, sadness, surprise, and trust. Sentiment analysis is performed with R programming using syuzhet and dplry packages. For each Sentiment type, the range of scores is 1 to 8. We first selected all the interviews where a respondent has talked about WhatsApp usage in any form. From these interview transcripts, those portions were manually picked where details around WhatsApp usage are being discussed, this gave us the dataset for content analysis. These segments of conversations were classified majorly into five different categories that were frequently being discussed: video calling, chat with close connections, communication with social connections, job search, and education-related communication, and work-related communication. Content analysis was then performed on the filtered data.

3.3 Thematic Analysis

The thematic analysis provides a controlled way to understand and structure the ideas emerging from ethnographically collected data (Aronson 1995). Through a thematic analysis, we identify, organize, and find meaningful patterns in our data and understand the shared experiences concerning the particular research questions for the study (Braun and Clarke 2012). We followed the following steps:

Step1. Familiarizing with the data: we evaluated the transcripts and memos and wherever needed, the audio files repetitively while trying to read the assumptions that the respondent had at the time of interviews.

Step 2. Initial codes: Initial codes were generated by highlighting the relevant text sections. This part led us to statements and emotions that were shared commonly, and those that stand out as exceptions.

"Take WhatsApp for example. I used to scold my kids for using it. Some scandal took place in our village because of WhatsApp, there were some boys… A girl went to a hotel with her friend. The guy asked her to send the video on WhatsApp which got sent to two groups. It became an issue as there were so many members of the groups. Then the girl who was married had to face divorce. So I used to be scared of all these things. I used to tell my kid not to use WhatsApp, it contains dirty stuff. Later I got to know that things don't work this way. Whatever we put there is there only. My son, both my kids, keep on telling me that I should try and understand things first before I scold them. The whole world is using these things."

The statement talks about the initial perception that was generated possibly during various conversations that the respondent had had with her peers and surrounding people about an unfortunate incident in the village. It also talks about how interactions with her kids later restructured her biases towards the usage of these web platforms.

Step 3. Structuring the data in sub-themes: from the codes, we identified different patterns, clubbed them, and created a hierarchy. We looked for patterns that were indicated by various "conversation topics, vocabulary, recurring activities, meanings, feelings, or folk sayings and proverbs" (Taylor and Bogdan 1989).

Step 4. Structuring themes: various components of ideas and experiences that were meaningless in exclusion are bridged together to make sense in a collective view in this stage (Leininger 1985). The sub-themes were linked to themes.

Step 5. Relevant themes and their names: We identified those themes that were relevant to our research questions and named them to suitably depict the emotions that they carry. These represented respondents' views that indicated the social structure and its interactions with their thought process. During this process, a background of literature guided us while understanding the pattern (Aronson 1995).

4   Analysis and Findings

4.1   Word Cloud

A word cloud with the responses of the qualitative interviews discussing the WhatsApp application is shown in Fig. 2. A word cloud highlights the most repeatedly used words in the responses, and the size of the word shows how frequently the word was used in the conversations. Word cloud provides us with a preliminary filter to refine the broader concepts from the text (DePaolo and Wilkinson 2014). The words situated close to each other represent that they are often used in the same or related context. For example 'communication', 'network', 'information', 'connected' are in close connection, depicting one aspect of WhatsApp usage being staying connected in a network supporting information flow.

Fig. 2. Word Cloud showing the ideas reflected upon in the responses

Another aspect can be seen in the upper left part of the diagram where words like 'friends', 'family', 'kids', 'status', 'group', 'conversation' are connected closely. These indicate the conversations between close friends and family. In the upper-right part of the figure words like 'work', 'document', 'job', 'publicity' 'classes' 'share' can be seen in close connection, indicating another prominent usage of WhatsApp in connection with a job, work and education. We identify five broader concepts that we use as a guideline in the emotion analysis below.

4.2 Polarity Analysis

The second technique of content analysis was sentiment analysis which is performed in two different ways: polarity analysis and Emotion Analysis. Figure 3 shows the results of the polarity analysis conducted using NVIVO12. The diagram shows that a majority of the views given by the respondents are 'moderately positive' in nature. The number of 'moderately negative' sentiments deducted by the software are relatively few. Strong reactions, both positive and negative are fewer in number yet significant. These results show the overall acceptance of WhatsApp usage in rural areas. Rural people have more positive sentiments regarding WhatsApp usage than negative sentiments. We further investigate these sentiments through Emotion analysis.

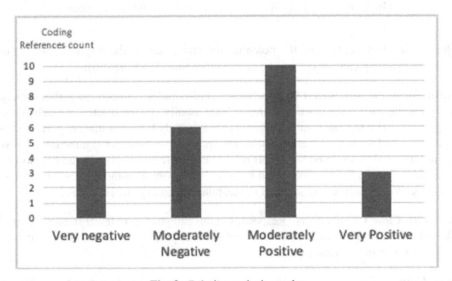

Fig. 3. Polarity analysis results

4.3 Emotion Analysis

Figure 4 shows the graphical representation of results from Emotion analysis performed on different categories of WhatsApp usage, which were earlier defined manually. Using R programming the text in these categories was rated between 0–8 on eight different emotions anger, anticipation, disgust, fear, joy, sadness, surprise, and trust. Also, overall positive or negative sentiment is indicated on the same range of value here. The categories were guided by the word cloud, results for each of the five categories are explained below.

WhatsApp Video Calling. Overall sentiments are positive for video calling. Among emotions, trust value is high, respondents have largely shown trust in the WhatsApp

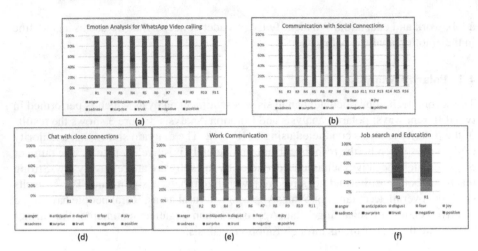

Fig. 4. Emotion analysis for various categories of WhatsApp usage

video calling feature. One of the potential reasons given by the respondents for this finding is that they can see the person on the other side (See Fig. 4(a)).

Communication with Social Connections. This includes connections within society, within people with same caste or ethnicity who usually stay connected through WhatsApp groups. The messages in these groups are generally forwards that are perceived as informative and relevant. Overall sentiments are positive, however significant negative sentiments are also observed here. This might be since these are considered time killing engagement. Anticipation is observed high in the responses in these categories. Small areas in yellow depict fear in some of the responses (see Fig. 4(b)).

Chat with Close Connections. Responses in this category were fewer in number since talking to close connections, call or video calls are the preferred mode. Among emotions trust along with joy and anticipation are prominent (See Fig. 4(c)).

Work Communication. Trust along with high anticipation is shown in the responses in this category. Work communication includes one to one or group interactions where the exchange of documents and information is common. This also includes usage of WhatsApp for business publicity and day to day tasks. The sentiments are mostly positive, and the graph shows joy and surprise emotions as well (See Fig. 4(d)).

Job search and Education. The responses on this category show a good mix of sentiments, both positive and negative sentiments can be seen in the graph. Positive sentiments still can be seen in the majority. Students and employment seekers use the application and join a group where they can communicate and get relevant information like study material, details about new openings, process, and date of application, etc. (Fig. 4(e)).

4.4 Thematic Analysis

Our thematic analysis results in eight different themes around WhatsApp namely usage, concerns, emotions, stigmas, resistance, addiction, constraints, and motivators (See Fig. 1). Ideas in these themes are discussed below.

Usage. Usages of WhatsApp for the people in this area are categorized into three major categories. The forms of social capital bonding, bridging, and linking social capital directly reflect in these three usage patterns. The first category includes communication with family and friends (bonding) which majorly include video calling and sending and receiving photographs of the members and responding to those. Video calling also provides indirect access to less educated people who are not comfortable using other text-based features of the application. For example, an elder lady who uses a keypad phone otherwise gets access through her kids who make video calls to her relatives for her:

> *"Kids do make a call for us to our family, relatives. I talk to my mother and father...A video call, there is our picture on the screen and theirs as well. I: So they make the call for you or you do it yourself? R1: They make the call I only talk. I: What more do you do? R1: We just talk, how are you doing, what did you cook, what did you do all day and things like that. What else to do?"*

The second category is that of social connections which usually include distant relatives, friends from the same locality, people from the same caste or ethnicity among others (bridging). The most common information flow is in the form of forwarded messages. This also works as a source of information for current affairs and news, also local information flow. Even after being time-consuming, people continue to be a part of these groups for the sake of connectedness.

> *"More than half is Jhutha Prachar (false advertising) on WhatsApp. Small things blow up. They write small things in such a big way to make it viral."*

The third category includes work, employment search, and education-related usages in this context (linking). Students and job seekers join these groups usually created by e-Mitra and coaching centers who keep on sending details on vacancies for a job, examinations, and study content on these groups. Many of the people instead of going on different websites to look for options rely on these groups for the majority of the information in this regard. Some of the local business owners use WhatsApp groups to market their products in nearby areas.

Emotions. The emotions associated with WhatsApp are a mixture of positive and negative. Though people have accepted usage in their day to day life, there are different notions around it including gender-based biases and stigmas, apprehension and fear of doing something wrong with it, and exposure to misinformation, inappropriate content especially for young teens, frustration because of it being time-consuming and being a popular 'time pass'. Positive notions include a sense of connectedness, empowerment-based on the ability to use, and to learn and based on the information gained. When used for connecting with close friends and family it provides joy, belongingness, and contentment.

Concerns. The concerns around WhatsApp usages are majorly formed by collective notions based on experiences of people around or based on the stories that float across the afternoon and evening chit-chats in the village. These concerns include 'fake news', inappropriate content, misuse of the platform, addiction, and too much time consumption. Also, the inadequate network is another concern in those areas, though mobile internet works fine across the majority of the parts of the village.

Stigmas. The stigmas that exist there in the local rural society are reflected in their usage of WhatsApp as well. One example being gender inequality, in the majority of households a young adult or sometimes teenage male is the first one to get mobile phone access. Females still carry keypad mobile phones so that they can talk to the family. Even when they do have a smartphone, they are expected to use it with restraint.

"Video calling as well the kids they do, I don't pay much attention to that. I: You never used it? R1: No I haven't...I: And your daughter has a smartphone... R1: No my daughter doesn't do that either... never..." (sounded more like she ought not to indulge in all this).

Resistance. Resistance towards learning as well as usage post-learning is more evident in older generations. One of the major reasons is that adoption is still new in these areas and people in their circle are not using similar technology. Various stigmas discussed above also cause resistance.

Addiction. Addiction is not that common among the surveyed individuals; however, people do have the habit of having to check messages on their device, mostly in the evening hours. Interviews display a realization that these habits can lead to addiction.

Constraints. Apart from lack of access, lack of education forms major constraints for text-based applications. Learning to use these applications take many efforts for uneducated people even to use the video calling options. The stigmas and concerns sometimes work as constraints towards access and usage.

Motivators. Though WhatsApp is a text-based technology, it contains features that let people overcome the barriers that they traditionally experience. Pictures, video, and video calling options are usable even for indirect users. A sense of connectedness, information access, a sense of empowerment, joy of connecting to the close family motivates such users often. Another motivating factor is the possibility of saving money through different usages.

5   Conclusion and Implications

Our study illustrates and appraises the core sentiments associated with the usage of WhatsApp in a rural area of north India. The combination of sentiment analysis with thematic analysis of the interviews conducted leads us to identify the key sentiments into play, then deepen our awareness of them through an examination of the eight thematic constructs. Our findings depict a mixture of positive and negative sentiments, each associated with various types of users and with the past experiences lived by interviewees. Putnam's concepts of bridging, bonding, and linking social capital serve to illuminate people's use of the messaging service, providing a basis for further investigation of the multiple topical trends in the analysis.

Our analysis reveals that the social constructs around which respondents' opinion cluster play an important role in shaping people's habits and usage of WhatsApp. Though these connections are quite evident in places, the indirect influence on other aspects needs to be explored step by step. For example, while the surveyed individuals show anticipation towards distant connections, bonding social capital in close connections is reflected in terms of trust, anticipation, and joy. Sentiments of fear and anger are also reflected indicating the concerns and stigmas around the usages, these sentiments recur among users who are less acquainted with the new technology (e.g. older people) and those whose awareness of instant messaging is mostly indirect.

There are two orders of implications from this study. Firstly, the stylized facts reported here – of which we have sought to reach primary sensemaking through Putnam's theory – display a high degree of heterogeneity, hence providing a first picture of the range of sentiments associated with new technology in a rural area. These sentiments – and the relations of their variety with different categories of users within the same context – require greater analyses to understand the roots of their formation, and to appraise their implications for usage of WhatsApp and other instant messaging services. The stylized picture produced in this study constitutes a solid basis to do so, in further analyses that will focus on sentiment formation – building causal theory on the roots of sentiments – and the consequences of the associations of specific sentiments with technology usage.

Secondly, this study serves as a means to throw light on the advantages of using mixed methods in ICT4D. Mixed methods, which traditionally see a limited application in our discipline, have recently been taken up in the Information Systems (IS) discipline (e.g. Zachariadis et al. 2013) as a means to illuminate the same phenomenon through multiple, complementary angles. Our study has sought to do so by combining the quantitative insights of sentiment analysis with the qualitative features of thematic analysis, hence providing primary explanations for the quantitative results displayed. This has led us to observe a quantitative picture of the data collective and, at a second stage, provide qualitative explanations for it, hence integrating two methods that do not find large complementary applications in ICT4D to date.

It is the benefits of this mixed-method application that we want to throw light on as we conclude the paper. In a domain like ICT4D, where interpretive research predominates, mixed methods offer the possibility to explore the same phenomenon under two concomitant lights, which illuminate each other by providing complementary insights on the same observation. The importance of doing so, already illustrated in IS at large (Zachariadis et al. 2013), is enhanced in ICT4D by the importance of appraising users' view of phenomena, to avoid the design-reality gaps (Heeks 2002) that lead to failure. We hope, on these grounds, that our study can serve as a basis for wider applications of mixed methods to ICT4D, with a view of generating more in-depth appraisals of user perspectives in their context of generation.

References

Aharony, N.: What's App: a social capital perspective. Online Inf. Rev. **39**(1), 26–42 (2015)

Aharony, N., Gazit, T.: The importance of the WhatsApp family group: an exploratory analysis. Aslib J. Inf. Manage. **68**(2), 174–192 (2016)

Aronson, J.: A pragmatic view of thematic analysis. Qual. Rep. **2**(1), 1–3 (1995)

Balkrishan, D., Joshi, A., Rajendran, C., Nizam, N., Parab, C., Devkar, S.: Making and breaking the user-usage model: WhatsApp adoption amongst emergent users in India. In: Proceedings of the 8th Indian Conference on Human Computer Interaction, pp. 52–63, December 2016

Braun, V., Clarke, V.: Thematic analysis. In: APA Handbook of Research Methods in Psychology, Research Designs: Quantitative, Qualitative, Neuropsychological, and Biological, vol. 2, pp. 57–71. American Psychological Association (2012)

Bijarnia, S., Ilavarasan, P.V., Kar, A.K.: Comparing SERVQUAL for transportation services in the sharing economy for emerging markets: insights from Twitter analytics. In: Rana, N.P., et al. (eds.) Digital and Social Media Marketing. ATPEM, pp. 127–134. Springer, Cham (2020). https://doi.org/10.1007/978-3-030-24374-6_9

Bijarnia, S., Khetan, R., Ilavarasan, P.V., Kar, A.K.: Analyzing customer engagement using Twitter analytics: a case of uber car-hailing services. In: Pappas, I.O., Mikalef, P., Dwivedi, Y.K., Jaccheri, L., Krogstie, J., Mäntymäki, M. (eds.) I3E 2019. LNCS, vol. 11701, pp. 404–414. Springer, Cham (2019). https://doi.org/10.1007/978-3-030-29374-1_33

Bourdieu, P.: The forms of capital (1986)

Chamlertwat, W., Bhattarakosol, P., Rungkasiri, T., Haruechaiyasak, C.: Discovering consumer insight from Twitter via sentiment analysis. J. UCS **18**(8), 973–992 (2012)

Coleman, J.S.: Social capital in the creation of human capital. Am. J. Sociol. **94**, S95–S120 (1988)

DePaolo, C.A., Wilkinson, K.: Get your head into the clouds: Using word clouds for analyzing qualitative assessment data. TechTrends **58**(3), 38–44 (2014)

Devanuj, Joshi, A.: Technology adoption by "emergent" users: the user-usage model. In: Proceedings of the 11th Asia Pacific Conference on Computer Human Interaction (APCHI 2013). Association for Computing Machinery, New York pp. 28–38 (2013)

Digital Empowerment Foundation Publication Page. https://www.defindia.org/wp-content/upl oads/2018/10/WhatsApp-Rural-Study_V3.pdf. Accessed 29 May 2020

DiMaggio, P., Hargittai, E., Neuman, W.R., Robinson, J.P.: Social implications of the Internet. Ann. Rev. Sociol. **27**(1), 307–336 (2001)

Galloway, L.: Can broadband access rescue the rural economy? J. Small Bus. Enterp. Dev. **14**(4), 641–653 (2007)

Gazit, T., Aharony, N.: Factors explaining participation in WhatsApp groups: an exploratory study. Aslib J. Inf. Manag. **70**(4), 390–413 (2018)

Güven, S., Steiner, M., Ge, N., Paradkar, A.: Understanding the role of sentiment analysis in contract risk classification. In: IEEE Network Operations and Management Symposium (NOMS), pp. 1–6. IEEE, May 2014

Harwood, T.G., Garry, T.: An overview of content analysis. Market. Rev. **3**(4), 479–498 (2003)

Heimerl, F., Lohmann, S., Lange, S., Ertl, T.: Word cloud explorer: text analytics based on word clouds. In: Proceedings of the Annual Hawaii International Conference on System Sciences, pp. 1833–1842 (2014)

IMRB   Homepage.   https://imrbint.com/images/common/ICUBE™_2019_Highlights.pdf. Accessed 29 May 2020

Kayser, V., Blind, K.: Extending the knowledge base of foresight: the contribution of text mining. Technol. Forecast. Soc. Chang. **116**, 208–215 (2017)

Kenny, R., Kenny, C.: Superfast broadband: is it really worth a subsidy? Info **13**(4), 3–29 (2011)

Kleine, D.: ICT4WHAT?—using the choice framework to operationalise the capability approach to development. J. Int. Dev. **22**(5), 674–692 (2010)

Leininger, M.M.: Ethnography and ethnonursing: models and modes of qualitative data analysis. In: Qualitative Research Methods in Nursing, pp. 33–72 (1985)

Leong, L.W., Ibrahim, O., Dalvi-Esfahani, M., Shahbazi, H., Nilashi, M.: The moderating effect of experience on the intention to adopt mobile social network sites for pedagogical purposes: an extension of the technology acceptance model. Educ. Inf. Tech. **23**(6), 2477–2498 (2018). https://doi.org/10.1007/s10639-018-9726-2

Lin, N.: Building a network theory of social capital. In: Social Capital, (pp. 3–28). Routledge (2017)

Liu, B.: Sentiment analysis and subjectivity. In: Handbook of Natural Language Processing, vol. 2, pp. 627-666 (2010)

Liu, B.: Sentiment analysis and opinion mining. In: Synthesis Lectures on Human Language Technologies, vol. 5, no. 1, pp. 1–167 (2012)

Mir, U.B., Kar, A.K., Dwivedi, Y.K., Gupta, M.P., Sharma, R.S.: Realizing digital identity in government: prioritizing design and implementation objectives for Aadhaar in India. Gov. Inf. Quarterly **37**, 101442 (2019a)

Mir, U.B., Kar, A.K., Gupta, M.P., Sharma, R.S.: Prioritizing digital identity goals – the case study of aadhaar in India. In: Pappas, I.O., Mikalef, P., Dwivedi, Y.K., Jaccheri, L., Krogstie, J., Mäntymäki, M. (eds.) I3E 2019. LNCS, vol. 11701, pp. 489–501. Springer, Cham (2019b). https://doi.org/10.1007/978-3-030-29374-1_40

Mittal, A., Goel, A.: Stock prediction using Twitter sentiment analysis 15 (2012). Standford University, CS229 (2011 http://cs229.stanford.edu/proj2011/GoelMittal-StockMarketPredictionUsingTwitterSentimentAnalysis.pdf)

Nie, N.H., Hillygus, D.S., Erbring, L.: Internet use, interpersonal relations, and sociability. Internet Everyday Life, 215–243 (2002)

Pang, B., Lee, L.: Opinion mining and sentiment analysis. Found. Trends® Inf. Retrieval **2**(1–2) 1–135 (2008)

Parmar, M., Maturi, B., Dutt, J.M., Phate, H.: Sentiment Analysis-Interview Transcripts (2018)

Putnam, R.D.: Bowling Alone: the Collapse and Revival of American Community. Simon and Schuster, New York (2000)

Putnam, R.D.: Bowling together. Am. Prosp. **13**(3), 20–22 (2002)

Rambocas, M., Pacheco, B.G.: Online sentiment analysis in marketing research: a review. J. Res.Inter. Market. **12**(2), 146–163 (2018)

Rathore, A.K., Kar, A.K., Ilavarasan, P.V.: Social media analytics: literature review and directions for future research. Decis. Anal. **14**(4), 229–249 (2017)

Rathore, A.K., Ilavarasan, P.V., Dwivedi, Y.K.: Social media content and product co-creation: an emerging paradigm. J. Enterp. Inf. Manag. **29**(1), 7–18 (2016)

Sánchez-Moya, A., Cruz-Moya, O.: "Hey there! I am using WhatsApp": a preliminary study of recurrent discursive realisations in a corpus of WhatsApp statuses. Procedia-Soc. Behav. Sci. **212**, 52–60 (2015)

Scott, N., Garforth, C., Jain, R., Mascarenhas, O., McKemey, K.: The economic impact of telecommunications on rural livelihoods and poverty reduction: a study of rural communities in India (Gujarat), Mozambique and Tanzania (2005)

Selouani, S.A., Hamam, H.: Social impact of broadband internet: a case study in the Shippagan Area, a rural zone in Atlantic Canada. J. Inf. Inf. Tech. Organ. **2**, 79–94 (2007)

Singh, P., Dwivedi, Y.K., Kahlon, K.S., Pathania, A., Sawhney, R.S.: Can twitter analytics predict election outcome? An insight from 2017 Punjab assembly elections. Gov. Inf. Q. 101444 (2020)

Statista Page. https://www.statista.com/statistics/280914/monthly-active-whatsapp-users-in-india/. Accessed 29 May 2020

Taylor, S.J., Bogdan, R.: Introduction to Qualitative Research Methods: The Search for Meanings. Wiley, New york (1984)

Thapa, D.: Exploring the link between ICT intervention and human development through a social capital lens: the case study of a wireless project in the mountain region of Nepal. Universitet i Agder/University of Agder (2012)

Venkatesh, V., Sykes, T.A.: Digital divide initiative success in developing countries: a longitudinal field study in a village in India. Inf. Syst. Res. 24(2), 239–260 (2013)

Williams, D.: On and off the'Net: scales for social capital in an online era. J. Comput.-Mediated Commun. 11(2), 593–628 (2006)

Woolcock, M.: The place of social capital in understanding social and economic outcomes. Can. J. Policy Res. 2(1), 11–17 (2001)

Zachariadis, M., Scott, S., Barrett, M.: Methodological implications of critical realism for mixed-methods research. MIS Q. 855–879 (2013)

Enrolling Actors in a Social Information System: The Incremental Development of Unique Registry in Brazilian "Bolsa Família" Program

Nadja Piedade de Antonio[1], Marcelo Fornazin[2,3]($\boxtimes$), Renata Mendes de Araujo[4,5], and Rodrigo Pereira dos Santos[1]

[1] PPGI – Programa de Pós-Graduação em Informática, UNIRIO – Universidade Federal do Estado do Rio de Janeiro, Rio de Janeiro, Brazil
{nadja.antonio,rps}@uniriotec.br
[2] National School of Public Health of Oswaldo Cruz Foundation, Rio de Janeiro, Brazil
marcelo.fornazin@ensp.fiocruz.br
[3] Computer Science Department, Federal Fluminense University, Niterói, Brazil
[4] Mackenzie Presbyterian University, São Paulo, Brazil
renata.araujo@mackenzie.br
[5] Graduate Program in Information Systems, University of São Paulo, São Paulo, Brazil

Abstract. Although the Brazilian "Bolsa Família" Program (BFP) was largely discussed due to its economic and social outcomes, little is known about the Information Systems (IS) that support BFP. In the context of BFP, CadÚnico system emerged as the registry for citizens who seek to qualify for BFP income transfers, as well as it is an important source of information for other public policies. This paper presents a case study of BFP's evolution over decades through the CadÚnico development. We analyze how the CadÚnico system evolved in Brazil from a fragmented, offline databases in the early 2000 to a unified, online registry essential to BFP operation. Based on enrolment operations, the paper explains how CadÚnico first attracted other ministries from the Federal Government and later attracted municipalities to data registering. By analyzing BFP IS, we bring more evidences to the political and incremental nature of IS development in developing countries.

Keywords: Bolsa Família Program · Social programs · Brazil · Critical-interpretative case study · Actor-Network Theory · Enrolment

1 Introduction

The Brazilian "Bolsa Família" Program (BFP) is an income transfer program that regularly delivers money to nearly 14 million families in condition of poverty or extreme poverty in Brazil [1]. BFP began in 2003, after the Brazilian Federal Government decided to integrate existing fragmented income transfer programs; today, it is one of the largest income transfer programs in the world [2]. By means of BFP, the Government regularly

J. M. Bass and P. J. Wall (Eds.): ICT4D 2020, IFIP AICT 587, pp. 157–168, 2020.
https://doi.org/10.1007/978-3-030-65828-1_13

transfers money to families, aiming to eradicate poverty and hunger and to reduce economic and social inequalities within the country. BFP management is decentralized, i.e., Federal Government, states and municipalities have attributions in its execution [1].

Despite BFP being a widely discussed social program and considering the importance of Information System (IS) to operate social and welfare programs [3–5], with a few exceptions [6–9], little is known about the role of IS in the implementation of BFP. One of the essential IS for running the BFP is the Federal Government's Unique Registry for Social Programs, called "Cadastro Único" (CadÚnico) in Portuguese. CadÚnico is an IS that registers data from citizens to enable them to receive BFP money transfers. It also allows the government administration to track healthcare and children education conditions, as well as to understand the socioeconomic reality of its members and the population in general.

Due to BFP's magnitude, managing its resources is a great technological challenge, especially in a developing country of continental dimensions and heterogeneities, such as in the case of Brazil. Enabling a program on this scale involves technological elements (e.g.: network connectivity, data processing and storage in a country with infrastructural deficiencies), social issues (e.g.: registering low-income people that sometimes are illiterate and often have difficulty to use technology), and political issues (e.g.: negotiation with city halls, provision of service at distant locations and training people for data registration at municipalities). In this context, this paper hence addresses the following research question: How did CadÚnico system evolve over time to support a social program (BFP) in a developing country such as Brazil, with its continental dimensions?

In order to present our argument, we conducted a longitudinal case study on CadÚnico's development. This paper therefore aims to explain how BFP evolved technologically and socially throughout the last 20 years. We operate the "enrolment" category to describe how actors were attracted to the BFP.

The paper is structured in six sections. After this introduction, Sect. 2 discusses the importance of IS for welfare programs. Section 3 defines Actor-Network Theory and enrolment category. Section 4 describes the research method, data gathering and analysis procedures based on an interpretative research. Section 5 presents the CadÚnico case study based on two movements of enrolment: first movement - enrolling the ministries, and second movement - enrolling the municipalities. Conclusion and directions for future research are presented in Sect. 6.

2 The Role of IS Social and Welfare Programs

Social Programs are very important to promote social and economic development. Income transfer programs in middle and low-income countries contribute to improvements in the population's health and education conditions [3, 10, 11].

Fukami and McCubbrey [4] describes the 7-year deployment obstacles of the Colorado Benefits Management System (CBMS), an information system aiming at replacing six aging legacy systems supporting welfare programs in the State of Colorado, USA. The purpose of investing in CBMS was to centralize citizens' applications through data integration and web access. However, for 7 years and after different IT managers, CBMS was not able to be deployed in its full capacity, bringing great losses, including legal proceedings against the state. The scalability of CBMS was hampered by political issues, budget restrictions, lack of planning, unclear accountability and lack of trained people in serving citizens.

There is also a strong understanding of social programs data as the basis for effective statistical analysis and business intelligence IS for public policies decision making. These issues bring new design implications for the welfare programs as well as challenges to their operation.

In DC context, Conditional Income Transfer Programs (CITP) emerged and expanded in the 90's, being integrated to Social Protection Systems in most Latin American countries. CITPs have been called "Social Protection Networks", composed by a set of compensatory interventions focused on combating poverty and extreme poverty. These interventions are the main mechanism to address the so-called intergenerational poverty in the Latin American countries [10].

The importance of management IS to social and welfare programs, and the sociotechnical nature of their IS are reported in research literature. Oliveira *et al.* [6] carried out a study whose main objective was to analyze the effectiveness of IS as an element of federative coordination, also evaluating the management, control and transparency processes related to the use of three IS implemented since 2008 in Brazil: (i) the System Horus, in the area of Health; (ii) Sisjovem, the system responsible for the activities of the Projovem Adolescent Program, in the area of social assistance; and (ii) the interactive School Development Program (SDP), in the area of education. Analyzing their use in the public sector, IS have been considered a strategic tool to improve the efficiency of public services, generating greater savings for the government administration, greater level of transparency and more quality for meeting citizens' demands. Oliveira *et al.* [6] cited, as an inspiring case, CadÚnico as a BFP's IS integrated with other IS of social programs, such as Sisjovem. According to the authors, CadÚnico has tools that allow the generation of numerous social indicators used by the government administration and by researchers to analyze the impacts of the program and formulate new policies.

2.1 The BFP and CadÚnico

The BFP began on October 2003 and serves families living in poverty and extreme poverty. The program started transferring money to 5 million people and after 10 years, the number of beneficiaries almost tripled to around 14 million people, as shown in Fig. 1. The BFP Budget increased from the R$ 2.3 billion spent by the former program "Bolsa Escola" in 2002 to R$ 29 billion in 2014.

According to the Ministry of Citizenship (2020) [1], BFP has three main axes: i) Income supplement - every month, families served by the Program receive a cash benefit, which is transferred directly by the Federal Government guaranteeing the most immediate poverty alleviation; ii) Access to rights - families must fulfill certain commitments (conditions), which aim to reinforce access to education, health, and social assistance offering conditions for future generations to break the cycle of poverty. The conditions do not have a punitive logic; they exist to guarantee that basic social rights reach the population in situation of poverty or extreme poverty. iii) Integration with other social actions - BFP has the capability to integrate several social policies, for example

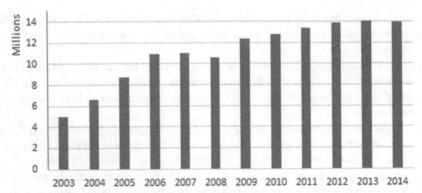

Fig. 1. Number of Bolsa Família Beneficiaries. Data gathered from MSD's system for evaluation and information management [13].

healthcare and education, in order to help people overcome the families' situation of vulnerability and poverty.

The functioning of BFP raises some complexities: Brazil is a continental country organized as a federative republic where Federal Government, 27 state governments and 5571 municipalities are autonomous political entities and public policies are negotiated between the three levels of government administration. For example, Federal Government does not have the workforce and resources in every municipality to register individuals in the BFP. Due to this, the Federal Government negotiates with municipal governments through the mayors' association to register individuals using municipal resources. The intersectoral nature of BFP adds more complexity, once program's decisions are based on information gathered from different sectors of government administration, such as, education and public health. The Brazilian social policies are decentralized, that is, schools and primary care are usually managed by municipalities by means of their educational and health departments, respectively. Therefore, these departments share information on social services to fulfill the BFP registry. In addition, Brazil is a heterogeneous country where some people live urban metropoles, peripheries, rural areas, semi-arid regions and rainforest. Thereby, different strategies are necessary to reach individuals throughout the country.

Considering the aforementioned complexity, BFP management is shared among the Federal Government and municipalities. At the federal level, the social program is managed by Ministry of Social Development (MSD), and Caixa Econômica Federal (CAIXA), a Brazilian's public bank, maintains the information technology resources and transfers the money its beneficiaries. Municipalities are responsible for registering families - those seeking to be included in the program go to a service center in their city to provide their information for registration in CadÚnico – the BFP management information system. All the information is digitally registered in the CadÚnico and centralized in a database at the MSD for eligibility analysis.

CadÚnico started on 2001 and supported the increase in Bolsa Família beneficiaries. Today, besides the nearly 14 million beneficiaries, there are other 14 million people registered in CadÚnico, totaling around 28 million registrations, according the MSD's

System for Evaluation and Information Management [14]. This number comprises beneficiaries, and people that registered but did not fulfil the requirements, people that are waiting to receive the benefit, and former beneficiaries that do not need the aid from BFP anymore. CadÚnico is also an instrument of transparency and accountability for BFP. Individual data is available on the Transparency Portal [15] of Federal Government, and through the MSD's System of Evaluation and Information Management [15].

Considering the BFP context, some studies analyzed the access to the program. Feitosa [7] carried out a study about how citizens are codified in BFP and CadÚnico. Jayo [8] analyzed the banking correspondents which provide banking services on behalf of CAIXA to several distant locations in Brazil, and Santos [9] described the impacts on financial inclusion indicators of a bank agency installed in a boat on Marajo Island, in the Amazon region. These research studies offer distinct contributions in order to understand the access to BFP in many heterogeneous places of Brazil. This paper proposes a different approach focused on how the BFP IS evolved from the perspective of the Brazilian government administration. In order to analyze CadÚnico's development, we take inspiration in the Actor-Network Theory [23, 24, 26, 27] and chose to describe it based on the idea of *enrolment* [24] of actors, as we explain next.

3 Actor-Network Theory

The Actor-Network Theory (ANT) approach has inspired research in IS field since 1990. However, from 2000 onwards, its use was intensified, as several IS tracks, including ICT4D, started to report research inspired by this approach, such as: digital inclusion [16, 17]; e-government [18, 19]; health IS [20, 21] and geographic IS [22].

ANT-inspired studies often observe a longitudinal approach [16–22], the aim of such research being to study the movement, formation of groups and translations, rather than collecting information about a specific moment. Most of the ANT research addresses controversies of technical artifact construction referring to complex environments with multiple actors having opposing preferences, whereby the political dimension of an IS implementation is present. Some works analyzed how actor networks are mobilized to develop sustainable IS in developing countries [18, 20]. It can also be seen that these papers depict complex settings, as well as the role of technical artifacts and other factors in network stabilization.

The movement to attract other actors are described as moments of translation [23], namely: problematization, interessement, enrolment, and mobilization. Moments of translation [23] have been widely used in IS research [16–19]. In these processes, systems are understood to be similar to an Obligatory Passage Point, where the other actors tend to converge during the course of the translation. It is important to stress that consensus building in ANT is not a simple endeavor that can be taken for granted as several negotiations, also referred to as *translations*, are needed to succeed in the deployment of an IS.

Here, we focus in the enrolment of actors. Callon [23] define enrolment as the "the device by which a set of interrelated roles is defined and attributed to actors who accept them". The enrolment is therefore depicted as "the group of multilateral negotiations, trials of strength and tricks that accompany the interessements and enable them to succeed". According to Callon and Law [24]: "The theory of enrolment is concerned with the ways in which provisional order is proposed and sometimes achieved". CadÚnico system's unique registration had to make numerous translations to be able to leave several fragmented bases and offline databases in the early 2000 and built a unified and online registry essential to BFP's operation. In the case of BFP, we will show how MSD and CadÚnico enrolled ministries and municipalities to construct the BFP.

We therefore aim to extend Feitosa's [7] argument by adding some evidence to the incremental and evolving nature of CadÚnico. We analyzed ten years of CadÚnico development and observed how the political configuration on BFP registry infrastructure changed over time.

4 Research Method

This research was designed as a longitudinal case study based on the critical-interpretative approach [25, 26]. The ANT approach was chosen to analyze the case's trajectory, involving heterogenous actors. While ANT does not attempt to be a critical approach, "tracing the network and the actions of its constituents, combined with a refusal to make a priori distinctions or grant status, enables a critical light to be shone on the assumed, the mundane and the status quo" [27].

In this case study, we gathered and analyzed data related to BFP from 2001 to 2012. Data was gathered through a period of eighteen months based on semi-structured interviews (conducted in two rounds) and public documents related to BFP. The first round of interviews were conducted from March to December 2018 and approached six technicians and managers at CAIXA, located in Rio de Janeiro, Brazil. The second round covered nine interviews at the MSD in Brasília, on December 2018. Interviews lasted 1 h 30 min on average and most of them were recorded with interviewees' consent. The interviewees' were CadÚnico managers and BFP businesswomen, as well as IS coordinators and developers. Generally, interviewees have more than 10 years of work experience in BFP or CadÚnico. In addition to the interviews, we had access to reports and data published on Internet, and material provided by the interviewees.

This paper considers the research quality criteria proposed by Klein and Myers [28]. Interviews transcripts and notes were successively read so that the story became clear to the researchers. After carrying out this process successively, a coherent narrative was achieved to write a plausible manuscript. Multiple interpretations were considered, since different people in distinct positions at CAIXA and MSD were interviewed. Concerning contextualization, we presented the historical and social background of BFP, based on interviews, documents from public agencies and newspaper articles.

To address the abstraction and dialogical reasoning criteria, we conducted a dialogue with the research field, associating the findings in the field through interviews. We also asked some participants to read and confirm the reports after the interviews. The case presented here does not aim to be directly generalized to other contexts, but by means of transferability we hope the findings presented in this paper might help other researchers and managers to think about their theoretical and practical questions.

5   The Case of CadÚnico

During the decade after the promulgation of the current Brazilian Federal Constitution, a social-liberal government proposed opening the Brazilian market while focusing on social services. During the second term of the former president Fernando Henrique Cardoso (1998–2002), the Federal Government conducted pilot projects of conditional income transfers. "Bolsa Escola" program transferred money to families with children attending school and was managed by Ministry of Education. "Bolsa Alimentação" was an instrument for the Union's financial participation in supplementing family income to improve access to food and was managed by the Ministry of Health. The program especially targeted pregnant women, nursing mothers, and children up to six years of age. "Auxílio Gás" was managed by the Ministry of Mines and Energy and consisted of an aid for the purchase of gas cylinders. The aid addressed nutrition issues indirectly simply because poor people were unable to regularly purchase gas cylinders for food preparation. The three social programs together assisted 5.5 million families and were managed by different ministries while CAIXA technologically supported all the programs.

In 2001, the Federal Government published a law establishing the Unique Registry for Social Programs, called in Portuguese as "Cadastro Único" (CadÚnico). As its name suggests, CadÚnico was designed with the aim of unifying several IS that previously registered social benefits. Similarly to Fukami and McCubbrey's study [4] of CBMS, BFP also faced difficulties in the development and implementation of its various supporting IS, such as: different interests, different databases and decentralized management. These issues are reported in following paragraphs.

5.1   First Movement – Enrolling Other Ministries

We observed that, before BFP, each social program was managed by a different ministry, that is, the programs were fragmented among the government administration sectors. This fragmentation in different ministries hindered dialogue between internal government actors to manage benefits in the same direction, as they would have to negotiate, and each ministry had its own priorities. Additionally, each social benefit had its separate registration and a beneficiary could have several registrations for different benefits. An excerpt from the interview follows: "Registration was precarious. There was no CadÚnico. The register was decentralized. We had an IS that attached all the benefits within it" (Respondent 2–8 years in BFP).

The various existing programs in the previous years used different numbers to identify and select the target audience, which in turn made it difficult to coordinate actions, fragmented the service and reduced its efficiency. As the name Unique Registry suggests, designing CadÚnico intended to unify several IS that previously registered social benefits in a fragmented way. In order to unify the fragmented registries, the system was split into two, the CadÚnico and the novel Information System for Benefits Payment (SIBES), which is not object of this paper. The former would hold people information while the later, after the analysis of conditions, would transfer money to the beneficiaries.

In the year 2003, Luís Inácio Lula da Silva ascended to the Presidency, changing the political group in charge of Federal Government. The new government created MSD, which proposed the BFP in order to eradicate extreme poverty in Brazil through a regular aid offered to every family in the condition of extreme poverty. At that time, the income transfers which were previously pilot projects, gained political projection as one of the main goals of the new term. Thus, the Federal Government put conditional income transfers in the core of its agenda by centralizing BFP in MSD, including IS that supported the previous social programs. About enrolling other ministries to promote the BFP and CadÚnico, an excerpt from the interview follows:

"When the unification of social programs took place, the Federal Government's transition team that carried out the study and unification of the programs worked physically inside the Bolsa Escola building. Bolsa Escola was the largest cash transfer program that existed among the four programs that were unified. They considered it important to have profound knowledge of the dynamics of this program to understand what to expect, how it worked etc. The inception of the unification of the programs had been built, but not the operation of the new unified program. An effort was made within Ministry of Education and Culture (MEC) to make employees available to help the operationalization of the new unified social program together with the transition team. When the ministry that would serve the program was defined, part of the staff permanently migrated from MEC to MSD. During 2003 and 2005, I also worked at the MEC in parallel (...). In 2003 there was no MSD yet, there was not even an e-mail server. Extraordinary Ministry of Food Security and Fighting Hunger came first and only in 2005 that it migrated to MSD" (Respondent 8–17 years in MSD).

By the end of year 2003, there were 6 million people receiving the money transfers from BFP. They were all registered in CadÚnico. CAIXA technologically supported the former social programs and had the infrastructure to enable the payment of these benefits. Moreover, CAIXA was the bank that operated social security in Brazil. Therefore, CAIXA held the skills and infrastructure to hold a national registry for social programs as well to deliver the money to its beneficiaries. It was hence chosen as the financial operator of BFP and started a relationship with MSD.

CadÚnico was then delivered to the municipalities that opted to offer "Bolsa Família". Every city in Brazil started to register families seeking access to the monthly aid. Law unified the registry, but the registering procedures were still fragmented in the various municipalities, as explained: *"The database was decentralized. A person could be in several places, because people moved from city to city, and there was no such control in the registry"* (Respondent 4–15 years in CadÚnico). Interviewees referred to this third period as "CadÚnico offline" because there was no internet connection in all municipalities to support registration procedures directly to the centralized base at that time. Municipalities had to register families' information in a local system and later send it the database to MSD.

5.2 Second Movement – Enrolling the Municipalities

The following excerpt summarizes the technological challenge of the CadÚnico development in the first years: *"In 2005, we barely had a computer to work with. In addition, we barely had access to CadÚnico. The very first CadÚnico database I had access to was delivered just in January 2005. The system was offline and installed in 5,571 municipalities. The base was problematic. The data was transmitted to CAIXA and had a return file for each municipality. The municipality analyzed the issues and all inconsistencies, treated and sent them to CAIXA. Even though it was unified, there were multiple registrations. When the city hall's management changed, the previous management erased the entire previous base. The municipality then had to ask CAIXA for a new base. This generated a great deal of rework for city halls"*. (Respondent 6–13 years in CadÚnico).

During the period known as CadÚnico offline, it was possible to notice several issues related to the continued management of CadÚnico, according to the following excerpt: *"A study of the CadÚnico's database was carried out and many problems and multiplicities were identified. There was no flag of active and inactive registrations. CAIXA had to limit access to the CadÚnico base nationwide. Everyone stayed without work waiting for the end of the appointments at the base. From the moment it made this appointment, MSD launched Law 360/2005 to update its registration. The MSD remunerated the municipalities to promote the registration update"* (Respondent 6–13 years in CadÚnico).

There was an urgent and necessary action to systematize the process to avoid issues, such as the constant extinction of the base during the municipalities' mayor transition. Law 360/2005 was published after marking the bases to promote the registry update and offered incentives for data quality improvement to municipalities. With the reward for registry improvement, municipalities promoted the registration update in their communities. This was the first moment of political promotion of CadÚnico's system to the municipalities. In 2006 the number of people assisted by BFP was around 10,5 million, almost double from 2003 figures when CadÚnico started.

CadÚnico's transformation was imminent. The offline data transfer from municipalities to centralized CadÚnico incurred in data and money losses to MSD and CAIXA, since this process was susceptible to errors. CadÚnico needed an online infrastructure to unify registries, and to share them among all government levels.

In 2010, CadÚnico started to be online and data fragmentation was eliminated. The move from offline to online has brought a great improvement to CadÚnico. The most significant change was the possibility to transfer citizens' data from one municipality to another. This digital transfer carries several political articulations followed by technological improvements so that this movement could take place and reach CadÚnico online. This change eliminated data inconsistencies which occurred during the CadÚnico offline. At that time, BFP served 12.8 million families.

After the move from offline to online version, MSD released a new instrument to enroll municipalities in the CadÚnico maintenance, called DMI-M (Decentralized Management Index - Municipalities). DMI-M was launched through Law 754/2010 initiating a second moment of political action for municipalities to update CadÚnico. The municipality signed a term with MSD to comply with two registration indicators (updated and valid registration) and two social indicators referring to the conditions recommended by BFP (health and education). As the DMI-M increased, the more financial aid the municipality received from MSD. In 2012 the number of BFP beneficiaries reached the mark of 14 million people and since then this is the average number of people benefited by BFP. Moreover, CadÚnico holds data of more people, 28 million on average.

The various efforts to enroll municipalities, including on-line registering and DMI-M, were successful instruments since they aligned interest of MSD and municipalities for the qualification of CadÚnico.

6 Conclusion

This paper reports an investigation of the trajectory of CadÚnico, a registry that supports the BFP by drawing on ANT enrolment to discuss how CadÚnico incrementally aligned a network of political actors over fifteen years.

As described in previous sections, CadÚnico system was built as a response to unify several fragmented IS (the reason for its name). The former fragmented registers limited the scaling of the novel social program "Bolsa Família", but also offered a problematization of the new "unified register" CadÚnico.

The CadÚnico system was built in Brazil through five different government terms over 18 years and this shows its incremental and resilient nature. It was initially built by decision of the Federal Government; certainly, a crucial condition for its success. Nevertheless, its implementation did not take place without gradual growth, since negotiations and change of roles where necessary for its establishment. First, ministries were enrolled in CadÚnico and BFP. They changed their roles from managers of former social projects to partners of MSD, as now they monitor health and education indicators, for example, based on CadÚnico information. Later, municipalities enrolled in data registering in CadÚnico. Here BFP improved infrastructure, trained employees and used financial instruments to align local interest to the national agenda. Therefore, municipalities registered families and maintained the registry updated to assist people and have access to funding for local social services.

This analysis was carried out through a longitudinal case study, considering the quality criteria and using multiple sources of evidence. Our analysis shows that, despite CadÚnico's success, it was not enough to provide a good technological infrastructure with connectivity, computers and databases. It was necessary to go beyond articulating a network of actors to make possible the identification and registration of millions of impoverished families in Brazil. Thus, CadÚnico comprised a series of legal and political operations to attract city halls to register families in their respective municipalities.

As such, in this paper, we bring a theoretical contribution to refine the understanding of social IS in Brazil and in a specific scenario, by means of translation movements of the actors articulated themselves so that the CadÚnico could be transformed from offline to online IS. Through the interpretative approach method, the IS was studied in its context of production and use, and came up with critical and important knowledge for understanding social IS.

As a managerial and social contribution, this paper can help managers of the public agencies to get a starting point to reflect on how IS are produced within organizations, as well as to understand how different IS work using ANT concepts. This paper also proposes a new approach to observe and manage IS that can assist in their development process.

A limitation of our work was the lack of financial resources and time to conduct more interviews, considering the countless IS that operationalize BFP. We therefore hope to bring to light an unavailable knowledge - the story of the most important IS which supports a social program of enormous magnitude such as BFP

As a research agenda, we suggest theorizing about IS that promote social services to citizens in the Brazilian context, considering the peculiarity of this very heterogeneous scenario. We expect future works to promote a stronger dialogue with established literature, for example, Information Infrastructure studies. Finally, based on this work, we concluded that CadÚnico is a vital condition for the BFP to have an updated registration and promote improvement in the lives of beneficiary families.

This paper was finished during the covid-19 pandemic, a time when CadÚnico is mentioned in many political discussions. Brazilian Congress passed a bill that offers an emergency relief income to help millions of informal workers left with no income by the social distancing measures adopted in the country to fight de pandemic. The emergency income is a two-month payment of approximately half minimum salary for every Brazilian citizen in poverty condition, and targets nearly 60 million people. An important part of the 28 million people registered in CadÚnico were able to receive the emergency income, while the remaining people spend days in lines to fulfill the information to qualify to the benefit. This catastrophe, besides the horror spread throughout the world, shows us the importance of IS to keep citizen information updated and ready to offer responses to unexpected situations.

Acknowledgments. The authors gratefully acknowledge the financial support of Oswaldo Cruz Foundation Strategy for the 2030 Agenda. Renata Araujo is also supported by the Brazilian National Research Council grant #313210/2019-5.

References

1. Brazil: Ministry of Citizenship. https://desenvolvimentosocial.gov.br/servicos/bolsa-familia. Accessed 02 June 2020
2. Shei, A., Costa, F., Reis, M.G., Ko, A.I.: The impact of Brazil's Bolsa Família conditional cash transfer program on children health care utilization and health outcomes. BMC Int. Health Hum. Rights **14**(1), 10 (2019)
3. Keuning, S.: SESAME: an integrated economic and social accounting system. Int. Stat. Rev. **65**, 111–121 (1997)
4. Fukami, C.V., McCubbrey, D.J.: Colorado benefits management system: seven years of failure. Commun. Assoc. Inf. Syst. **29**(5), 97–102 (2011)
5. Harrison, T.M., Canestraro, D., Pardo, T., et al: Applying an enterprise data model in government: transitioning to a data-centric information system for child welfare in the US. In: Proceedings of the 20th Annual International Conference on Digital Government Research (2019)
6. Oliveira, L.C.P., Faleiros, S.M., Diniz, E.H.: Sistemas de Informação em Políticas Sociais Descentralizadas: uma análise sobre a coordenação federativa e práticas de gestão. Revista de administração Pública **49**, 23–46 (2015)
7. Feitosa, P.H.F.: O Cidadão Codificado: A Digitalização da Cidadania em Bancos de Dados de Interesse Público. MsC Dissertation. Federal University of Rio de Janeiro, Brazil (2010). https://www.cos.ufrj.br/index.php/pt-BR/publicacoes-pesquisa/details/15/2163
8. Jayo, M.: Correspondentes bancários como canal de distribuição de serviços financeiros: taxonomia, histórico, limites e pontencialidades dos modelos de gestão de redes. Ph.D. thesis, Getulio Vargas Foundation, Brazil (2010). https://bibliotecadigital.fgv.br/dspace/handle/10438/8108

9. Santos, R.P.: O papel da tecnologia da informação e comunicação na inclusão financeira da população ribeirinha da Ilha de Marajó: o caso Agência Barco. MSc Dissertation. Getulio Vargas Foundation, Brazil (2015). https://bibliotecadigital.fgv.br/dspace/handle/10438/14978
10. Silva, M.O.S.: Caracterização e problematização dos Programas de Transferência de Renda Condicionada (PTRC_ na América Latina e Caribe. In: Silva, M.O.S. (ed.) Bolsa Família in tackling poverty in Maranhão and Piauí. Programas de transferência de renda na América Latina e Caribe, pp. 85–234. Cortez, São Paulo (2014)
11. The Economist, How Africa is creating welfare states. https://www.economist.com/middle-east-and-africa/2019/02/21/how-africa-is-creating-welfare-states. Accessed 29 May 2020
12. Braa, J., Hanseth, O., Heywood, A., Mohammed, W., Shaw, V.: Developing health information systems in developing countries: the flexible standards strategy. MIS Q. 31, 1–22 (2007)
13. FH deu bolsa a 5 milhões e Lula a 7 milhões. Jornal O Globo. https://oglobo.globo.com/politica/fh-deu-bolsa-milhoes-lula-7-milhoes-3054879. Accessed 02 June 2020
14. Sistema de Avaliação e Gestão da Informação. https://aplicacoes.mds.gov.br/sagi. Accessed 02 June 2020
15. Portal da Transparência, Brazilian Government. www.portaltransparencia.gov.br/beneficios/bolsa-familia. Accessed 02 June 2020
16. Teles, A., Joia, L.A.: Assessment of digital inclusion via the actor-network theory: the case of the Brazilian municipality of Piraí. Telemat. Inform. 28, 191–203 (2011)
17. Andrade, A.D., Urquhart, C.: The affordances of actor-network theory. ICT Dev. Res. 23(4), 352–374 (2010)
18. Heeks, R., Stanforth, C.: Understanding e-Government project trajectories from an actor-network perspective. Eur. J. Inf. Syst. 16(2), 165–177 (2007)
19. Cavalheiro, G.M., Joia, L.A.: Examining the implementation of a European patent management system in Brazil from an actor-network theory perspective. Inf. Technol. Dev. 22(2), 220–241 (2015)
20. Braa, J., Monteiro, E., Sahay, S.: Networks of action sustainable health information systems across developing countries. MIS Q. 28(3), 337–362 (2004)
21. Sahay, S., Saebo, J., Braa, J.: Scaling of HIS in a global context: Same, same, but different. Inf. Organ. 23(4), 294–323 (2013)
22. Rajao, R.G.L.: The site of IT actor-network and practice theory as approaches for studying IT in organisations. In: Vilodov, S.O., Scolai, P., Rajão, R., Faik, I., Higgins, A. (eds.) Heterogeneities, Multiplicities and Complexities; Towards Subtler Understandings of Links Between Technology, Organisation and Society, pp. 92–105. UCD School of Business, Dublin (2008)
23. Callon, M.: Some elements of a sociology of translation: domestication of the scallops and the fisherman of St Brieuc Bay. In: Law, J. (ed.) Power action and belief a new sociology of knowledge, pp. 196–223. Routledge, London (1986)
24. Callon, M., Law, J.: On interests and their transformation: enrolment and counter-enrolment. Soc. Stud. Sci. 12(4), 615–625 (1982)
25. Pozzebon, M.: Conducting and evaluating critical interpretive research: examining criteria as a key component in building a research tradition. In: Kaplan, B., Truex III, D.P., Wastell, D., Wood-Harper, A.T., DeGross, J.I. (eds.) Information Systems Research: Relevant Theory and Informed Practice, pp. 275–292 (2004)
26. Mitev, N.N.: Postmodernism and criticality in information systems research: what critical management studies can contribute. Soc. Sci. Comput. Rev. 24(3), 310–325 (2006)
27. Doolin, B., Lowe, A.: To reveal is to critique: actor-network theory and critical information systems research. J. Inf. Technol. 17(2), 69–78 (2002)
28. Klein, H.K., Myers, M.D.: A set of principles for conducting and evaluating interpretive field studies in information systems. MIS Q. 23(1), 67–93 (1999)

Business Innovation and Data Privacy

Exploring Gender Gaps: How Nigerian Micro Business Owners Use Mobile Apps for Business

Adebowale Owoseni[1]($\boxtimes$) (iD), Kutoma Wakunuma[1] (iD), Adedamola Tolani[2] (iD),
and Hossana Twinomurinzi[3] (iD)

[1] Centre for Computing and Social Responsibility, School of Computer Science and
Informatics, De Montfort University, Leicester LE19BH, UK
adebowale.owoseni@dmu.ac.uk

[2] School of Computing, University of South Africa, Pretoria, South Africa

[3] Department of Applied Information Systems, University of Johannesburg,
Johannesburg, South Africa

Abstract. This exploratory study examined how men and women who own micro businesses in Lagos, Nigeria, use mobile apps for business from Amartya Sen's capability approach perspective and quantitative research methods. The two key findings suggest that women micro business owners make more use of mobile apps compared to men, and that they tend to exit micro businesses as they grow older indicating a possible influence of patriarchy in African contexts. Specifically, women seized opportunities presented by mobile apps to acquire *capabilities* to *function*; and they adapt mobile apps to enhance their *wellbeing* and *freedom* despite the restrictions and responsibilities in the patriarchal environments typical of low-income countries. The insignificant gender gap in certain mobile app usages presents new perspectives to debates on gender (economic) gaps, inequality, women empowerment, and technology uptake in low-income country contexts.

Keywords: Mobile apps usage · Gender gap · Micro-business owners ·
Micro-businesses · Capability approach

1 Introduction

Inequality in its various forms magnifies challenges [1] such as unemployment, poverty, and hunger. In the context of micro-businesses (MBs), inequality could manifest in form of economic empowerment of business owners [2]. MBs being the foundation of any economy [3, 4], it is important to understand how gender inequality affects micro business owners (MBOs).

Usually, economic challenges in MBs are addressed by encouraging strategic use of Information and Communication Technology (ICT) [5, 6]. However, the adoption and usage of ICT could create unintended inequality across gender, particularly in developing African country contexts, which are often patriarchal in nature [2, 7]. Hence the need to understand gender perspectives of ICT usage in MBs. Arguably, emerging ICTs such

J. M. Bass and P. J. Wall (Eds.): ICT4D 2020, IFIP AICT 587, pp. 171–182, 2020.
https://doi.org/10.1007/978-3-030-65828-1_14

as mobile apps are positively impacting how MBs are conducted [8, 9]. Nevertheless, few works of literature have considered the gender aspects when it comes to the usage of mobile apps and how it could influence gender gaps in Africa.

Moreover, considering Nigeria as an example of a low-income African country, 97.8% of MBs are not registered [10, 11], suggesting that they constitute the informal business sector. It is argued that more than half of the informal sector business owners are women [10]. This also aligns with the fact that women constitute more than 49% of 200.96 million Nigerians. As such, understanding how men and women use mobile apps for MBs in a patriarchal, but women populated environment could inform the discourse on gender (economic) gaps, jobs creation, poverty reduction and economic growth [2, 12, 13]. Thus, this exploratory study offers an insight into *how mobile app usage by MBOs reflect gender gaps in Lagos, Nigeria.*

The remainder of this article presents the theoretical framework, research objectives, underlying literature, research approach, results, discussions, and implications of findings.

2 Theoretical Framework: Capability Approach

The extent of freedom enjoyed by people in a community, arguably informs their perception of equality [14, 15]. Amartya Sen defines *freedom* as not only a measure of an individual's possession of the *means to achieve* such as money, cars, and houses, but also includes their *functioning* – the ability to become who they want to be, by doing what they like to do [16–18].

Arguably, mobile apps appear as the most widely accepted ICTs in low-income countries. Mobile apps tend to enhance individual's perception of freedom when adapted to solve contextual problems in fast-evolving environments [12], particularly as it applies to managing MBs. For example, knowledge about mobile apps could enhance the ability *to do* more business, doing more business could provide opportunities to earn more income and achieve some personal goals, which could result in improved self-esteem. In low-income countries, it is perceived that women make limited use of technology such as mobile apps [19], this situation influences women *functioning*, and potentially creates gender gaps [15, 20]. Understanding the mobile app usage capabilities of MBOs along gender differences in this regard could reveal the dimension of inequality and possible approaches to close the gap.

Although, other theoretical viewpoints such as social balance theory, and digital divide framework, appear relevant to ICT and gender discourse, the capability approach is suitable and applicable to explore human development, gender gaps and social practices [15, 16] on three grounds: First, the capability approach is a normative theory that considers individual perspectives; secondly, it recognises peoples functioning in formal and informal situations, and thirdly, it appreciates the diversity of individuals in a community while developing their individual capabilities [14, 15]. Within the context of this study, the capability approach was used to illustrate the freedom that comes from the use of mobile apps, particularly for women. Moreover, attention is drawn to unrealized freedoms from using mobile apps between gender and the contrast between men and women with their use of mobile apps for micro businesses.

3 Research Objectives

This research sought to explore how men and women who own micro-business in Lagos Nigeria use mobile apps for business. Specifically, the study seeks to answer the following research question: *How does mobile app usage by microbusiness owners reflect gender and freedom gaps in Lagos, Nigeria?*

4 Review of Literature

This section provides the underlying literature for this study in a low-income country context, it considers micro-businesses as economic development factor, mobile apps as ICT for enhancing micro-businesses, and the influence of gender in mobile app usage in micro-businesses.

4.1 Micro Businesses and Economic Development

It is difficult to adopt a generic definition for micro-business. MBs are autonomous business enterprises managed by owners, or co-owners in a personalized and mostly unstructured way [21–23]. The Nigerian Bank of Industry (BOI) defined micro-businesses as a business entity with a maximum of 10 employees, 5-million-naira total asset and 20-million-naira annual turnover [22]. MBs create economic balance because it creates jobs, prompt innovation and reduces poverty [3–5]. MBs exist across all sectors of the Nigerian economy either as artisans or "white-collar" consultants, thus the importance of MBs.

It is challenging to know the exact number of MBs in Nigeria because a significant number of MBs do not exist on any government register. Nevertheless, the Small and Medium Enterprises Development Agency of Nigeria (SMEDAN) suggests that approximately 74 million MBs exists in Nigeria, and the MBs engaged more than 85% of total labor and contributing more than 50% to the GDP [21, 22]. Notwithstanding, the contributions of MBs to the economy, the MB are overwhelmed with challenges such as infrastructural shortfalls, scarce capital, derisory market research, multiple taxation, and poor management (as exhibited in lack of focus, succession plan, proper bookkeeping, and business strategy, etc.) [4, 5]. Other challenges include the emergence of new technologies that could be disruptive [24].

4.2 Mobile Apps as ICT in Micro-businesses

The nature of MBs as entities with limited resources restricts ICT options to drive business [24]. Although MBs have much flexibility in adapting to change, they also carry the risk of extinction due to emerging technologies [25]. For example, the sale of airtime vouchers was a lucrative business two decades ago when mobile telephony (2G) was new in Nigeria. In recent times, the sale of airtime vouchers as a business is no longer needed because airtime could be purchased directly from Telco via Unstructured Supplementary Service Data (USSD) and mobile banking apps. This disruption is applicable to emergence Uber and extinction of cabdrivers.

Mobile apps are software installed on smartphones, mobile apps interact with the internet and the smartphone hardware like camera, fingerprint scanners and microphones to provide unique capabilities [26–28]. The adoption of mobile apps as a form of ICT by micro-business could enhance the management and the efficiency of business activities. Mobile apps allow users to work remotely, mobile apps defile the odds of working within a structured business hour, provides access to virtual (borderless) markets and reduces the risk of data loss when connected to cloud data storage infrastructure. The usage of mobile apps for business by MBs is cost-effective as the sunk cost is relatively negligible or bearable. Mobile apps used by MBOs in Lagos include social media apps, productivity apps, transport apps and payment apps [29] as illustrated in Fig. 1.

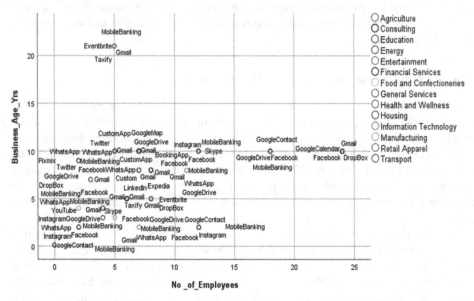

Fig. 1. Mobile apps used by MBOs in Lagos, Nigeria (Source [29])

4.3   Gender and Mobile Apps Adoption in Micro-businesses

Previous studies on gender and micro-businesses had broader perspectives of gender, businesses, and ICTs. For example, [30] focused on the understanding of the perception of business success by men and women. [31] investigated the uptake of ICTs by women who run small businesses. The outcome of the qualitative research affirms knowledge progressions from static webpages to dynamic online transactions, which lays groundwork for examining how women use other ICTs like mobile apps.

The women MBOs perceivably need to combine MB management with family demands like child-raising, home management and other tasks placed by African culture [2, 7]. The women MBOs would like to work remotely from home or transit, access virtual and borderless markets, and reduce the risk of data loss at relatively low cost. The adoption of mobile apps seems to meet these peculiar needs of women MBOs and perhaps responsible for increasing participation of women in micro-business [32]. There is limited literature with empirical reference as to how women MBOs use mobile apps compared to their male counterparts in low income country context. This exploratory study investigated *how mobile app usage by microbusiness owners reflect gender gaps in Lagos, Nigeria.*

5 Research Approach

5.1 The Study Area

The research was conducted in Lagos, Nigeria. Geographically, Lagos is the smallest state in Nigeria, nonetheless, it has the highest population density of 23 million people occupying 3 577 km^2 [33]. Approximately 30% of Nigeria's economic activities originate from Lagos [34] which, represents 60% of Nigeria's industrial and commercial activities. Lagos economy is diversified, unlike the larger Nigerian economy which depends severely on proceeds from the oil and gas industry. Lagos generates the highest internal revenue of all states in Nigeria. Thus, Lagos is financially viable and economically stable [34].

5.2 Data Collection

Using non-probability convenience sampling, the study administered face-to-face questionnaires to 2,500 MBOs in Lagos. To improved participant's responses and reduce data collection errors, 15 field officers were involved in the data collection activities that lasted for 4 weeks. The officers visited MBOs at their business locations, ask questions and input feedback in google forms. Apart from questions that retrieved MBOs' demographic details, respondents provided 5-point Likert-scaled responses to 15 questions that elicited feedback for mobile apps usage construct (see Table 1). With Likert scale measurement, data output could be subjected to a wider range of quantitative analyses [35]. 1159 responses were analyzable. The data collection had ethical approval from statutory University ethical committees.

5.3 Data Evaluation

This exploratory study examined the demographic data of MBOs before focusing on the influence on mobile app usage. The mobile app usage construct is measured along 15 predefined measured variables, while gender gap, and freedom are social constructs within the Nigerian context. The study used descriptive statistics to evaluate the 1,159 5-likert-scale responses. The statistical output includes response counts, mean, standard deviations, variance, kurtosis, skewness. weighted average, and percentage average, all grouped across men and women gender. The responses had Kurtosis and Skewness within an acceptable range of -2 to $+2$ [35], with very close variances between men and women for 14 out of 15 mobile app usage variables. Minitab 18 was used for the statistical evaluation.

6   Results and Discussion

This section presents the demography of all respondents, and thereafter groups the responses by gender and compares outcomes of men and women MBOs.

6.1   Exploring Gender Gaps in Demography of Micro Business Owners in Lagos

The demography consists of 540 women and 619 men respondents which summed up to 1,159 MBOs. Table 1 summarized background information of the participants.

Table 1. Demographic analysis of MBOs in Lagos (Source: Field Survey)

Demographic variable	Options	Frequency count (fc)			Frequency % (fc %)		
		W	M	T	W	M	T
Education Of MBOs	No formal education	19	24	43	1.6	2.1	3.7
	Secondary	205	282	487	17.7	24.3	42
	Diploma	98	90	188	8.5	7.8	16.2
	Bachelors	170	160	330	14.7	13.8	28.5
	Masters	46	59	105	4.0	5.1	9.1
	PhD	2	4	6	0.2	0.3	0.5
	Total frequency	540	619	1159	46.6%	53.4%	100%
Age of MBOs	<=20 years	97	33	130	8.4	2.8	11.2
	21–29 years	211	201	412	18.2	17.3	35.5
	30–39 years	164	250	414	14.2	21.6	35.7
	40–49 years	43	107	150	3.7	9.2	12.9
	50–59 years	24	21	45	2.1	1.8	3.9
	>=60 years	1	7	8	0.1	0.6	0.7
	Total frequency	540	619	1159	46.6%	53.4%	100%
Age of MBs	<=5 years	407	291	698	35.1	25.1	60.2
	6–10 years	88	181	269	7.6	15.6	23.2
	11–15 years	33	74	107	2.8	6.4	9.2
	16–20 years	10	43	53	0.9	3.7	4.6
	21–25 years	2	16	18	0.2	1.4	1.6
	>=25 years	0	14	14	0.0	1.2	1.2
	Total frequency	540	619	1159	46.6%	53.4%	100%

M = Men, W = Women, T = Total

Evaluating the demography along the gender construct, the results suggest three gender gap perspectives: 1) Women ownership of MBs at 20 years old is thrice that of men. For instance, 97 female and 33 male respondents were running micro businesses at age 20 years old. 2) A gradual decline in women ownership of MBs as they get older, for example, at 40–49 years, men's ownership is twice that of women. 3) As MBs existed for longer years, fewer women compared to men owned MBs, this is depicted by 181:88 ratio, representing men to women MB ownerships when MBs existed for 6–10 years.

These perspectives corroborate the normative or critical reasoning stance of the capabilities approach [15] with regards to individual's uniqueness to develop capabilities that enhance their freedoms. Women tend to own MBs in their early adulthood because they have less responsibilities for spouse(s) or child(ren), at about 20 years old, women arguably pride themselves in the prestige of being entrepreneurs, earning incomes, and fulfillment of financial independence. However, these freedoms seem to decline in their late thirties and early forties due to increased family demands and cultural pressures on women in a patriarchal community. Remarkably, men who did not own MBs in their early adulthood seemingly developed the capacity to manage MBs for longer years, from their thirties. This could be attributed to what Magidimisha and Steven [2] termed as different characteristics between men and women. Magidimisha and Steven [2] argued that women's double burden of looking after the home and having to carry out business activities (from home) could impact their capacity or freedom to sustain MBs which is not often the case with men. On the other hand, the men, as they grow older, tend to build more capabilities to meet financial and social demands of their dependents.

Furthermore, Fig. 2 categorizes MBOs along gender and 17 business areas, the figure indicated that women own more MBs than men in all business areas, except groceries. Although, there were high concentration of MBs in business areas that focus on frequent basic needs. For example, 25.97% were in beauty fashion and cosmetics, 18.55% in foods and hospitality and 17.17% in into groceries. Reflecting on these statistics from capability approach standpoint could suggest that women simply turn their socially assigned day to day responsibilities and activities into business ventures, thereby enhancing their functioning and freedom. These responsibilities include preparing food, managing events, dressing well, and looking good.

Based on the demographic evaluation of this study, the concept of gender gaps in the context of MBOs in Lagos Nigeria is not one-sided in favor of men or women. Rather it reveals the complexities, and diversity of individuals while developing their individual capabilities for freedom at different satages of life.

6.2 Exploring Gender Gaps in Mobile Apps Usage by Micro Business Owners

Mobile app usage examined across 15 variables suggests that women MBOs used mobile apps more than men in all variables except virtual meeting and online content creation. Women used mobile apps more than men at providing feedback to customers, generating referrals, managing job orders, advertisement, marketing, online search, payments, funds collections, and e-learning (Fig. 3).

The inclination of women to operate MBs from home (as home keepers and child minders) could be responsible for increased usage of mobile apps by women, because mobile apps enhances the MBOs capability to work remotely. This is could mean that the gender gap between women and men occasioned by the use of digital technology (such as mobile apps) is reducing. It is more telling when one considers that the total number

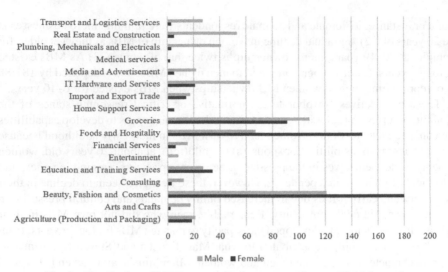

Fig. 2. Distribution of MBOs across business areas (Source: Field Survey).

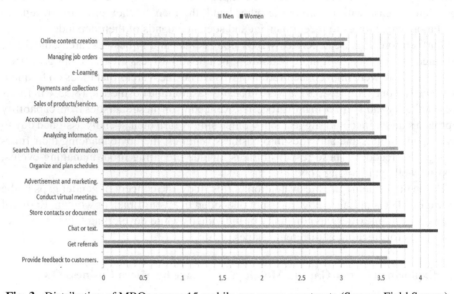

Fig. 3. Distribution of MBOs across 15 mobile app usage constructs (Source: Field Survey).

of women involved in the study were fewer than men but that they used the mobile apps more than their men counterparts. Women like men, can manage their own business. They, like men were not only using mobile apps to chat and text but to do activities like manage business referrals even more than men, manage contacts and documents, manage advertisement and marketing, analyze information, manage sales as well as manage payments and collections.

Therefore, as far as digital technology is concerned in low-income African country contexts (such as Nigeria), particularly in urban areas, women are seizing the opportunities presented by mobile apps to acquire capabilities to do what they want to do and become who they would like to be, notwithstanding the restrictions and burden of caring for their children, spouses and other family members. However, the argument as to whether mobile app usage is helping women MBOs to become *all* they would like to be remains unanswered. This reflects the reality of unrealized capabilities and unfreedoms. While perfection cannot be assumed in the use of digital technologies, it is necessary to consider factors that are responsible for the unrealized capabilities and how to address them. Some of these factors may include the poor adaptation of mobile apps to a wide range of business situations. An example is the adaptation of WhatsApp as e-commerce solution for selling foods, and planning events. Other factors could stem from poor infrastructure, such as poor electricity supply, poor internet connectivity, and cyber security issues.

7 Implications of Findings

In furthering the goal of this exploratory study which sought to understand how mobile app usage by MBOs in Lagos reflect gender gaps and freedom relative to Sen's capability approach, three main findings and their implications to ICT for development theories and practices are made.

First, the demography of MBOs seems to disprove a notion that women are usually at the receiving end of gender gaps or inequality, rather, the contrast between men and women regarding what they could do and achieve is a complex phenomenon that is difficult to generalize. Solving the problems of gender gaps and inequalities require problems solving approaches that consider the diversity of individuals and uniqueness of the community where they develop their individual capabilities to function.

Secondly, the descriptive statistics of MBOs suggests that women MBOs are more active in mobile apps usage than men MBOs. Women are leveraging on the use of technologies like mobile app to build their ability to function, to realise their dreams and experience sense of freedom. Moreover, Research findings suggest that policies driven by mobile app usage and focus on women MBOs will arguably produce better results because women MBOs seem to be more active in mobile apps usage. In addition, the understanding that at less than 20 years old, there are 3 women MBOs for every man MBO suggests the need for policies that will drive the development of entrepreneurial skills in men in early adulthood. Such policies should also consider the need to ensure female MBOs are kept in business as MBs and MBOs grows. Deliberate and strategic drive towards micro-business development in low income-country such as Nigeria promises an increased positive impact on the unemployment, poverty alleviation, and general well-being of a country with 200.96 million population, 60% are under 21 years old, 49.5% are female, and about 48% are female (less than 50 years). In addition, 25% are unemployed, and 48% are under-employed [10]. In the same vein, the tendency of women MBOs to use mobile apps more than their men counterparts could mean that testing beta-features of newly developed mobile apps with women MBO will likely provide better outcomes.

Thirdly, reflecting on this exploratory study from a normative viewpoint of capability approach, the problem of inequality (and ICT for development field) would benefit from more focused theoretical frameworks that explains associations between gender gaps and use of technology. This association would also consider how personal and community factors influence uptake of technology, and how the uptake enhances people's wellbeing, and their sense of freedoms or unfreedoms. This study attempted to conceptualize these relationships, and the results suggest that mobile apps are helping to close the gender and freedom gaps, although further research is needed. Nonetheless, it is identified that mobile apps could be instrumental in achieving the United Nations Sustainable and Development Goals (SDGs) goals that present roadmaps for addressing global challenges such as poverty, hunger, unemployment, inequality, peace and justice, environmental degradation and climate change [36]. Specifically, the 5th goal that aims to promote gender equality and women empowerment. According to the Sustainable Development Goals Report [37], in 2015, medium-high and high-technology sectors accounted for 44.7% of total manufacturing value added globally. The value added reached 34.6% in developing economies, up from 21.5% in 2005. The implication is that if technologies like mobile apps can be made more widely accepted in businesses which have large populations of women who make up more than half of a country's population, economic growth can become a reality not only for the countries themselves, but for women as well.

8 Conclusion

Motivated by the drive to understand how MBOs use the mobile app along gender construct in low-income country context and business environment perceivably edged by male ideals, this research adopted an exploratory research approach, quantitative methods, and Amartya Sen's capability viewpoint. Data from 1,159 MBOs was analyzed using descriptive statistics and the results suggest that gender gaps in the context of MBOs in Lagos Nigeria are not one-sided in favor of men or women. Women are making use of mobile apps to more than men, women are seizing the opportunities presented by mobile apps to acquire capabilities to function, they adapt mobile apps to do what they want to do and become who they would like to be, notwithstanding the restrictions and responsibilities women experience in male dominated environments.

The study recommends that policies makers could explore the use of mobile apps to enhance the development of MBs, and the capabilities of women, and that the strategic use of ICTs like mobile apps could also contribute to the United Nations SDG 5 on gender equality and women empowerment in low income country contexts.

This study contributes to the literature in Information Systems (IS) and micro-business management in low-income country contexts, and also initiates debate regarding theoretical frameworks that could explain associations between gender gaps, technology uptakes and people's capability and sense of freedoms.

8.1 Future Research

Future research could use confirmatory and explanatory approaches to investigate factors that influence how men and women MBOs use mobile apps in a low-income country context. This study was limited in its exploratory approach because it only considers data from Lagos only. Although Lagos is the economic hub of Nigeria, the data collected from Lagos may not entirely speak to micro-business realities in other states and regions in Nigeria.

References

1. World Business Council for Sustainable Development (WBCSD): The consequences of COVID-19 for the decade ahead Vision 2050 issue brief (2020)
2. Magidimisha, H.H., Steven, G.: Profiling South African gender inequality in informal self-employment. J. Gend. Stud. **24**(3), 275–292 (2015)
3. Eniola, A., Entebang, H., Sakariyau, O.B.: Small and medium scale business performance in Nigeria: challenges faced from an intellectual capital perspective. Int. J. Res. Stud. Manag. **4**(1) (2015)
4. Tom, E.Z., Glory, B., Alfred, U.J: An Appraisal of Nigeria's micro, small and medium enterprises (MSMEs): growth, challenges, and prospect. Int. J. Small Bus. Entrep. Res. **4**(4), 1–15 (2016)
5. Siyanbola, T.O.: Challenges of growth and development of manufacturing and Services SMEs in Nigeria. In: WEI International Academic, Harvard USA (2015)
6. Ilegbinosa, I.A., Jumbo, E.: Small and medium scale enterprises and economic growth in Nigeria. Int. J. Bus. Manag. **10**(3), 203–216 (2015)
7. Williams, C.O.: Patriarchy and the representation of women in Africa and Asia. In: 2nd International Conference on 'Africa-Asia: A New Axis of Knowledge', Dar es Salaam, Tanzania (2018)
8. Wakunuma, K, Siwale, J, Beck, R.: Computing for social good: supporting microfinance institutions in Zambia. Electron. J. Inf. Syst. Dev. Ctries. **85** (2019)
9. Mbogo, M.: The impact of mobile payments on the success and growth of micro- business: the case of Mpesa in Kenya. J. Lang. Technol. Entrep. Afr. **2**(1) (2010)
10. Nigerian Bureau of Statistics: Statistical Report on Women and Men in Nigeria. Nigerian Bureau of Statistics, Abuja (2017)
11. Nigerian Bureau of Statistics: Micro, small, and medium enterprises (MSME) national survey 2017 report (2017)
12. Aker, J., Mbiti, I.: Mobile phones and economic development in Africa. J. Econ. Perspect. **24**(3), 207–232 (2010)
13. Wamboye, E.F, Nyaronga, P.J.: The Service Sector and Economic Development in Africa First. Routledge, London and New York (2018)
14. Robeyns, I.: The capability approach in practice. J. Polit. Philos. **14**(3), 351–376 (2006)
15. Robeyns, I.: Sen's capability approach and gender inequality: selecting relevant capabilities. Fem. Econ. **9**, 61–92 (2003)
16. Sen, A.: Development as Freedom. Oxford Press, Oxford (1999)
17. Robeyns, I.: The Capability Approach, Stanford University, 3 October 2016. https://plato.stanford.edu/entries/capability-approach/. Accessed 23 Feb 2020
18. Robeyns, I.: The capability approach – a theoretical survey. J. Hum. Dev. **6**(1), 94–114 (2005)
19. Doss, C., Meinzen-Dick, R., Quisumbing, A., Theis, S.: Women in agriculture: four myths. Glob. Food Secur. **16**, 69–74 (2018)
20. Nussabaum, M.: Women and equality: the capabilities approach. Int. Labour Rev. **138**(3) (1999)
21. Small and Medium Enterprise Development Agency of Nigeria (SMEDAN) & Nigeria Bureau of Statistics (NBS). SMEDAN and National Bureau of Statistics Collaborative Survey: Selected Findings, NBS, Abuja (2013)

22. Bank of Industry: MSME's Definition, Bank of Industry. http://www.boi.ng/smedefinition/. Accessed 23 Feb 2020
23. Ngwu, B.: Small and medium enterprises (SMEs) in Nigeria: problems and prospects. St. Clements University (2005). http://stclements.edu/grad/gradonug.pdf. Accessed 20 Feb 2020
24. Ashrafi, R., Murtaza, M.: Usage and effects of information and communication technologies on small and medium-sized enterprises in Oman. In: International Conference on Information Resources Management (Conf-IRM), Ontario (2008)
25. Bankole, F., Bankole, O.: The effects of cultural dimension on ICT innovation: empirical analysis of mobile phone services. Telemat. Inform. **34**(2), 490–505 (2017)
26. Young, D.: Improving the Adoption Of Cloud Computing by Small and Medium Scale Enterprises in Nigeria. The University of South Africa, Pretoria (2015)
27. Cheng, Y., Tao, W., Gang, Y., Huaimin, W., Ming, W., Ming, X.: Personalized mobile application discovery. In: 1st International Workshop on Crowd-based Software Development, Hong Kong (2014)
28. Jun-Jie, H., Voon-Hsien, L., Keng-Boon, O., June, W.: What catalyses' mobile apps usage intention: an empirical analysis. Ind. Manag. Data Syst. **115**(7), 1269–1291 (2015)
29. Owoseni, A., Twinomurinzi, H.: The dynamic capabilities of small and medium-scale enterprises using mobile apps in Lagos, Nigeria. Electron. J. Inf. Syst. Dev. Ctries, 1–14 (2019)
30. Weber, P., Geneste, L.: Exploring gender-related perceptions of SME success. Int. J. Gend. Entrep. **6**(1), 15–27 (2014)
31. Sharafizad J.: Women business owners' adoption of information and communication technology. J. Syst. Inf. Technol. **18**(4), 331–345 (2016)
32. Françoise, O.-E., Gaëlle, T.T.: Female entrepreneurship and growth in Cameroon. Afr. J. Econ. Manag. Stud. **6**(1), 107–119 (2015)
33. Lagos State Government: Lagos State Development Plan 2012–2025. Lagos State Government, Lagos (2013)
34. Ministry of Economic Planning and Budget: Overview of Lagos State, Nigeria. Federal Government of Nigeria, Abuja (2014)
35. George D., Mallery, M.: SPSS for Windows Step by Step: A Simple Guide and Reference, Boston, Pearson (2010)
36. United Nations: The Sustainable Development Goals 2018. United Nations, New York (2018)
37. United Nations: Sustainable development goal 5: achieve gender equality and empower all women and girls. https://sustainabledevelopment.un.org/sdg5. Accessed 20 Feb 2020

What Enables and Restrains Business Entrepreneurship in Refugee Camps in Malawi? A Search for Technology-Related Causal Mechanisms

Suzana Brown[1]([✉]) [iD], P. J. Wall[2] [iD], Patience Desire[3], Dave Lewis[2], Lucy Hederman[2], and Chrystina Russell[3]

[1] SUNY, Incheon, Korea
suzana.brown@sunykorea.ac.kr
[2] Trinity College Dublin, ADAPT Center, Dublin, Ireland
{wallp2,hederman}@tcd.ie, dave.lewis@adaptcentre.ie
[3] Southern New Hampshire University, Manchester, USA
pdesire10@gmail.com, chrystina.russell@gmail.com

Abstract. This paper examines business entrepreneurship in the Dzaleka refugee camp in Malawi. In particular, the research seeks to discover the underlying causal mechanisms that both enable and restrain entrepreneurship in this context. We leverage a critical realist-based philosophical research approach and methodology to hypothesize these causal mechanisms, and a methodological approach based on critical realism is presented. The research finds that while technology is an important component in the overall environment required for business entrepreneurship to flourish within the refugee camp, the causal mechanisms identified suggest that technology is a not significant enabling or restricting mechanism in this case. Instead, we posit that other non-technology related mechanisms have a more significant enabling or restricting impact on business entrepreneurship in the Dzaleka refugee camp. This is somewhat surprising, as other recent research claims that technology is an integral component required for successful business entrepreneurship. The causal mechanisms that were hypothesized using our methodology are presented, and the implications associated with the lack of technology-related mechanisms in this case, and the associated consequences for future ICT4D related research, are discussed.

Keywords: Business entrepreneurship · ICT4D · Critical realism · Refugee · Causal mechanism · Malawi

1 Introduction

According to the United Nations High Commissioner for Refugees (UNHCR), in 2018 more than 70 million people around the world were forced to flee their homes because of war, persecution, violence and human rights violations (UNHCR 2019). One of the

© IFIP International Federation for Information Processing 2020
Published by Springer Nature Switzerland AG 2020
J. M. Bass and P. J. Wall (Eds.): ICT4D 2020, IFIP AICT 587, pp. 183–194, 2020.
https://doi.org/10.1007/978-3-030-65828-1_15

most affected regions is the African continent, with Sub-Saharan Africa hosting more than 26% of the total refugee population with some estimates putting this at 18 million people in this region. Approximately 4.4 million of these refugees have sought refuge in neighboring countries, e.g. in Rwanda which is currently hosting more than 162,000 refugees in 6 refugee camps. Hosting refugees in camps is supposed to be temporary, but the average time of displacement for a refugee is now over 17 years.

Self-reliance is an integral component of the UNHCR's Framework for Durable Solutions for Displaced Persons (UNHCR 2010). Self-reliance is also a key component in any strategy aimed at avoiding or addressing protracted refugee situations, enabling refugees and host countries to find durable solutions and providing a foundation towards achieving the Millennium Development Goals. Such self-reliance can also have a positive influence by bringing new skills and additional income to the local host community and economy. Uganda and Zambia provide examples of countries that have seen the kind of positive change that refugees brought to isolated and neglected areas (UNHCR 2010).

More recently, the United Nations Conference of Trade and Development (UNC-TAD), the International Organization for Migration (IOM) and the UNHCR developed a guide on the role of entrepreneurship for refugees (Zhan et al. 2018). The section of this guide which discusses technology exchange and innovative start-ups recommends the promotion of social innovation for refugees. The following are selected policy recommendation:

- Support initiatives that develop digital literacy.
- Invest in information and communications technology (ICT) backbone infrastructure in rural and remote rural settlements.
- Support eCommerce platforms for refugee businesses.
- Support platforms that facilitate collaboration between refugees.
- Support platforms for sharing knowledge and best practices to facilitate the adoption of successful innovations.

Surprisingly, very few studies discuss the potential for entrepreneurship resulting from immigration, i.e. refugee entrepreneurship and their influence on the host economy (Wauters and Lambrecht 2008). However, it is recognized that the issue is complex, and the approach should result in a more nuanced exploration of the entrepreneurial activities relevant to the context and institutionally bounded outcomes (Rindova et al. 2009). Therefore, more recent explorations do consider the benefits of immigrant entrepreneurship concerning the context in which it occurs and are further expanding this area by observing the different dimensions of social capital on the survival and success of refugee-entrepreneurial ventures (Bizri 2017).

Academic literature on refugee entrepreneurs typically gives examples of the various creative forms of entrepreneurship, but such activities have largely remained unexamined in depth. One study by Freiling et al. (2019) on refugee entrepreneurial activities collected 17 case studies in order to do cross-case analysis. Another type of published research explores the role that technology can play in facilitating and fostering entrepreneurship opportunities for refugees in their host country. For example, AbuJarour et al. (2019) conducted a series of interviews with Syrian refugees in Berlin to collect preliminary insights, and from these insights organized panel discussions at two of the larger information systems conferences (ICIS 2016; ECIS 2017). Among the research themes discussed at those conferences were accessibility to information and admissibility to labor markets and entrepreneurship opportunities. Other literature (Heilbrunn 2019) about entrepreneurship in refugee camps demonstrates how refugees initiate entrepreneurial activities in the context of pressure (Alexandre et al. 2019).

To our knowledge no other study identifies underlining enabling or restricting causal mechanisms that impact successful business entrepreneurship in refugee camps. In addition, none of the studies addresses broader issues such as the socioeconomic context of technology and business innovation. The context is where new technology and business model originated. There are two widely used perspectives regarding the context of ICT innovation process in developing countries. One is a transfer and diffusion perspective, while the other one is a socially embedded approach. The socially embedded innovation approach considers the transfer and diffusion approach overly simplified and inaccurate (Avgerou 2010). The focal point of socially embedded research is the process of innovation in situ (Westrup et al. 2003).

Our approach is centered on one particular refugee camp, Dzaleka camp in Malawi, and the active entrepreneurs within. This particular refugee camp was chosen for a variety of reasons and there are outlined in the following sub-section and also Sect. 3 below. The main goal of this paper is to discover the underlying causal mechanisms that both enable and restrain business entrepreneurship in that particular camp. From a philosophical perspective, we employ a critical realist-based philosophical approach and associated methodology to identify causal mechanisms that influence entrepreneurship in that setting. There are multiple benefits to using such an approach and methodology this context as detailed by Heeks and Wall (2018), one being the deployment of a triangulated approach that takes into consideration multiple stakeholder perspectives and encourages discussion of multiple methodologies.

1.1 Location

In response to a surge of forcibly displaced people fleeing genocide, violence and wars in Burundi, Rwanda and the Democratic Republic of Congo, the UNHCR established camp Dzaleka in 1994. Dzaleka refugee camp is located in Dowa District around 45 km from Lilongwe, the capital city of Malawi. It houses refugees from different countries such as the Democratic Republic of Congo, Burundi, Rwanda, Somalia, and Ethiopia. The UNHCR coordinates all activities in the refugee camp, along with many partners such as the Ministry of Homeland Security, Churches Action for Relief and Development, Welt Hunger Hilfe, World Food Program, and the Jesuit Refugee Services. According to the report of Welt Hunger Hilfe, an organization operating in this camp, as at February 2019 a total of 45,095 refugees are residing in Dzaleka.

1.2 Access to Technology in Dzaleka Refugee Camp

Residents of Dzaleka refugee camp have access to two cellular internet providers in the camp, namely Airtel and TNM. The voice bundle and the Internet bundle differ and because of the low-bandwidth Internet connection they are considered to be not economical for the refugees. The most affordable monthly Internet bundle is equivalent in value to 2 months of corn maize allotment from the UNHCR. Because of these prices, people buy specific bundles that are only for WhatsApp paying only 600 Kwacha per month (equivalent to 80 cents). Residents find Internet bundles expensive and the advertised speeds are often inaccurate. Despite this however, data sharing is not a common practice. There is no free Wi-Fi at the Dzaleka Refugee Camp, and instead residents buy dongles and use them at night because the Internet traffic is lower, and thus the speed of connectivity is faster. Currently, only a few organizations are educating the refugees about technology. One example is AppFactory which offers classes on phone application development. Also, the Jesuit Refugee Service provides lessons that include computer literacy and Jesuit Worldwide Learning provides online studies. These organizations do not provide free Wi-Fi, but students do have access to the Internet while participating in their programs.

2   A Critical Realist Philosophical Approach and Methodology

It has been suggested that the ICT4D body of work is dominated by positivist and interpretivist philosophical approaches (Walsham and Sahay 2006) and that while each of these approaches have their own unique strengths, they also contain many weaknesses that hinder ICT4D research in particular (Heeks and Wall 2018). The relative strengths and weaknesses of positivist and interpretivist philosophical approaches has been written about extensively, and thus we will not contribute to that debate in any meaningful way in this paper. We will however briefly outline the benefits of adopting a "third-way" (Allen et al. 2013, p. 835) research paradigm which goes beyond both positivism and interpretivism. One such third-way research paradigm is critical realism.

It is generally accepted that critical realism is time-consuming, complex, and difficult to operationalize (e.g. Reed 2009; Smith 2018; Fleetwood 2014). In addition, there is little methodological guidance available. The paradigm asserts that general elements of an independent reality exist, but our knowledge of specific structures and causal mechanisms is limited because of the difficulty of accessing them directly through three levels of stratification. These levels of stratification consist of the Real, the Actual and the Empirical domains of reality as proposed by Bhaskar (1975) as represented in Fig. 1. Causal mechanisms are best understood as "causal structures that generate observable events" (Henfridsson and Bygstad 2013, p. 911), with these mechanisms residing in the domain of the Real. This is obviously problematic as researchers seek mechanisms, but as mechanisms reside in the domain of the Real they are independent of human knowledge or our ability to perceive them. The Actual domain contains events which are generated from both exercised and non-exercised mechanisms. The domain of the Empirical contains the events that we as humans are able to experience and record as they are identified by interviewees and through observation by the researcher. Examples of events include the formation of groups and committees, appointment of leaders, approval of new rules and structures, and changes of ICT infrastructure.

This means that any methodology associated with critical realism must be designed to identify and gather events in domain of the Empirical. Using these events, researchers

	Domain		
	Real	Actual	Empirical
Mechanism	X		
Events	X	X	
Experiences	X	X	X

Fig. 1. The stratified ontology of critical realism as proposed by Bhaskar (1975, p. 13)

must then have a way to uncover, or hypothesize, the mechanisms residing in the Real. The most widely accepted way of doing this is by way of a process called retroduction. Retroduction literally means "stepping back" from the events that we as researchers can see and record in the domain of the Empirical, to the mechanisms that we must hypothesize from these observed events. Thus, retroduction is key to any critical realist-based methodology (Bhaskar 1975) and requires the researcher to take "some unexplained phenomenon and propose hypothetical mechanisms that, if they existed, would generate or cause that which is to be explained" (Mingers 2004, p. 94).

Despite these many philosophical and methodological challenges, this paper relies on the critical realist-based methodology as developed by Wall et al. (2019) and originally based on Margaret Archer's (1995) morphogenetic approach. This methodology recognizes that agents create causation and this causation can change agency, culture and structure in any particular case. This ability of agents to create causation can work towards either changing things or keeping them the same. Archer refers to this as morphogenesis (where change occurs) and morphostasis (where things stay the same). The first step in the methodology is to create a factual case description and a chorological account of events in as much detail as possible. From this, distinct morphogenetic/morphostatic (M/M) cycles are identified. M/M cycles can be most simply described as logical sections based on discrete time periods that the case can be broken down into. These M/M cycles are then analyzed to produce analytical histories of emergence which form the basis for retroduction. Theorization of mechanisms can then occur when causal influences in social structures, interactions and relationships have been identified.

The M/M cycles can be used to analyze the relationship between structure and agency in any context. Analysis is done over the discrete time intervals – i.e. the M/M cycles – which are used to identify emergent changes in structure, culture, and people, and their causal relationships. In the specific context of the refugee camps in Malawi, and ICT4D more broadly, these relationships are likely to complex and highly contingent on the ethical, social, cultural and political contexts applying in the particular case. This is discussed in more detail in the sections which follow.

3   Data Collection

Data collected consisted of semi-structured interviews of active entrepreneurs, focusing on the ones bringing changes into the community, and also with the businesses bringing technological and entrepreneurial innovation. Each interview had 15 semi-structured questions regarding their experience and motivation, and the major obstacles to their business with an emphasis on the role of ICT. Entrepreneurs were allowed to elaborate on questions they found most pressing and share some of their thoughts and recommendations. Conducting interviews started in October 2019 and were conducted on a face-to-face basis by a local resident who is currently a student at the Global Education Movement (GEM) that provides access to online degrees to refugee learners, an initiative by the Southern New Hampshire University (SNHU). The student speaks multiple languages and is trained by the SNHU faculty to conduct qualitative research. The interviews were conducted in French, English, Kinyarwanda, Kirundi, and Kiswahili which are all native languages of the camp residents. The translation was done by the same local student to keep subjects comfortable with the process, and the duration was between 45 min and 1 h for each interview. The local student is a refugee from Rwanda and has been residing in Dzaleka Refugee Camp since January 2015. Ethical approval for this research was granted by SNHU and is a home institution for one of the authors on this paper.

Dzaleka refugee camp is seen as a multicultural community because the people brought with them cultures and norms from their native countries. It has a large youth population interested in learning about technology and its use in studying and doing business. Very few camp residents own laptops, but a large number have smartphones. For example, 65% of the people who use smartphones are aged between 16 and 35. The demand for ICT products and services is very high within the camp. Even though there are many languages, Kiswahili is the most popular language in Dzaleka and doing business in the camp requires knowledge of Kiswahili.

It is important to note that Malawi's policies regulating the movement and the right to employment of refugees to make opportunities to earn a living outside the camp are very limited. Therefore, the majority of refugees are completely reliant on external assistance for survival. On the other hand, many refugees are trying to obtain online employment, and the government of Malawi is allowing refugees to operate businesses in the camp contingent upon them paying taxes. This has led to a variety of businesses in the camp, many of them related to the production and distribution of food and food services. The refugee camp currently has approximately 50 local businesses in operation. An attempt was made to interview all of them, but for various reasons we were only able to interview approximately half of 25 in total. Future iterations of this work will interview all active entrepreneurs in Dzaleka camp.

3.1   Entrepreneurs and ICT in the Refugee Camp

From this initial set of 25 interviews of active entrepreneurs in Dzaleka camp, a subset of three who specifically operate in the ICT field was identified. One of them is a female who started her business in 2010 repairing phones. Talking about her motivation she says;

> "... [I] got the idea of doing business from my mum. She told me that I am supposed to find something to do instead of waiting for her to give me something to do."

She credits her success to the circumstances of camp residents who cannot afford new phones, and therefore they need to repair them more than the regular population. When asked about ICT tools, she says;

"I use a few applications such as Google Chrome and YouTube in order to search [for] good phones and watch some tutorials on how to repair them. I advertise my phones and service on my WhatsApp status."

In addition, she identifies several obstacles including the need to increase her knowledge, the Internet being very expensive and slow, and inadequate ICT literacy among camp residents.

One male entrepreneur started his business in 2013 repairing and selling computers. He had a similar business in his home country, Burundi, before coming to the refugee camp. In own his words;

"I decided to put into action what I have studied before."

He uses many applications;

"... such as Adobe Audition, Microsoft office, Reiboot, YouTube, F.lux, Power Director, WhatsApp, Facebook and so on."

When asked about the growth of this business, he claimed;

"I have many customers because this world is growing on the technology side."

His main obstacle is a requirement for constant improvement because;

"...technology is keeping improving every day".

The third interviewee is also a male entrepreneur who started his business in 2015 teaching computer programming to youth and creating software. His background was in journalism and communication. He stated that he;

"...observed the need through the realization of being a victim as a refugee."

The goal was to change his life and support other people around him. He also uses many applications;

"...the android studio for android development, Eclipse, Netbeans, Notepad++ and Microsoft office package."

His motivation is based on what he calls *"the good cause of changing youth life"*. The main obstacles for this business are legal registrations and difficulty raising funding.

This interview data formed the basis for the retroduction of the mechanisms using the philosophical approach and associated methodology as very briefly described above. This resulted in three mechanisms being retroduced. These three mechanisms are discussed in the following section.

4   Causal Mechanisms Retroduced

The overall objective of this work was to use the philosophical base of critical realism and a unique methodology associated with Margaret Archer's morphogenetic approach to reveal mechanisms that explain how the interaction of different structural, cultural and agency factors can explain how these mechanisms have influenced business entrepreneurship in the Dzaleka refugee camp in Malawi. To reemphasize, we do this by relying on the research framework as developed by Wall et al. (2019) as based on Archer's (1995) morphogenetic approach. Sat its simplest level, this research framework uses data collected to identify events, with these events being used to retroduce mechanisms. Data was collected in this case primarily by semi-structured interview as detailed in the previous sections. This data was then analysed and used to prepare a detailed factual case study description leading to the development of a chronological account of events. These documents then gave rise to the identification of discrete M/M cycles which were identified empirically and based on Archer's morphogenetic approach which has three stages as follows (Archer 1995; Archer 1996):

- Stage one: The researcher identifies relevant antecedent social structural and cultural relations.
- Stage two: The researcher examines the activities of agents that are constrained and facilitated by the identified antecedent social structural and cultural relations.
- Stage three: The researcher examines the effect of the agential activities on the antecedent social structural and cultural relations. This effect may be to re-produce social structure and cultural system unaltered (morphostasis) or to modify or transform them (morphogenesis).

Analysis was then carried out over the discrete M/M cycle time periods, with each domain evaluated in time over each analytical cycle. This is at the core of the Wall et al. (2019) methodology and this approach was used to retroduce the mechanisms in this case. This methodology led to a total of three causal mechanisms being hypothesized. As previously mentioned, we were surprised these mechanisms were not strongly related to technology. This would seem to run counter to the literature, and specifically the work produced by UNCTAD and the UNHCR as referenced above which proposes that investment in ICT as a backbone infrastructure in rural and remote rural settlements, digital literacy, and the development of eCommerce platforms should be the key components of any policy underpinning business entrepreneurship in refugee camps.

4.1   Mechanisms Retroduced

This section will discuss the three mechanisms which were retroduced using the philosophical approach and methodology as outlined in the previous section. The mechanisms retroduced in this case are as follows:

- The refugees attitude towards, and their belief in, the importance of self-reliance. This attitude and belief is scaffolded by a strong family support system and includes the motivation of the entrepreneurs in the refugee camps to be successful.

- The ready and available workforce within the refugee camps who provide a customer base willing to buy goods and spend money. This includes the desire to learn new skills, and in particular technology based skills. Also included is the specific business environment and associated infrastructure within the Dzaleka refugee camp.
- The mobile telecommunications technology and associated infrastructure available within the Dzaleka refugee camp. This includes the innovative use of a variety of technologies and software platforms by the refugees to facilitate business, and also their desire to learn about this software.

It is important to state clearly that it is highly likely there are many more mechanisms that may be retroduced in this case, and the three mechanisms we present in this paper are not the only ones that have influenced the outcomes of the evolution of entrepreneurship in Dzaleka. We do appreciate that the three mechanisms retroduced by this iteration of our work are broad in nature, but we expect increasing levels of specificity of mechanisms in future versions of our work. This will happen when we obtain additional data, and in particular when we obtain additional data from different interviewees using alternative methods such as observation and focus group discussions. All of this will add depth and detail to the two key documents at the heart of our methodological approach – i.e. the detailed factual case study description and a chronological account of events – and will allow for the three already retroduced mechanisms to be further validated. It may also allow for additional new mechanisms to be retroduced. Furthermore, it is important to note that although there is currently significant overlap between the three mechanisms as presented in this paper, we do expect mechanisms to be more clearly bounded in our future work and for there to be less overlap between any existing and new mechanisms retroduced.

The first mechanism retroduced by this iteration of our work concerns the overall attitude of self-reliance and self-belief which is prevalent amongst the refugees we interviewed. This emerged clearly from the data, with the refugees strongly believing in themselves and their ability to innovate and be entrepreneurial. This innovative and entrepreneurial spirit was often scaffolded by a strong family support system. This is evidenced by one refugee who got the idea of doing business from her Mother who told her it was her own responsibility to find something to do instead of waiting for her to be given something to do by someone else. Action, as opposed to inactivity and dependence on others, was the default attitude amongst the refugees we interviewed. One refugee stated, "*I decided to put into action what I have studied before*" in order to create his business. Another refugee stated that his main goal was to change his own life and support other people around him. In almost all instances the refugees we spoke to were highly motivated and this was as a result of having the resilience and past experience of being able to survive in extremely resource constrained environments. This attitude of self-belief and resilience could be clearly seen amongst the entrepreneurs in the refugee camps in particular. They believed they had to create their own opportunities and could rely on their family support systems to help create such opportunities for both themselves and their families.

The second mechanism retroduced concerns the ready and available workforce and customer base available within the refugee camps. This may seem like an obvious mechanism, but it is important in this case and includes the business environment and associated infrastructure specific to the Dzaleka refugee camp as such infrastructure is a necessary prerequisite for entrepreneurship. One good example of this is the person teaching computer programming and creating software with the youth in the refugee camp. If there was no willingness to learn and consume what he is offering he would have no business. In his own words he *"observed the need through the realization of being a victim as a refugee"* and he acted on this need for his services and skillset. If this need and willingness to learn was not there it would be more difficult for entrepreneurship to flourish.

The third mechanism retroduced is the mobile telecommunications technology and associated infrastructure available within the Dzaleka refugee camp. We expanded this mechanism to include the manner in which people have leveraged the available technology to do business and how this overlapps with the refugee's desire to learn more about technology and create opportunities for themselves. This mechanism is evidenced by the innovative use of WhatsApp and Facebook to create new business opportunities. The mechanism also includes the somewhat surprising use of a wide variety of software applications and platforms in such a resource constrained environment. These include the android studio for android development, Eclipse, Netbeans, Notepad++, Adobe Audition, Reiboot, F.lux, Power Di-rector, and YouTube. It is clear that this mechanism also encompasses the manner in which refugees overcame a variety of technological obstacles such as the Internet being very expensive and slow and inadequate ICT literacy among many camp residents. For us, this represents a mechanism concerned with the power and potential of technology and how this can be leveraged for business and entrepreneurship as opposed to the actual technology itself.

As already mentioned, these three mechanisms have been retroduced from what we consider to be the first iteration of this work. There is highly likely to be many other mechanisms present in this case and we intend to uncover these mechanisms as we collect additional data and use alternative data collection methods. Based on this iteration of the work, it is important to note the significance of the mechanism concerning the attitude of self-reliance and motivation of the entrepreneurs in the refugee camps as this is perhaps most influential of the three mechanisms we present. It is also worth noting the high level of overlap between this mechanism and the other two mechanisms retroduced in this case. Furthermore, we consider this mechanism to be the primary determinant of the success or failure of business entrepreneurship in the Dzaleka refugee camp.

5 Summary and Conclusions

This research adopts a critical realist perspective to identify the underlying causal mechanisms that both enable and constrain business entrepreneurship in the Dzaleka refugee camp in Malawi. A critical realist-based philosophical and methodological approach was used to retroduce three mechanisms that explain how the interaction of different structural, cultural and agency factors have influenced this case. These mechanisms were not primarily technology related, but instead consisted of the attitude of self-reliance and motivation of the entrepreneurs in the refugee camps, and the available workforce, customer base, and overall business environment and associated technological infrastructure available in the refugee camp.

Considering the notion of self-reliance is becoming an integral part of many strategies aimed at enabling refugees and host countries to find durable solutions, we believe we make an important contribution to this debate by identifying mechanisms which confirm that self-reliance is indeed key to successful entrepreneurship in such instances. However, the other mechanisms we hypothesize would seem to run counter to the existing body of knowledge in this area which suggests that business entrepreneurship in this context is also driven by technology. We found no such mechanism, but we did hypothesize mechanisms to support the assertion that the technology itself is not a significant causal mechanism in such environments. Instead, it is the potential and the innovative use of such technology that is important for entrepreneurship in this case.

Based on our preliminary results to date we call for additional work in Dzaleka refugee camp in Malawi to either support or counter our initial findings. Furthermore, we call for more critical realist-based approaches and methodologies which examine refugee entrepreneurship in general. This is important, as such mechanism-based explanation is likely to influence where scarce resources are allocated in refugee camps into the future.

References

AbuJarour, S.A., et al.: ICT-enabled refugee integration: a research agenda. Commun. Assoc. Inf. Syst. **44**, 874–890 (2019)

Allen, D.K., Brown, A., Karanasios, S., Norman, A.: How should technology-mediated organizational change be explained? A comparison of the contributions of critical realism and activity theory. MIS Q. **37**, 835–854 (2013)

Alexandre, L., Salloum, C., Alalam, A.: An investigation of migrant entrepreneurs: the case of Syrian refugees in Lebanon. Int. J. Entrep. Behav. Res. (2019)

Archer, M.S.: Realist Social Theory: The Morphogenetic Approach. Cambridge University Press, Cambridge (1995)

Bhaskar, R.: A Realist Theory of Science. Harvester Press, Hassocks (1975)

Bizri, R.M.: Refugee-entrepreneurship: a social capital perspective. Entrep. Reg. Dev. **29**(9–10), 847–868 (2017)

Freiling, J., Harima, A., Heilbrunn, S.: Refugee Entrepreneurship: A Case-Based Topography. Machmilan, New York (2019)

Heilbrunn, S.: Against all odds: refugees bricoleuring in the void. Int. J. Entrep. Behav. Res. (2019)

Henfridsson, O., Bygstad, B.: The generative mechanisms of digital infrastructure evolution. MIS Q. **37**, 907–931 (2013)

Heeks, R., Wall, P.J.: Critical realism and ICT4D research. Electron. J. Inf. Syst. Dev. Ctries. **84**(6) (2018)

UNHCR: IASC Framework on Durable Solutions for Internally Displaced Persons, The Brookings Institution – University of Bern Project on Internal Displacement, April 2010

UNHCR (2019). https://www.unhcr.org/news/press/2019/6/5d03b22b4/worldwide-displacem ent-tops-70-million-un-refugee-chief-urges-greater-solidarity.html

ICIS: International Conference on Information Systems (ICIS 2016), Dublin, Ireland, 11–14 December 2016

ECIS: European Conference on Information Systems, Guimarães, Portugal, 5–10 June 2017

Rindova, V., Barry, D., Ketchen, D.: Entrepreneuring as emancipation. Acad. Manag. Rev. **34**(3), 477–491 (2009)

Wall, P.J., Lewis, D., Hederman, L.: Identifying generative mechanisms in a mobile health (mHealth) project in Sierra Leone: a critical realist framework for retroduction. In: Nielsen, P., Kimaro, H.C. (eds.) ICT4D 2019. IAICT, vol. 552, pp. 39–48. Springer, Cham (2019). https://doi.org/10.1007/978-3-030-19115-3_4

Walsham, G., Sahay, S.: Research on information systems in developing countries: current landscape and future prospects. Inf. Technol. Dev. 12(1), 7–24 (2006)

Wauters, B., Lambrecht, J.: Barriers to refugee entrepreneurship in Belgium: towards an explanatory model. J. Ethnic Migr. Stud. 34(6), 895–915 (2008)

Zhan, J., Bolwijn, R., Farinelli, F.: Policy guide on entrepreneurship for migrants and refugees (2018)

Check Your Tech - Considering the Provenance of Data Used to Build Digital Products and Services

Dympna O'Sullivan$^{(\boxtimes)}$ and Damian Gordon

School of Computer Science, Technological University Dublin, Kevin Street, Dublin 8, Ireland
{dympna.osullivan,damian.x.gordon}@tudublin.ie

Abstract. Digital products and services are producing unprecedented amounts of data worldwide. These products and services have broad reach and include many users and consumers in the developing world. Once data is collected it is often used to create large and valuable datasets. A lack of data protection regulation in the developing world has led to concerns about digital colonization and a lack of control of their data on the part of citizens in the developing world. The authors of this paper are developing a new digital ethics curriculum for the instruction of computer science students. In this paper we present two case studies we have developed with a focus on data ethics in a developing world context. Each case study is accompanied by a list of specific questions to be used by the instructor to allow students to evaluate the implications of introducing new digital products and services in a developing world context as well as a generic case studies checksheet that allow deeper reflection on the intended and unintended consequences of introducing new technologies.

Keywords: Digital ethics · Digital colonization · Computer science education

1 Introduction

The World Economic Forum predicts that the digital universe will reach 44 zettabytes by 2020 [1]. The current number of smartphone users in the world is 3.5 billion, on average, Google processes more than 40,000 searches every second, there are 2 billion active Facebook users and 156 million emails are sent each day. In 2020 there are projected to be 200 billion Internet of Things devices. A significant proportion of this data is generated by users in the developing world. The ITU report from 2019 reports that 47% of individuals in the developing world have internet access, and in the least developed countries 19 percent of individuals were online in 2019 [2].

Introducing new technologies into developing countries is generally a positive development, leading to new infrastructure and new business models that stimulate economic development. One consequence of the significant pace of technological development is the creation of large digital datasets. Large datasets are of huge economic value and form

© IFIP International Federation for Information Processing 2020
Published by Springer Nature Switzerland AG 2020
J. M. Bass and P. J. Wall (Eds.): ICT4D 2020, IFIP AICT 587, pp. 195–204, 2020.
https://doi.org/10.1007/978-3-030-65828-1_16

the backbone of many computing applications, particularly those that use machine learning, predictive analytics and business intelligence. Such techniques allow applications to synthesize billions of data points and make inferences about users, how they behave now and how they will behave in the future. As technology companies have come to utilize data in products and services, extensive data protection laws and privacy regulations emerged to ensure ethical use of that data. These same protections, however, do not exist uniformly in the developing world. These conditions have led to accusations of digital colonialism, which has been defined by Kwet as "the decentralized extraction and control of data from citizens with or without their explicit consent through communication networks developed and owned by Western technology companies" [3].

Digital colonialism is one facet of a larger field of digital ethics that seeks to understand the impact of technology on our societies and the environment at large [4, 5]. It encompasses a range of issues and concerns from privacy and agency around personal information, digital literacy, big data including governance and accountability, the dominance of a small number of large network platforms, pervasive technology, the Internet of Things, surveillance applications, Artificial Intelligence and algorithmic decision making. It concerns how people, organizations, society and technology interact. With digital ethics comes the added variable of assessing the ethical implications of things, which may not yet exist, or things, which may have impacts we cannot predict.

The authors of this paper are leading an Erasmus+ project, Ethics4EU [6] that seeks to explore these issues via the teaching of ethics in computer science curricula. Research in the last decade shows that there is a paucity of ethics teaching in computer science, unlike other science disciplines [7]. One of the core project objectives is the development of a wide variety of educational content for the instruction of digital ethics to university students. Given the ethical issues surrounding digital data, a number of resources are being developed in this area. In this paper we present sample educational content that was developed as part of the project, specifically synthesized or fictionalized case studies, that focus on data collection from users in developing countries. The case studies are designed to serve as a way to improve computer science students' ability at consequence scanning – a way to consider the potential consequences - intended and unintended - of a new technological product or service on people, communities and the planet [8].

2 Methods

A case study is a suitable vehicle for examining this topic as case studies explore specific real-world phenomena that focus on interpreting events, and exploring the societal context in which the case occurs [9]. The qualitative nature of these cases can be seen as novel when introduced in computer science courses which are typically more quantitative in nature. They can be used to both explore and evaluate specific problems and challenges of introducing new technologies into developing countries, as well as exploring digital ethics in a more general context. The materials allow for detailed examination of technological, organizational and social implications.

In this section we introduce two case studies we have developed as a part of a wider curriculum on digital ethics for computer science students. The case studies concern the impact of the introduction of new technology on persons and society in the developing world with a specific focus on how data is collected and used by third parties as part of the introduction of new digital products and services. Each case study comprises a detailed narrative and set of questions (or "Talking Points") to be used by an instructor in delivering the content. We also introduce a general checksheet that can be used by students to evaluate scenarios involving the development of new digital products and services.

Please note that these case studies have been developed specifically as teaching tools; each is based on a synthesis of several real cases, and are designed to generate detailed and diverse discussions by student groups about the ethics of these scenarios. The use of synthesized case studies has a long history in the teaching of Law courses [10], sometimes to circumvent issues like confidentiality and legal privilege, which are clearly very important considerations when discussing Data Ethics scenarios. To highlight the fictitious nature of the case studies, fictional placenames and company names are very often used to underscore the fact that these case studies are fictional.

Synthesized case studies closely resemble a teaching approach that is already used in Computer Science, the "toy problem", which is an approach used in the teaching of computer programming, where a scenario is created as an expository device to help students explore challenges around a specific topic [11]. These problems often distil some key features or challenges into simplified scenarios, and sometimes they combine several distilled features into one problem that would be unlikely to occur in a real world setting, but are very useful in teaching students about the challenges in a specific domain. Thus, these case studies are designed to highlight specific features or challenges that serve as the basis for the talking points to discuss with the students.

The first case study focuses on how new technology can result in divisions between a nation and external agencies, whereas the second case study explores how new technology can create divisions within a nation, and particularly how historical and cultural factors can play an important role in people's perspectives on technology, and its impact.

2.1   Case Study 1: The Online Avalanche in Ishmaelia

Description

Ishmaelia[1] is a developing country in East Africa, and in the past ten years its people have fallen in love with the online world; whether it is social media, search engines, or subscription television services; they cannot get enough of it. These online services are being provided mainly by a consortium of international companies, predominantly founded and based in the United States of America. The ease of using these services and technologies has had a very detrimental impact on the country's local media, which is slowly fading away. Concurrently, much of the content that has already been created by the local media outlets has been bought up by these large organizations, and can only be accessed by subscribing to their services.

The Consortium argue that they are "*spending billions of euro in creating vital technological infrastructure that is bringing Ishmaelia into the 21st Century*". It is true that they are collectively, and individually, providing a great deal of Internet infrastructure,

---

[1] "Ishmaelia" is a fictional African country created by Evelyn Waugh for his 1938 novel "Scoop".

as well as cloud-based data centres, and specialised software. They have also been digitising archives of newspapers and indigenous film, television and radio; and are also working closely with a number of national museums and universities to digitise (and preserve) important historical and archaeological artefacts that they are making freely available to scholars.

They also sponsor a number of national sports teams and individual athletes. One of the key goals of the Consortium is to harvest the vast quantity of data that is being generated by the people of Ishmaelia when they interact with these services. This data is a very valuable commodity, and can be used by the Consortium to expand their global reach; the data can also be processed to generate further consumer services, as well as being sold onto third-party organisations for marketing purposes. Ultimately, this results in the Consortium generating a large profit, the majority of which is transferred to the United States, and does not stay in Ishmaelia.

Over the past 18 months, the government of Ishmaelia have been trying to encourage the development of indigenous technology companies by providing taxation breaks and small state grants. They have had some very minor successes with this initiative, but in general these indigenous companies are not succeeding since the Consortium won't allow them access to their Internet infrastructure, and the government of Ishmaelia cannot afford to roll out its own publicly-funded Internet infrastructure. Those few companies that have been successful have had to emulate the marketing tactics, and data collection strategies of the Consortium.

The *Ishmaelian Digital Rights Activitsm Group* (IDRAG) is a growing political body who are deeply concerned with the digital trends that are occurring in their country, where they feel their people's personal information is being exploited by outside organizations. They also feel that their people's privacy is at risk from services that collect a range of information each time a service is accessed, including: geographical information, specific device information, a record of all of the other applications the users have launched (whether these applications are Consortium-owned or not), and a record of all key-clicks and mouse-clicks done while the application is running. According to IDRAG, this is essentially "*constant, 24 h surveillance of everything you do, think, read and buy*". They also point out that the Consortium have an unfair advantage, since not only do they have they technological infrastructure already in place, but they are also collecting more and more data that allow them to create services that are increasingly attractive to consumers. IDRAG has been working with the few successful indigenous technology companies to develop alternative services using Open Source Software as foundation for development.

The Consortium is aware of the bad publicity that they are engendering (in spite of the many good works they have contributed to this country), they have therefore decided to create a suite of educational services that they will make freely available to primary and secondary schools. This will include the development of a sophisticated virtual learning environment, as well as creating a rich collection of educational content (including free textbooks) that is localised to national needs and this will also be supplied freely. The Consortium is about to start to roll out this initiative, and is also supplying free hardware, free installation, and free support service in exchange for having full access to all the data generated by these educational systems.

Suggested Talking Points

1. Given that the Consortium have created the majority of Internet infrastructure in Ishmaelia, don't they have the right to refuse indigenous technology companies access to it? Why?
2. If the people of Ishmaelia are no longer supporting their own local media, should the government intervene to stop their existing media being bought up by the Consortium? Why?
3. When accessing the Consortium's services, the *Terms & Conditions* clearly state that all of the data generated, as well as other contextual data, is being copied to Consortium servers, what they are doing is clearly legal, but is it ethical? Why?
4. IDRAG has been working with the few successful indigenous companies to develop alternative services, and they call on the government to provide them with substantial funding to complete this project, if you were the official who had the decision-making power in this scenario, would you fund this initiative? Why?
5. IDRAG are arguing that the new educational services are simply a way of Ethics Washing, as well as a way of collecting more data about people (starting at a younger age), and this new service is also getting children accustomed to the Consortium' specific software so that they will be more likely to use this type of software in the future. IDRAG call on the government to stop this rollout. If you are the official in charge of making this decision, will you stop the rollout or not? Why?

2.2   Case Study 2: Mobile Mania in Qumran

Description

Qumran[2], a developing country in the Middle East, that was historically part of the British Empire, and was a British protectorate until the late 1970 s. As a consequence of these historical ties, most of the population have some proficiency in the English language. Qumran has seen an explosion in the use of smartphones in the past seven years. The country hasn't got a significant landline infrastructure, but with the advent of affordable Wifi and smartphones, internet usage is growing rapidly. A national survey was recently undertaken, and it found that Internet usage is currently at 57% of the population. There is a sharp divide in terms of age profile of users, with almost 90% of educated, younger adults (18- to 34-year olds) using these services; in contrast, amongst older adults (older than 34 years old) having a rate of 29% usage.

The first section of the survey asked respondents what services they access using the internet, and there was almost unanimous agreement that it serves as a very easy way to keep in touch with family members and friends who are geographically dispersed. A typical survey response stated that *"I can keep up with friends and family who are in other parts of the county, and I can see what they are up to. I also get to hear all the gossip from everyone as well"*.

---

[2] "Qumran" is a fiction Middle Eastern country created by Antony Jay and Jonathan Lynn for their 1982 episode of "Yes Minister" entitled "The Moral Dimension".

The younger adults who participated in the survey also highlighted the significant educational benefits of Internet usage, commenting on the access to an enormous repository of resources, including online courses, MOOCs, textbooks, newspapers (from around the world), and magazines. They also noted that since the majority of Internet content is in English, they are ideally situated to get the most out of this content (as many of this age group are highly proficient English speakers). This demographic also use these services for online shopping, to access government services, and social media.

The older adults are cognizant of the benefits of Internet usage, but amongst this demographic there is a growing concern evidenced in the second section of the survey (as well as in the national media, and by some politicians) that there may be notable drawbacks to Internet usage. Of particular concern is their perception that the Internet is responsible for the erosion of the Qumrani culture, where younger people are eschewing traditional dress, customs and values; and seem more concerned about the latest gossip concerning American celebrities than they are about local and national issues. According to the survey, the most egregious aspect of this concern is the upsurge in the use of the English language which had been in the decline after the Qumrani Secessionist Revolt of 1978, and subsequent withdrawal from British protectorate status, but is now popular again because of prevalence of English language on the Internet.

Also in the second section of the survey 64% of the older adults expressed significant concern about the nature of the personal data they are required to share to access these services, including their date of birth, sometimes photographs, and sometimes credit card details for services that claim to be free. They also identified the issue of how their data is being used by these technology companies, how it is being collated with other people's data, and how it is being shared with third-party organizations. In contrast only 25% of younger adults expressed similar concerns, and in fact many younger adults expressed the opposite opinion, many commented that their "*personal data is a fair exchange for access to these important services*".

In spite of these disagreements, there was general agreement on the negative impact of the Internet on morality in the third section of the survey. Even some of the most ardent advocates in the younger adult demographic rate the influence of the Internet on morality as being "*Neutral or Slightly Negative*", whereas 73% of older adults rate its influence as "*Somewhat or Significantly Negative*". Older adults highlighted specific concerns about the impact of the Internet on children, including the amount of time they spend using it, the lack of censorship of adult materials that they may inadvertently access, and the perceived increase in narcissism and perceived decline in empathy in children. They also expressed the view that since the Internet can be accessed anonymously, it can lead to immoral behaviour such as cyberbullying, digital piracy, and identity theft.

Another area of significant agreement was in the final section of the survey on the importance of Internet access for commercial activities, and the majority believe that the Internet will be crucial for the future growth of the Qumrani economy. Some of the key benefits that the survey participants mentioned include: the possibility of remote working, improved productivity, online accounting systems, eMarketing, and new business opportunities. As such, the government have decided to develop a comprehensive Computer Growth Policy, which includes the development of online government services, as well as giving instructions to all of the colleges and universities to allocate more places for students doing computer science courses, and finally they have decided to reduce their Corporation tax to attract large multinational technology companies to house their offices and Data Centres in Qumran.

Suggested Talking Points

1. Do the older adults in the survey have a reason to be concerned about the use of Internet access by younger adults who seem to be rejecting traditional Qumrani culture (particularly given the historical context)? Why?
2. Do the older adults in the survey have a reason to be concerned about the use of Internet access by children who have access to such a wide range of uncensored content? Why?
3. Do you think the statement *"personal data is a fair exchange for access to these important services"* is reasonable? Why?
4. Do you think that children who undertake illicit activities online such as digital piracy end up undertaking illicit or immoral activities in the real world? Why?
5. Do you think the Qumrani government is making the right choice by attempting to attract multinational technology companies? Why?

As well as the set of case study specific questions (or "Talking Points") presented at the end of each case study, we have also developed a generic case studies checksheet that allows a student to examine any scenario using a range of criteria that describe digital products are services - the data collected and used, the features of the product or service, the organization, stakeholders (developers, consumers, society at large) and the consequences of the technology - intended and unintended. The checksheet is intended for deeper reflection on specific aspects of the case studies and is to be used in conjunction with the "Talking Points" outlined above. The Case Studies checksheet is based on work by Yin [12] and is shown in Fig. 1.

CASE STUDIES CHECKSHEET

A task sheet for students to work through several times and internalise.

*Name of Case Study:*_____

Evaluation criteria	Notes
What is the case study about?	Introduction:
What is the organisation?	Introduction:
What are the technology issues?	Introduction:
Who are the principal actors?	Introduction:
What types of data were collected?	Data Collection:
From which sources did they come?	Data Collection:
How was the data recorded?	Data Collection:
What was the situation previously?	Main Features:
What interventions have been introduced?	Main Features:
What were the general outcomes of this intervention?	Main Features:
Are there any legal, social or ethical issues associated with this intervention?	Main Features:
Is there a chronological or other logic sequence for analysis?	Main Features:
What is the nature of the organisation?	Organisation:
What is its history?	Organisation:
How is it structured?	Organisation:
How has it changed as a result of intervention?	Organisation:
Who are the principal actors in detail?	People (Ecology):
What are their positions within the organisation?	People (Ecology):
What are their technical skills?	People (Ecology):
Does the target population for this intervention include more people?	People (Ecology):
What technology was present? What software? What hardware?	Technology:
What technical level of expertise exists within the organization?	Technology:
What new technology has been introduced for this intervention?	Technology:
How has the new technology effected the organisation?	Technology:
What are the possible consequences of this technology - intended and unintended?	Technology:
How successful has the intervention been?	Evaluation:
What new outcomes have been identified?	Evaluation:
What went well in this intervention?	Evaluation:
What did not go well in the intervention?	Evaluation:
What alternative approaches could have been taken?	Evaluation:

Fig. 1. Case studies checksheet

3   Discussion and Conclusion

New digital products and services are being introduced into the developing world at a rapid pace. Many of these technologies are developed by external technology companies and collect large amounts of data about users and consumers who use the products and services. In this paper we have presented educational content that we have developed in order to examine some of the implications of the introduction of such new technologies and specifically on the issues around data generated and collected by new digital products and services. We have presented two case studies, a set of case study specific questions ("Talking Points") and a generic case study checksheet to be used in the instruction of computer science students to allow them to reflect on the consequences - intended and unintended - of new technologies for use in developing world contexts. Although the content is developed for computer science students it could be adapted for other educational disciplines.

All of the synthesized case studies that are being designed as part of the Ethics4EU project are created in pairs. The first usually more straightforward, focusing on tensions between external and internal factions (in this case, The Consortium versus the Ishmaelian culture), whereas the second one is always more nuanced and often looking at internal tensions between two factions (in this case, the older Qumrani people versus the younger ones). In this way, they work well as individual case studies, but also when taken as a pair they provide an interesting contrast.

After piloting these case studies with a small classgroup, some benefits of the synthesized case studies became clear; students commented that because they knew the scenarios were fictitious, they felt more comfortable elaborating new details about the cases, and they also felt more comfortable hypothesizing motivations of particular actors in the scenarios. They also commented that the case studies opened their eyes to some of the problems associated with technology that they had not thought of before. A few commented that the use of pre-existing fictional placenames made them curious to follow-up on those references, and to explore some literature.

In future work we intend to develop a larger range of educational content for the instruction of digital ethics. Content will focus on pertinent issues such as privacy, computer security, surveillance and facial recognition, the Internet of Things, AI and algorithmic decision making including biases such as racial and gender biases often present in large datasets and the environmental implications (specifically the carbon footprint) of storing excessive quantities of data in data centres.

We intend to evaluate the educational materials with students in the classroom, gathering feedback from students on the educational instruments and evaluating their before and after understanding of the ethical issues raised in the case studies. We also intend to develop an additional instrument for assessing the ethical implications of introducing new technologies for the developing world based on Hofstede's Cultural Dimensions Theory [13].

The theory is a cultural model that attempts to represent the social values of different countries using six dimensions (the dimensions are: *Power Distance, Individualism, Masculinity, Uncertainty Avoidance, Time Orientation,* and *Indulgence*). This model is commonly used to assist computer science students in the design of online content [14], and would therefore be something that the students would be already familiar with, and they would readily be able to apply this model in the context of these case studies.

Acknowledgements. The authors of this paper and the participants of the Ethics4EU project gratefully acknowledge the support of the Erasmus+ programme of the European Union. The European Commission's support for the production of this publication does not constitute an endorsement of the contents, which reflect the views only of the authors, and the Commission cannot be held responsible for any use which may be made of the information contained therein.

References

1. World Economic Forum, How much data is generated each day. https://www.weforum.org/agenda/2019/04/how-much-data-is-generated-each-day-cf4bddf29f/. Accessed 06 Mar 2020
2. Measuring digital development Facts and figures 2019, International Telecommunication Union Publications. https://www.itu.int/en/ITU-D/Statistics/Documents/facts/FactsFigures2019.pdf. Accessed 06 Mar 2020
3. Kwet, M.: Digital Colonialism: US Empire and the New Imperialism in the Global South. Race Class **60**(4), 3–26 (2019)
4. Russo, F.: Digital technologies, ethical questions, and the need of an informational framework. Philos. Technol. **31**(4), 655–667 (2018). https://doi.org/10.1007/s13347-018-0326-2
5. Floridi, L.: Foundations of information ethics. In: The Handbook of Information and Computer Ethics, pp. 1–23. Wiley (2009)
6. Ethics4EU, Erasmus+. www.Ethics4EU.eu. Accessed 06 Mar 2020
7. Spradling, C., Soh, L.K., Ansorge, C.: Ethics training and decision-making: do computer science programs need help?. In: Proceedings of the 39th SIGCSE Technical Symposium on Computer Science Education, pp. 153–157 (2008)
8. Doteveryone, Consequence Scanning, An Agile Practice for Responsible Innovators. https://www.doteveryone.org.uk/project/consequence-scanning/. Accessed 06 Mar 2020
9. Martin, D.A., Conlon, E., Bowe, B.: A constructivist approach to the use of case studies in teaching engineering ethics. In: Auer, M.E., Guralnick, D., Simonics, I. (eds.) ICL 2017. AISC, vol. 715, pp. 193–201. Springer, Cham (2018). https://doi.org/10.1007/978-3-319-73210-7_23
10. Dyer, B., Hughson, M.A., Duns, J., Ricketson, S.: Teaching note: creating a corporations law case study. Legal Educ. Rev. **8**, 161 (1997)
11. Pearl, J.: Heuristics: Intelligent Search Strategies for Computer Problem Solving. Addison Wesley, Boston (1984)
12. Yin, R.K.: Case Study Research and Applications: Design and Methods. Sage Publications, Thousand Oaks (2017)
13. Hofstede, G.: Culture's Consequences: International Differences in Work-Related Values. SAGE Publications, Thousand Oaks (1984)
14. Ahmed, T., Mouratidis, H., Preston, D.: Website design guidelines: high power distance and high context culture. Int. J. Cyber Soc. Educ. **2**(1), 47–60 (2009)

Data Privacy and Protection: The Role of Regulation and Implications for Data Controllers in Developing Countries

Mohammed Agbali, Abubakar A. Dahiru$^{(\boxtimes)}$![ORCID], G. Daniel Olufemi, Inuwa A. Kashifu, and Olatunji Vincent

National Information Technology Development Agency, 28, P/H Crescent Area 11, Garki, Abuja, Nigeria

{magbali,odaniel,kinuwa,volatunji}@nitda.gov.ng,
d.a.abubakar@rgu.ac.uk

Abstract. Advances in new technologies present challenges to general expectations relating to collection, usage and cross-border control and transfer of personal data in recent times. Data has become the critical component of the fourth industrial revolution in global economies involving governments, businesses, and individuals. This paper considers the recent introduction of Data Protection Regulation in Nigeria (NDPR), which can be adjudged to have novel compliance structures globally. Using a qualitative approach, and further enabled by the institutional theory as a framework the paper examines the implications of the NDPR requirements for Data Controllers and Processors in key sectors of the economy. Findings from the study shows that there are five key components of the NDPR that can compel, motivate or support organizations to make significant structural changes such as standardization of processes, practices and IT assets to show conformity and/or gain legitimacy. The study equally identified the factors that facilitate or inhibit the adoption and implementation of the conditions of the NDPR categorised in line with the three pillars of the institutional theory framework. These findings projects policy direction in enhancing the institutionalisation of NDPR measures across key sectors. It will also inform businesses on necessary cause of action and changes to ensure privacy and protection of personal data collected from data subjects.

Keywords: Data protection · Data privacy · Regulation · Data controllers · Data processors · Institutional theory · Framework · ICT · NDPR

1 Introduction

Globalisation and phenomenal growth of Internet and Web access are complicating the challenges of personal data privacy and protection around the world. Vulnerabilities due to data collection in both public and private sectors are at a potentially remarkable stage. For instance, governments collect and process personal information from population census, birth certificate, voters register, and drivers' license records. On the other

J. M. Bass and P. J. Wall (Eds.): ICT4D 2020, IFIP AICT 587, pp. 205–216, 2020.
https://doi.org/10.1007/978-3-030-65828-1_17

hand, private corporations such as telecommunications operators, fund managers, and commercial banks increasingly build capacities for compiling databases of customer information aided by unlimited capability of new technologies with ease of tracking and retrieval.

With globalization and rapid technological advancements, there is obviously increased capability for organizations or businesses to collect, analyse, store, transfer and interlink data for various purposes including direct marketing and personalized services [1]. In this regard, with identification technologies in the form of radio-frequency identification (RFID) and social media platforms such as Facebook, Instagram and other networks, data privacy and protection are currently being challenged [2].

In Europe and North America, developments in personal data processing technologies evolved with data privacy legislation and several other initiatives to improve the level of privacy protection. The first data privacy act by German Federal State of Hessen dated back to 1970 and was followed by the adoption of Swedish Data Protection act in 1973 [3]. Similarly, the United States government formulated the popular Fair Information Practices (FIPs) since 1973 [4]. The development of modern data protection laws started with the Convention for the Protection of Individuals regarding Automatic Processing of Personal Data, 1981 (aka Convention 108). The Convention enumerated the core principles of data processing which are still the basis of modern data protection laws today. The next major intervention is the European Union Data Protection Directive, 1995. Similarly, while issues around protection of citizen's telephone conversation, correspondence, telegraphic communications, etc. are covered under section 37 of the 1999 constitution of the Federal Republic of Nigeria [5], the National Information Technology Development Agency (NITDA), pursuant to Section 6(c) of the NITDA Act 2007, issued a Data Protection Guideline in 2013. However, upon the issuance of the EU General Data Protection Regulation (EUGDPR) in 2016, and other international developments on privacy protection, NITDA issued the Nigeria Data Protection Regulation (NDPR) [6] on 25th January 2019.

In Nigeria, Data Privacy and Protection regulation has been evolving since the introduction of the NDPR which is a subsidiary legislation. The NDPR aims to safeguard the rights of citizens and people living in Nigeria to data privacy and protection in order to foster the integrity of commerce and industry in the volatile data economy. It also aims at enhancing the secure exchange of data; improve business operating environment and create sustainable jobs [6]. The NDPR applies to public and private entities processing data of Nigerians.

In this paper, we examine the implications of data privacy and protection regulations in the context of a developing country – Nigeria, with particular attention to data intensive businesses. These businesses include financial service providers such as banks/fund managers, telecommunications companies, health-care service providers and a host of other operators that need to take into account the Nigeria Data Protection Regulation (NDPR) requirements as it relates to their businesses. To address this issue, a research question was raised '*what are the implications of the new NDPR for data controllers in Nigeria'?*

We provide answers to this question through a comprehensive systematic literature review and analysis of feedback obtained from audit reports filed by entities as well as expert's interviews. We found five key components of the NDPR that can compel, motivate or support organizations to make significant structural changes such as standardization of processes, practices and IT assets to show conformity and/or gain legitimacy. We equally identified the factors that facilitate or inhibit the adoption and implementation of the conditions of the NDPR categorised in line with the three pillars of the institutional theory framework adopted for this study. The findings are discussed and enumerated to inform policy makers on the implications of their approaches towards ensuring compliance. It will also educate businesses on necessary cause of action and changes to ensure privacy and protection of personal data they solicit from data subjects.

The remaining part of the paper is organized into distinctive sections as follows: Sect. 2 presents related works in the field of privacy and data protection. Section 3 summarizes the concept of institutional theory. Section 4 discusses the methodology adopted for this study. Section 5 presents the result and discussion of the findings. Finally, Sect. 6 concludes the paper.

2 Related Work

The growing dependence by businesses on information technology (IT) to manage their data has led to increase in information security and privacy risks implications. The term 'privacy' is a multifaceted concept currently gaining traction in the field of computing. According to Nissenbaum [7], privacy is a contextual integrity and one of the most enduring social issues associated with information and communication technologies (ICT). The author opined that privacy is breached if personal data is used or made available outside its intended context. Data protection on the other hand refers to the processes of safeguarding the confidentiality of data including ensuring its privacy and protecting it from compromise. According to Friedewald et al., the concept of data protection is both broader and more specific than the right to privacy [2]. Art. 8 of the EU Charter of Fundamental rights is the first legislative attempt to distinguish data protection from privacy. According to Lynskey [8], the right to data protection provides individuals with more rights than right to privacy. The enhanced control introduced by data protection serves two purposes- a) it proactively promotes individual personality rights which are threatened by personal data processing and b) reduces the power and information asymmetries between individuals and those who process their data. In this regard, data protection is not intended only to make the protection of privacy real but also seeks to protect other rights relating to conscience, non-discrimination and a host of other concerns or interests.

Article 12 of the United Nations Universal Declaration on Human Rights provides- *no one shall be subject to arbitrary interference with his privacy, family, home or correspondence, nor to attacks upon his honour and reputation. Everyone has the right to the protection of the law against such interference or attacks.* The declaration is a statement of intent of every member of the United Nations, including Nigeria. Article 8 of the European Convention for the Protection of Human Rights and Fundamental Freedoms guarantees the right to respect for private and family life, home, and correspondence. The African Charter on Human and People's Rights on the other hand does not provide for the right to privacy. This lacuna has been justified on the basis that Africa has more pressing rights issues such as child labour, slavery, terrorism etc. However, it has been argued to the contrary that invasion of privacy by telecommunication companies on behalf of government is repressing fundamental rights to expression, beliefs and life.[1] The courts have ruled that illegal monitoring of employees' usage of computer such as private mails, browsing sites and social media activities is a breach of right to privacy[2]. Unlawful storage of data is also held to be a breach of privacy.[3]

The growing concerns about automated personal data systems therefore resulted in the introduction of data privacy measures, regulations, and conventions in the western countries such as United States of America (USA) through the US Department of Health, Education, and Welfare as well as in Europe through the Organization for Economic Co-operation and Development (OECD) and EU [1]. For instance, in a move to standardize the protection of personal data privacy, the European Union (EU) enacted the Data Protection Directive in 1995 [9]. The directive which among other things prohibits corporations and governments from using personal data for any purpose other than original purpose without permission, took effect in 1998 [10].

Organizations are facing ever increasing regulatory interventions (e.g., GDPR, CCPA, NDPR, PIPEDA, HIPAA, etc.) that may lead to significant structural changes such as standardization of processes, practices, and IT assets to show conformity and/or gain legitimacy. According to UNCTAD, 107 countries (of which 66 were developing or transition economies) have put in place legislation to secure the protection of data and privacy [11]. Noteworthy is the growing level of adoption in comparing Europe, Asia and Africa.

3 Institutional Theory

The manner in which organisations respond to changes is often dependent on the socio-political, economic and technological influences exerted by the environment in which they operate as posited by Weerakkody et al. [12]. Thus, the impacts of such external forces on organizational behaviour have been studied by many researchers using the institutional theory. The core concept of institutional theory is that organizational structures and processes tend to acquire meaning and achieve stability in their own right, rather than on the basis of their effectiveness and efficiency in achieving desired ends, such as the mission and goals of the organization [13]. Few studies have focused on using the theory to understand the impact of IT-enabled change in organizations [12]. According to DiMaggio & Powell, institutions exert three types of isomorphic pressures or effects, viz. coercive, normative, and mimetic [14]. Jennings and Greenwood [15] suggest that the notion of institutional pressures is akin to the concept of institutional pillars proposed by Scott, which comprises of *"regulative, normative and cultural cognitive elements that, together with associated activities and resources, provide stability*

---

[1] Privacy International at the 62nd Session of the African Commission on Human and People's Rights (ACHPR).

[2] Barbulescu v. Romania (No. 61496/08).

[3] Roman Zakharov v. Russia (No. 47143/06).

and meaning to social life" (p. 48) [16]. The basic similarity in all institutional theo-retical claims however, is that something identified at a higher level is used to explain processes and outcomes at a lower level of analysis [17].

In this research, the strength of the institutional theory is employed to determine the various implications of data privacy and protection regulations on data intensive businesses in the context of a developing country – Nigeria. Specifically, Scott's [16] three key pillars that can make up or support institutions viz. *regulative, normative and cognitive* are employed.

Table 1. Institutional theory framework

	Regulative	*Normative*	*Cultural-Cognitive*
Basis of compliance	Expedience	Social obligation	Taken-for-grantedness Shared understanding
Basis of order	Regulative rules	Binding expectations	Constitutive schema
Mechanisms	Coercive	Normative	Mimetic
Logic	Instrumentality	Appropriateness	Orthodoxy
Indicators	Rules Laws Sanctions	Certification Accreditation	Common beliefs Shared logics of action Isomorphism
Affect	Fear Guilt/ Innocence	Shame/Honor	Certainty/Confusion
Basis of legitimacy	Legally sanctioned	Morally governed	Comprehensible Recognizable Culturally supported

Source: *Institutions and Organizations pp. 51 [16]*

Institutionalization, through the lenses of the regulative pillar can be viewed as a sta-ble system of rules that can be informal or formal backed by monitoring and sanctioning powers and accompanied by feelings of fear or guilt and/or innocence or incorruptibility. In normative systems, not only are goals and/or objectives defined, appropriate methods of pursuing them are also defined. Norms and values can vary depending on what the position is or who the actors are. Thus, the appropriate goals or activities assigned to par-ticular actors or positions leads to the creation of roles or normative expectations of how specific actors are required to behave. Cognition can be described as the psychological result of perception and learning and reasoning. Scott [16], DiMaggio and Powell [14], and other organizational scholars have stressed the centrality of cognitive elements of institutions as being the *"shared conceptions that constitute the nature of social reality and the frames through which meaning is made"* [16] p. 57.

In summary, the three pillars – *regulative, normative and cognitive,* all have their distinctive features and ways in which they operate as shown on Table 1. However, Scott pointed out that in most empirically observed institutional forms, a combination of the pillars are observed at work which can lead to the formation of a stable social system [16].

This research contributes to the few studies that have applied institutional analysis as a theoretical lens for studying the implications of IS/ICT regulations on organizations. For instance, institutional theory has been used by Appari et al to explain the variability in regulatory compliance prevalent in the US healthcare sector [18]. In their explanation of firms' response to information security and privacy issues, Greenway and Chan argue that information security research could leverage socio-organizational theory, like the institutional theory, to frame inquiries [19]. Similarly, D"Arcy and Hovav advocate application of institutional theory to study the relationship between organizational characteristics and security best practices [20]. In a developing country context, Dahiru et al have also used the theory to determine the associative interaction between exciters and inhibitors to technology adoption [21].

4   Methodology

The research methodology adopted by this study is a qualitative one. A systematic literature survey backed by a pilot study was conducted in Nigeria between November 2019 and January 2020. During this phase, the focus of the study is to obtain the implications of data protection and privacy laws/regulations on data intensive businesses across key sectors in Nigeria. Considering the broadness of the topic as well as potential legal and economic implications, a systematic literature review was initially conducted to provide insights into the topic and to collect adequate qualitative data [22]. Further, using the selected theoretical underpinnings of the institutional theory, a data collection instrument was developed to allow for expansion of the research and to provide an evaluation mechanism. The pilot study was carried out in line with the design emphasised by Naoum [23]. As Naoum posited, lessons drawn from feedback in a pilot study helps the researcher to refine and check the instrument before the main data collection exercise.

4.1   Research Context

Considering key criteria, Nigeria is Africa's largest economy [24]. In addition, Nigeria launched one of the most vibrant campaigns towards enforcement of data privacy and protection on African content in recent time. Data collection and analysis were carried out in Nigeria cutting across key sectors including telecommunication, banking and finance, and regulatory agencies. These sectors were selected based on their direct involvement in the personal data processing and management to enhance the quality of data used in this study. As technology researchers involved in various stakeholders' awareness programmes, the research team was able to access qualitative data through top quality interviews in both public and private sectors.

4.2 Data Collection

The study relied on gradual but systematic literature reviews including audit reports and face-to-face interviews using a semi-structured interview guide. The systematic literature survey was conducted to elicit information required to meet the objective of this study. During the face-to-face interviews, selection of participants was made based on participant's degree of involvement in the ongoing data protection and privacy revolution in Nigeria. The selection process also employed snowballing approach that facilitated researcher's contact with data privacy and protection experts across key sectors in Nigeria. In this pilot study, seven data intensive organizations were considered in both public and private sector and a total of eleven participants were interviewed. The participants included two executive directors, and three general managers, four senior managers and two CTOs. Participants profile are summarized in Table 2. All the interviews were conducted in English language with note taking and audio recording and lasted for 45 to 55 min.

Table 2. Profile of interview participants

Sector	Profile			
	ED	GM	SM	CTO
Telecommunications	0	2	1	0
Banking/Finance	1	1	2	2
Regulatory Agencies	1	0	1	0
Total	**2**	**3**	**4**	**2**

4.3 Data Analysis

Data relating to Privacy and Protection advances were analyzed using institutional theory discussed in the previous section. Data Privacy and Protection issues in this study were evaluated within each domain (as shown in Table 2) on the basis of qualitative data elicited through interviews and credible documents relating to NDPR. In view of the relatively small number of participants involved in this pilot study, results from the interviews were analyzed using qualitative manual method.

5 Results and Discussion

In this section, we describe the most important findings based on the feedback from experts' interviews, pertinent literature and audit reports. Considering the early stage of Data Protection regulation in Nigeria, the analysis focused on laying out the key issues relating to implications of Personal Data Protection for data controllers in key sectors. We achieved this through useful inputs obtained from experts in terms of Personal Data Protection implications in the context of Nigeria.

The recent adoption of NDPR brings about new obligations compelling all data controllers handling Nigerian personal data to review their existing data privacy and protection policies to ensure compliance with NDPR. To guide these tasks, this paper identified key implications of NDPR for data controllers. The 5 key components of NDPR identified in the analysis are summarised in Table 3.

Table 3. NDPR implications for data controllers

NDPR implications	Requirements
Data Controllers to Designate a Data Protection Officer	Data Controllers are required to appoint competent person or outsource data protection to verifiably competent firm to ensure adherence to NDPR
Considering conditions for data processing in international context	Data Controllers are obliged to ensure that Data Subject consent explicitly to the proposed transfer, after being informed of possible risks of such transfer to a third country. Data Controllers must ensure that Data Subject is manifestly made to understand through clear warning of the specific implications of data protection likely to be violated as a result of such transfer to third country
Ensuring Data Subject's right to data portability	Data Controllers are required to ensure that data subject reserve the right to have personal data transmitted directly from one controller to another
Provision of measures for dealing with data breaches	Data Controllers are obliged to secure personal data against all foreseeable hazards and breaches such as theft, cyberattack, viral attack, manipulation of any kind, and damage by natural elements
Reckoning with penalty for dealing with default	Under NDPR, regulatory authority (NITDA) has powers to impose administrative fine on defaulting Data Controllers. Issues of non-compliance could cost Data Controllers a fine of up to 10 million Naira or 2% of Annual Gross Revenue of the preceding year

Awareness of NDPR implications is key and can be viewed as the starting point for the NDPR requirements for implementation amongst data controllers. In this area, findings of this study only confirmed the awareness at the top-management level. For instance, when prompted to confirm the level of awareness of NDPR and the potential implications on their organization, participants of this study confirmed that only their top management is aware of the regulation and implications of not adhering to data protection laws, procedures and policies. Although the interviewees tend to confirm awareness at the management level, only one participant from the banking sector confirmed compliance and steps taken to engage Data Protection Compliance Organization (DPCO). This is an indication of the need for additional awareness creation and sensitization. Implementation of NDPR in Nigeria indicates the need to designate DPCOs in various organizations, which may have considerable impacts on controllers' technical competence and may need the hiring of more expertise.

Organizations involved in data processing in international context are also required to put in place security measures including rules for the onward transfer of personal data to foreign country or international organization. This principle is related to a host of other principles enunciated in the NDPR for data processing regarding data minimization, specific purpose, lawful and legitimacy, accuracy as well as storage and security of personal data (Art. 2.1a to 2.1d). Adherence to these principles can be considered reasonable. However, interviewees from the banking sector expressed concern regarding data they share with their partners in card sub-sector that maintain data centres worldwide, where in most cases, location of such centres remain unknown to them. This is in alignment with previous studies by Dahiru et al. [21] that indicated how data is transferred to international 3rd parties without recourse to its sensitivity.

Implementation of NDPR also introduces a new right to data portability. This right imposes new capability on Data Controllers to ensure there is capability to provide data subject their personal data in compatible format when the need arises. One of the underpinning principles of the NDPR is that Data Controller must comply with basic minimum standards of information security management. In this regard, Data Controllers and Data processors are to ensure Confidentiality, Integrity and Availability. Interviewees have all indicated that their organizations have created a new role for Data Protection Officer within the organization and have appointed or are in the process of appointing an officer to fulfill that role.

Regarding data breaches, implementation of NDPR imposes new obligation for Data Controllers to notify the regulatory authority and data subjects of any data breaches without delay. In this regard, Data Controllers need to put in place notification mechanisms which may require serious changes to the existing systems especially in the area of new technologies. When asked to indicate whether or not their organizations have a register for data breaches and security incidence, interviewees across the sectors investigated indicated "*NO*" suggesting that they do not currently have an internal data protection policy in place to support implementation of this NDPR commitment.

Finally, implementation of the NDPR requires that Data Controllers and Data Processors reckon with sanctions in their processing principle for failure to do so may cost them a fine of up to 10 million Naira (Approx. USD27,000, or €24,000) by the regulatory authority. Response from interviewees indicate that while organizations are concerned about fines in monetary terms, they are more worried with brand image damage, and marketing and publicity. Thus, to ensure compliance and avoid these sanctions, Data Controllers have started to review their privacy and protection measures to keep to this requirement.

Further, the analysis of the audit report and feedbacks from experts' interviews led to identification of several factors arising from the adoption and implementation of NDPR in Nigeria. While some of the factors are positive and favourable in facilitating the implementation of NDPR conditions, some are negative, and hence inhibiting the implementation of NDPR measures. These identified factors are categorised in line with the three pillars of institutional theory framework as shown in Table 4.

Table 4. Institutional Factors in the Adoption of NDPR

Institutional pillar	Facilitators	Inhibitors
Regulative	Well-articulated policies and guidelines	Lack of organizational plans and initiatives regarding NDPR
	NDPR Compliance monitoring	Absence of legal framework and policy
	Risk Assessment mechanism	Insufficient technical staff & training
	Capacity building for senior managers on NDPR	
Normative	Awareness and sensitization of key stakeholders	Lack of industry-wide direction on how to achieve NDPR objectives
	Monitoring & Evaluation of NDPR Implementation	Absence of review mechanism for NDPR
	Funding with regards to NDPR enforcement	Absence of budgetary provision for NDPR
Cultural-Cognitive	Involvement of key Stakeholders in the implementation of NDPR	Resistance to change and risks of leaving personal data unprotected
	Communicating the benefits of Personal Data Protection to stakeholders	Not realizing the importance of NDPR

As Scott [16] pointed out, in most empirically observed institutional forms, a combination of the pillars are observed at work. Concerning the regulative pillar, formulation of well-defined policies appears to be the strongest factor facilitating the level of compliance with NDPR measures amongst stakeholders. Thus, formulation of such policies received inputs from key actors through series of stakeholders' engagements. Inhibiting factors under the same pillar include insufficient human capacity especially in technical areas and adequate training organized by top management.

Regarding the normative pillar, it is important to note that some of the data controllers are willing to conform to industry best practices and recognize the opportunities therein, however, data subjects are not yet conversant with the newly acquired rights as a result of the introduction of the NDPR. The findings from this study therefore suggest the need for continuous awareness for data subjects and adequate training for data controllers at organizational level. A major inhibiting factor highlighted under this pillar relates to absence or lack of funding for NDPR activities.

Regarding the Cultural-Cognitive pillar, involvement of key stakeholders in NDPR implementation and communicating the benefits of Data Protection to stakeholders were highlighted as facilitating factors. Under the same pillar, resistance to changes and risks of leaving personal data unprotected are highlighted as inhibiting factors. It is therefore imperative to learn how to deal with the cultural changes inherent in data privacy and protection initiatives such as NDPR.

6 Conclusion and Future Work

This study attempts to identify Data Protection Regulation requirements and implications for Data Controllers and Processors in the context of a developing country - Nigeria. The research study analysed these implications using the institutional theory framework. Although the NDPR was launched in January 2019, most Data Controllers and Processors are yet to realise the complexity of its implications.

The identified implications of the new changes introduced by NDPR adoption and implementation were collated with 5 key aspects prioritised by Data Controllers for compliance in order to avoid sanctions from regulatory authority for non-compliance. Specifically, the research projects that controllers need to pay attention to awareness creation and designate DPOs for proactive implementation of NDPR requirements. NDPR also specifies procedures for data processing in international context. Thus, Data Controllers must consider this requirement when transferring personal data to third countries or international organisations. Similarly, the NDPR introduces obligations that require Data Controllers to ensure data portability. Data Controllers also need to ensure uniform standards or interoperability of their procedures for seamless transmission of data. Regarding data breaches, Data Controllers equally the appointment of a DPO that will support the compliance through the development of an internal data protection policy and a robust data breach reporting mechanism. Finally, as the NDPR also imposes sanctions for non-compliance, Data Controllers need to review their strategies and reckon with sanctions and adequate budgetary provision to support compliance when planning.

As part of the major contributions of this paper, some guidelines believed to facilitate the institutionalisation of NDPR measures across organisations were pushed forward. Evidence from this study as presented in the previous section suggests that use of institutional theory can help in interpretation of different level of NDPR adoption and implementation by Data Controllers. It can also help to project policy direction enhancing the institutionalisation of NDPR measures across key sectors. It is imperative therefore to extend the scope of this study in the future to cover more organisations in order to determine the extent to which the NDPR implementation facilitates and support the digital economy transformation in Nigeria.

References

1. Tikkinen-Piri, C., Rohunen, A., Markkula, J.: EU general data protection regulation: changes and implications for personal data collecting companies. Comput. Law Secur. Rev. **34**(1), 134–153 (2018)
2. Friedewald, M., Wright, D., Gutwirth, S., Mordini, E.: Privacy, data protection and emerging sciences and technologies: towards a common framework. Innov. Eur. J. Soc. Sci. Res. **23**(1), 61–67 (2010)
3. Roos, A.: Core principles of data protection law. Comp. Int. Law J. South. Afr. **39**, 102 (2006)

4. Gellman, R.: Willis ware's lasting contribution to privacy: fair information practices. IEEE Secur. Priv. **12**(4), 51–54.Ge (2014)
5. Law of the Federal Republic of Nigeria: Chapter 4, Section 37 fundamental right of citizens to private and family life (2004)
6. Nigeria Data Protection Regulation (2019). Art 1.1. https://nitda.gov.ng/wp-content/uploads/2019/01/Nigeria%20Data%20Protection%20Regulation.pdf
7. Nissenbaum, H.: Privacy as contextual integrity. Wash. Law Rev. **79**, 119 (2004)
8. Lynskey, O.: Deconstructing data protection: the 'added-value' of a right to data protection in the EU legal order. Int. Comp. Law Q. **63**(3), 569–597 (2014)
9. Steinke, G.: Data privacy approaches from US and EU perspectives. Telemat. Inform. **19**(2), 193–200 (2002)
10. Birnhack, M.D.: The EU data protection directive: an engine of a global regime. Comput. Law Secur. Rev. **24**(6), 508–520 (2008)
11. United Nations Conference on Trade and Development UNCTAD (2020). Data Protection and Privacy Legislation Worldwide. https://unctad.org/en/Pages/DTL/STI_and_ICTs/ICT4D-Legislation/eCom-Data-Protection-Laws.aspx. Accessed 18 Feb 2020
12. Weerakkody, V., Dwivedi, Y.K., Irani, Z.: The diffusion and use of institutional theory: a cross-disciplinary longitudinal literature survey. J. Inf. Technol. **24**(4), 354–368 (2009)
13. Miles, J.A.: Management and Organization Theory: A Jossey-Bass Reader. Wiley, Hoboke (2012)
14. DiMaggio, P.J., Powell, W.W.: The iron cage revisited: Institutional isomorphism and collective rationality in organizational fields. Am. Sociol. Rev., 147–160 (1983)
15. Jennings, P.D., Greenwood, R.: 6bConstructing the iron cage: Institutional theory and enactment'. Debating Organization: Point-Counterpoint in Organization Studies, 195 (2003)
16. Scott, R.W.: Institutions and organizations: ideas and interests (2008)
17. Clemens, E.S., Cook, J.M.: Politics and institutionalism: explaining durability and change. Annu. Rev. Sociol., 441–466 (1999)
18. Appari, A., Johnson, M. E., Anthony, D.L.: HIPAA compliance: an institutional theory perspective. In: AMCIS 2009 Proceedings, p. 252 (2009)
19. Greenway, K.E., Chan, Y.E.: Theoretical explanations for firms' information privacy behaviors. J. AIS **6**(6), 171–198 (2005)
20. D''Arcy, J., Hovav, A.: An Integrative framework for the study of information security management research. In: Gupta, J., Sharma, S. (eds.) Handbook of Research on Information Security and Assurance, pp. 55–67. Idea Group Publishing (2009)
21. Dahiru, A.A., Bass, J.M., Allison, I.K.: Cloud computing adoption in sub-Saharan Africa: an analysis using institutions and capabilities. In: International Conference on Information Society (i-Society 2014), pp. 98–103. IEEE, November 2014
22. Glaser, B.G., Holton, J.: Remodeling grounded theory. Paper presented at the Forum Qualitative Sozialforschung/Forum: Qualitative Social Research (2004). Author, F.: Article title. Journal **2**(5), 99–110 (2016)
23. Naoum, S.G.: Dissertation Research and Writing for Construction Students, 3rd edn. Routledge, Abingdon (2013)
24. National Bureau of Statistics: Nigeria Economy Largest in Africa (2019). http://nigerianstat.gov.ng/

Implementation of Agile Methodology in Developing Countries: Case Study in Lebanon

Scarlet Rahy$^{(\boxtimes)}$ and Julian M. Bass (ID)

University of Salford, Greater Manchester, UK
S.Rahy@edu.salford.ac.uk, J.Bass@salford.ac.uk
http://www.salford.ac.uk

Abstract. Researchers have become interested in agile approaches to information systems development, because of their potential to improve product quality and increase productivity. While often associated with project orchestration in software development, agile methods have a wider potential application within ICT4D.

Our interest, in this research, is to explore how practitioners in developing countries describe factors that either enable or impede the adoption of agile information system development methods. We chose Lebanon to investigate this question, because it is a center for outsourcing software development in Middle Eastern countries. We employed a qualitative research approach by conducting 31 semi-structured recorded interviews with practitioners in three Lebanese software development companies. We employ an analytical model which interlinks institutional theory, the capability approach, and ICTs to explore creating software using agile methodology.

The analysis revealed positive reinforcement between three factors that improve the effectiveness of agile methods including the inclusive and detailed sprint planning, rich variety of stakeholder communication tactics, and teams that embrace a rich variety of communication technologies that overcome challenges presented by geographical distance. On the other hand, we also discovered impediments to agile adoption including team and management misunderstandings of agile methodology and the current political and economic crisis in the country.

The model revealed the low investment of companies in ICT. The lack of knowledge of agile ceremonies roles and artefacts created gaps in the implementation process. Also, the model highlighted bottlenecks that should be crucially tackled such as the lack of customer involvement and risk mitigation towards external factors.

Keywords: Agile methodology · ICT4D · Institution theory · Capability approach · Developing countries · Lebanon

1 Introduction

The agile methods are based on values and philosophies developed in the Agile Manifesto [9], which promotes continuous customer involvement and encourages feedback.

© IFIP International Federation for Information Processing 2020
Published by Springer Nature Switzerland AG 2020
J. M. Bass and P. J. Wall (Eds.): ICT4D 2020, IFIP AICT 587, pp. 217–228, 2020.
https://doi.org/10.1007/978-3-030-65828-1_18

Agile information systems development is associated with the potential improvement of team productivity and software product quality [2]. Agile is increasingly expanding its influence from software development project planning to applications within the information and communication technology for development (ICT4D). Thus, researchers have become interested in the study of this field.

As in the global market, the demand for software development in developing countries is rising. Software development providers aim to enhance the quality and productivity of their development process. This study chooses Lebanon as a research site since Lebanon falls in UNDP's list of development aid recipient countries and is a source for outsourcing software in the Middle East and Gulf region [13, 15].

This paper describes and analyzes Agile Software Development in the developing country's software development industry using a model originally presented in [7]. The model created by [7] introduces an analytical framework for information and communication technology drawing on the capabilities approach and institutional theory. This combination uses institutional theory, focusing on roles, norms and organizational structures, and the capabilities approach, focusing on the achievement of goals and desires to account for the technology driven change in institutions in developing countries. It highlights the inhibitors and exciters between the model's different elements to create an analytical framework for ICT4D.

Three dimensions connect each of the elements that constitute the analytical platform. We explore how the human capabilities and their understanding of agile affect the roles and organization's structure in relation to agile implementation of ceremonies and artefacts in ICT context. This paper fills the gap and answers the below research question: What do practitioners in developing countries describe as factors that either enable or impede the adoption of agile?

The study employs a qualitative research approach by conducting 31 semi-structured interviews with practitioners in three Lebanese software development companies. We employ an analytical model which interlinks institutional theory, the capability approach, and ICTs to explore creating software using agile methodology. The model aids in identifying the inhibiters and exciters in the process.

This paper is structured as follows: first we present a literature review on agile software development and the research model. Then, we illustrate the methodology used to gather and analyze data. Then, we present an implementation of the model in the studied context followed by a discussion. Finally, conclusions and future work are presented.

2   Agile Software Development in Developing Countries

The agile methodology promotes continuous involvement of the customer in the development process [14]. In addition to software engineering, agile development has attracted attention in information systems and project management disciplines [11]. Agile methods are associated with increased level of productivity [12]. Conventionally, agile methods are comprised of ceremonies, such as stand-up meetings, retrospectives and customer demos, artefacts, which fall under five categories: feature, sprint, release, product and development programmed governance [5] and roles, which include self-organizing teams, product owners, and scrum masters. Agile practices may be tailored by practitioners to fit their context, large scale, regulated or disciplined environment [6].

2.1 Agile Implementation in Developing Countries

Developing countries have been implementing agile methods in their software development process. Practitioners are aware of the benefits of agile and stress on the importance of its implementation [18]. Gaps between the developers and the end-users hinder the development process [3, 10]. This is due to the end-user's IT skill level and communication pattern with developers [3].

For instance, a study conducted in Egypt revealed the positive effects on the software development process and customer satisfaction when adopting agile methodology [16]. Simultaneously, challenges were detected such as, high pressure on developers, inadequate use of effort estimation, and lack of sprint planning. Also, a study of an in-house software development for a Lebanese university revealed the lack of support from the educational sector [21, 22] and poor ICT structure [21]. The country's poor ICT infrastructure and lack of government plan for the IT industry stand as barriers to growth [24]. There is scarcity in the literature studying the benefits of implementing agile, its challenges, practices, and information flows in the Lebanese context. Thus, there is a large scope for conducting new studies to understand agile in developing countries, through studying the Lebanese context. This research aims at providing an understanding of agile software development in developing countries in relation to the Technology Institutions and Capabilities model's elements.

Agile teams in developing countries have the potential to enhance their software development industry through effectively applying agile methods. The analysis of geographically separated teams in Kenya and The Netherlands showed how teams may use their differences in order to benefit and learn from each other's experiences [17]. Team members at The Netherlands learned and enhanced their agile process by observing agile being implemented in Kenya.

2.2 Research Model

This research is based on the conceptual model, Technology Institutions and Capabilities model (TIC) created by [7] is shown in Fig. 1. The framework identifies a relationship between institutional theory, the capability approach, and ICT. In the context of the model, ICT is the technology used to 'deliver human centered development', the capability approach looks into the freedom given to individuals to expand their abilities using ICT, and institutional theory focuses on structure, technology, and institutional driven change. The bidirectional arrows between the model's elements represent the influences and interrelationships. The positive ones are labeled as exciters and the negatives ones are labeled as inhibitors. The model is used here to identify the strength and weakness of agile software development implementation in developing countries.

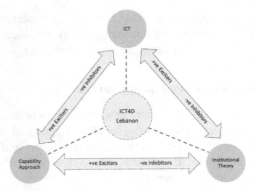

Fig. 1. Technology Institutions and Capabilities model adapted from Bass et al. (2013)

3 Methodology

The foundation of this research is based on the model presented by [7]. This model enables us to present a framework that combines institutional theory and the capability approach in relation to ICT and analyze the influences along the three different elements. This research used a case study approach, guided by [19], to explore the practitioner's perception on agile implementation in the Lebanese software development industry. The case study replicates the investigation in three different software development companies. Interviews were conducted with 31 respondents who were ensured confidentiality and anonymity. The following section introduces the research sites, data collection and data analysis process.

3.1 Research Sites

The agile software development industry is spreading across developing countries. Lebanon is considered as a case study for this research since it's a developing country and it outsources software to Middle Eastern and gulf countries [13, 15]. Thus, we chose practitioners involved in agile software development form 3 different research sites. The three sites were labelled LEB1, LEB2, and LEB3 to protect their anonymity.

LEB1 is a Lebanese based software development company providing solutions in areas of banking, analytics, technology, academy, insurance, retail, healthcare, and multimedia. LEB1 has its main headquarters in Mount Lebanon, and two other branches in North Lebanon, and Bekaa Valley. LEB2 is a software development company that provides technological solutions for clients in Lebanon and abroad. LEB2 develops on-demand and customized software using agile. LEB3 is a Lebanese based software development company that develops apps and websites for its clients.

3.2 Data Collection

The primary source of data collection is face-to-face interviews conducted in person. A list showing the participants' research sites, roles, and respective location is found in

[8]. The participants' selection was done with the help of company representatives. The interviews ranged from 30 min to 1 h and 10 min with 45 min being typical. The data collected was obtained from semi-structured open-ended interviews. Probing questions were used to encourage participants to discuss any new topics that were not included in the interview guide. The interview guide and consent form used for interviews may be viewed at [4]. All interviews were recorded after obtaining the practitioners' consent. Field notes were taken during the interviews by the researcher. Then, interviews were transcribed manually since it ensures correct transcription and reminds the interviewer of the social and emotional aspects that occurred during the interview [23] thus effectively conducting the data collection stage [1].

3.3 Data Analysis

For the transcribed interviews, we performed open coding, applied constant comparison methods, identified core categories, and memoed the data. All transcribed data was imported to an analyzing tool Nvivo 11. Open coding includes the analysis of data and exclusion of prior judgment to produce the maximum number of concepts. Line-by-line open coding approach was used on the transcribed interviews. Codes from each interview were compared from codes arising from the same and other interviews. This constant comparison technique enabled the grouping of codes that constitute concepts. Then, each key point is assigned a code titled with a phrase that summarizes it. From these, interview concepts arise and are grouped into categories which then form the main categories. We then chose the topics that align with the model of our choice. We chose the core categories and perform selective coding according to the framework of the model explained in the previous section. Our analysis involves mapping of our case onto the conceptual model supported by textual description.

4   Findings

We now explore how the TIC model can be used to understand agile implementation in Lebanon. This will enable us to explore how each of the model's elements when strengthened can decrease the inhibitors and increase the exciters in each case.

In our scenario, the capabilities approach is the people's ability to fully understand and correctly implement agile. ICT is software development methods used along with the agile ceremonies implemented and artefacts created. Institutional theory includes the roles of the employees and the structure of the organization. Figure 2 reveals the model adapted to the Lebanese context. Each of the three dimensions is explained thoroughly and the respective inhibiters and exciters are shown.

4.1   Dimension A: Capabilities to Institutions

A major obstacle towards applying agile is understanding what agile methodology is. Using the TIC analytical framework, we find this as an inhibitor from capabilities to building the software development institution. Being a new concept in the Lebanese software development industry, understanding agile is a major struggle for employees.

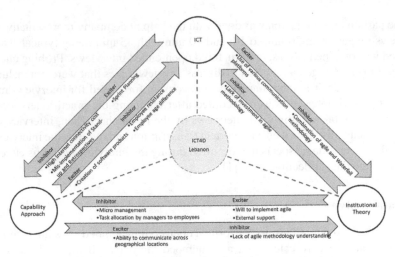

Fig. 2. TIC model adapted to the Lebanese context

First of all, implementing agile was suggested by either employees who discovered the agile concept while researching or the CEO who heard about the concept in a different company having no prior experience or knowledge. S6 explained: "*While I was research-ing for a project, I found out about agile. I presented this concept to the team leader and he liked the idea. So the company decided to turn into agile.*" Understanding agile and its importance was especially difficult for non-developers. A2 explained: "*Business development and marketing team didn't understand agile's importance*".

On the other hand, the ability to communicate across diverse geographical loca-tion acts as an exciter from capabilities to institutions. Interviews revealed that teams were located in different geographical locations while working on the same project. These team members come from different culture, tradition, and religion, which highly affects the person's character in Lebanon. Communication between these members is smooth. Surprisingly, from all the interviewed practitioners, who worked with outsourced employees or with team members in different company branches, none claimed that they are currently facing communication difficulties. Team members would join for meetings virtually through different communication platforms. A1 explained: "*Every morning at 9, everyone had to participate in the stand up and the employees outside the office would join in virtually.*" Different communication platforms were used to communicate with employees who are outside the office such as slack, email, calls, video conferencing. A6 said: "*Every time we needed something from someone we used slack, whether they are in the office or outside. The communication was very easy.*" Sometimes, urgent matter arise and employees from different geographical locations will have to join at the head-quarters. Managers try to minimize the movement between branches to decrease time loss time; since the branches are located in different districts, no public transportation is available in Lebanon, and traffic jams are major.

4.2 Dimension A: Institutions to Capabilities

In the opposing direction, micro management by the CEO and allocation of tasks by the managers are inhibitors from institutions to capabilities. First, dealing with the pressures of the upper management is one of the main challenges faced by employees. A2 said: *"Honestly, the biggest challenge faced is the upper management."* Practitioners revealed how the CEO was micro-managing and continuously involved in the process.

In regards to communication, the CEO requested to know all the details of every project. So the CEO would request a morning meeting to be informed of all the details. V9 expressed their opinion on these meetings: *"Instead of taking 20 to 30 min for each daily meeting, we would use it for our work to be done."* These morning meeting will last longer than advised. Managers complained from the CEO's interference in how they lead their team and plan and execute their upcoming tasks. A4 described: *"I am not given the space to implement the work independently. So I had the CEO assign tasks to my team without me knowing. He was deciding our next steps even if I didn't know."* Thus, A4, team manager, and A7, team member, described how they would use WhatsApp and Slack in order to communicate without being interrupted by the CEO. They would plan their overall tasks and daily to-do lists.

Second, managers and team leaders assign tasks to the team members. V7 explained: *"We assign the global tasks for each team and then each team leader will assign the tasks to his team."* Occasionally, team leaders discuss the task distribution with their team members. This creates occasional tension between the team leaders and project managers. Also, when tasks are imposed, tension between team members rise and they prefer to choose the tasks they want to work on. As A7 describes: *"I dislike the idea that our leaders allocate the tasks. I would like to choose the tasks I have to do."* S6 added: *"It would be motivating if I chose my own tasks from each sprint."* When tasks are allocated, some team members object and some team leaders disregard it.

Conversely, the upper management are open to implement agile. This demonstrates positive intentions towards this method. Also, external support is provided through the Beirut Digital District (BDD) which is a project that aims at creating a hub for the digital community in Lebanon. Occasionally, BDD conducts workshops on agile software development. Few practitioners mentioned that they attended these workshops.

4.3 Dimension B: Capabilities to ICT

The employee age difference and resistance are inhibitors flowing from capabilities to ICT. First, the age difference between employees is a challenge for managers to overcome. An employee who has just joined the company may be more qualified than another employee in a senior position. V4 gives an example: *"My challenge is how to say to a senior that a junior developer will be your supervisor."* This difference in ICT knowledge creates tension between certain employees.

In addition, the employees' resistance has been a subject in the management world for decades. In our studied companies, resistance was detected from the employees as well as the upper management. Employee resistance was detected when implementing new methods or when assigning certain tasks. V1 claimed *"Maybe they feel they are overwhelmed with the work load they have; they feel it is out of their roles and responsibilities; or they have some tension with other team members.*" Employee resistance was also detected when implementing agile methods especially amongst non-developers. A2 explained: "*The business development team and the marketing team do not understand the importance of agile.*" Upper management resistance appeared when implementing new agile methods. A2 continued: "*Honestly the upper management was my main struggle towards reaching agility.*"

On another hand, software products being created from the Lebanese companies to local and international markets are exciters from the capabilities to the ICT sector. The numerous success stories revealed by practitioners show how much the team's capabilities is enhancing the industry.

4.4 Dimension B: ICT to Capabilities

The inhibitors that flow from ICT to capabilities are the high internet connectivity costs and the improper implementation of agile ceremonies. In developing countries such as Lebanon the internet access is characterized by high costs and low quality. This sometimes hinders the process and increases the time for a certain task to be completed.

Through the interviews, it was apparent that practitioners either didn't implement standups or implemented them incorrectly. For instance, LEB1 didn't implement the standup meetings with the team members. Instead, morning meetings were held with the CEO, top managers and team leaders. V6 explained: "*In this meeting, we put all our active items. The CEO starts and then asks each team leader what they have for the day.*" V8 indicated that the morning meeting takes around 30 min and: "*They should have a different formulation. We discuss the project in general. It is sometimes repetitive.*" Another example is the stand-up held at LEB3 where all the members of the company, even the employees who weren't present in the company premises, would join in using Zoom. The time for each standup took from 20 to 30 min which was a "*tiring way to start the day* [كنا نهلك من الصبح]", according to A4. Similarly to LEB1, the CEO used to take the lead in the standup. After an all-inclusive meeting, the product owners and team leaders weren't able to conduct their own standup with their team members: "*It was impossible for me to do that again with my team.*"

In addition, through our interviews, confusion was detected on retrospectives, even in the same company. When asked about retrospectives, 21 interviewees didn't know what retrospectives are. So, as the interviewer, I had to explain what happens during retrospectives and how they are conducted. S1 responded: "*We did not do retrospectives; we didn't have formal evaluations. We just informally say what was wrong.*" As for the interviewees who responded to the question regarding retrospectives, they lacked a clear understanding of what they are. Every response was different from the other and misconception on retrospectives were clear even in the same company.

On the other hand, implementing sprint planning, an agile ceremony, acts as an exciter from the ICT to capabilities. Sprint planning was done by all interviewed practitioners. All practitioners identified its importance towards the success of the sprint.

4.5 Dimension C: ICT to Institutions

The lack of understanding of agile act as an inhibitor from ICT to institutions. This lack of knowledge led practitioners to implement a combination of methods, Waterfall and agile methods or tailored agile methods with traditional project management methodologies, and ineffective end-user involvement. As mentioned by V1: *"Inside the agile iteration we use the Waterfall methodology by respecting the sequence of processes."* The sequence is explained by collection of requirements, design, development, testing and delivery. Another example, the upper management needed to see a global picture of the requirements. The overall requirements were given in the traditional project management methods. V9 explained: *"We get the requirements from the project manager."* In addition, although the companies have no direct control over the end-user, the end-user's lack of involvement hinder the process. V15 expressed: *"I've noticed with Lebanese clients is the staff's availability and commitment is not always as promised."*

The various communication platforms used are seen as exciters from ICT to institutions. Communication is highly encouraged at the agile implementing software development companies. Diverse communication channels are open for employees at the company. The usage of communication channels depends on the needs and message delivered. If it is a simple update, then instant messaging platforms are used. If it is formal, then emails are sent and meetings are held. V4 explained: *"Sometime, I have to send just an informal message; I use WhatsApp."* A1 indicated that slack is one of the major communication platforms used. When practitioners need to communicate and are present in different geographical locations, they use online video conference call applications that are available free of charge.

4.6 Dimension C: Institutions to ICT

The lack of investment from institutions in agile software development acts as inhibitors towards building an agile environment. Of the three research sites, non had a certified agile coach who guides employees through agile implementation or a scrum master. A2 was responsible for implementing agile in LEB3 with no prior experience or certification. In LEB1, agile was tailored according to trial and error methods. V1 explained: *"Unfortunately, we base our work on research that we do on our own. We never had a coach specialized in agile methodology. We do our own research and we let ourselves be guided at the same time by the real needs on the ground."* The employees didn't thoroughly understand the concept of agile. For instance, some interviewee had no knowledge on what agile ceremonies and artefacts were. They knew general concepts such as individual interactions over processes and working software over comprehensive documentation.

5 Discussion

Since agile information systems development is associated with the potential improvement of team productivity and software product quality, we aim to explore how practitioners in developing countries describe factors that either enable or impede the adoption of agile information system development methods.

We use the TIC model to understand the exciters and inhibitors in each dimension in the agile software development industry in developing countries through our case study in Lebanon. We identified virtuous and vicious circles that enhance or diminish the role of agile methodology in the software development industry. The study identifies positive reinforcements between factors that improve the effectiveness of agile methods. An example of a virtuous circle is the exciter: inclusive and detailed sprint planning (ICT to capabilities) leading to the creation of software products (capabilities to ICT). The various communication tactics act as exciters when used along with a rich variety of communication technologies between teams across different geographical locations. Although our case isn't cross-country with no time difference, yet employees cross long distances in personal cars with no public transportation available. These exciters enable team members to overcome distance and religious and cultural differences.

Inhibitors create vicious circles that undermine the agile software development process. For example, lack of agile methodology understanding (capabilities to institutions), leads to task allocation by managers to employees (institutions to capabilities). In addition, we were able to identify loops that hinder the correct implementation of agile methodology. For instance, the combination of agile and waterfall methodology (inhibitor from ICT to institutions) leads to the task allocation by managers to employees (inhibitor from institutions to capabilities) which in turn lead to employee resistance (inhibitor from capabilities to ICT). These closed loops obstruct agile implementation.

We had a difficulty assigning a satisfying illustration of an exciter from institutions to ICT. In our case, this may be due to the current economic and political crisis in the country. Also, the recognition of the institution's role in support of ICT is less fortified.

Our findings are consistent with previous research conducted in Ethiopia, which show novice agile practitioners tend to mix plan-based and agile methods [18]. Also, companies experience gaps when implementing agile practices with missing roles, ceremonies and artefacts due to lack of staff, knowledge and finances. We also, found that, like in Egypt, novice agile practitioners find effort estimation challenging [16]. However, a surprising finding from our research was the enthusiastic adoption of communication technologies to overcome challenges of geographical distance

The software development industry in Lebanon needs to tackle in parallel the social and technical issues [10]. The relation between ICT and capabilities approach in the model stress the latter. This reveals the need to mitigate for the social bottlenecks that companies face. These include the lack of involvement of the end-user in the development process [3, 20] and the political and economic issues the developing countries face, especially Lebanon in the current situation. The end-user gives the requirements to the development team then reduces the contact with them and responds late to requests. In the final stages of the project, Lebanese customers tend to inform the development of changes which causes frustration and stress among developers and lateness in delivery date. In addition, the political and economic situation in Lebanon carries high risks ranging from employee transportation, internet connectivity, and employee motivation leading to possible delays in delivery of software.

5.1 Limitations

A limitation of this research study is that the research sites were dictated by the availability of research sites and willingness to participate in this study; similarly for research participants. Thus, the study was conducted in a relatively small number of research sites. Yet the constant comparison technique used allows the accommodation of more data from new contexts; especially through the replication of the study in other developing countries. Further, using the TIC model as a basis for our analysis aided in the analysis of agile implementation in relation to the three elements. Difficulties were encountered when identifying an exciter from institutions to ICT. To achieve rigor and generalizability in qualitative research, four critical factors have been identified [23]: construct, internal and external validity, and reliability. They were achieved through collecting data using multiple sources of evidence, specifying unit of analysis, replication of the study, and use of a universal interview guide for participants, respectively.

6 Conclusion

Agile software development can enhance product quality and improve team productivity. In our study, we explore the practitioners' perceptions of the factors that enable or impede agile methods in developing countries through observing three companies in the Lebanese software sector.

Our study uses a qualitative research approach. The case study replicates the investigation in three research sites resulting in 31 semi-structured open-ended interviews with agile software development practitioners. The research employs the TIC model which interlinks institutional theory, the capabilities approach, and ICT to explore ICT4D. This model aids in understanding of agile software development process in developing countries through highlighting impediments and stimulators of the process.

The analysis reveals positive reinforcements which include detailed and inclusive sprint planning, a wide range of communication tactics used by stakeholders, and different communication technologies used to facilitate communication across geographical locations. In addition, the analysis of the model revealed impediments that demonstrate how, from an institutional perspective, there was low investment in ICT. A lack of agile process knowledge created implementation process gaps across the roles, artefacts and ceremonies of agile. In addition, we discovered from analyzing the impediments between ICT and capabilities the need to tackle the technical and social bottlenecks that include lack of customer involvement and risk mitigation of the critical political and economic situation. Future work will investigate adaptation of agile ceremonies in the Lebanese context and observe the challenges faced and benefits achieved.

References

1. Adolph, S., Hall, W., Kruchten, P.: Using grounded theory to study the experience of software development. Empir. Softw. Eng. **16**(4), 487–513 (2011). https://doi.org/10.1007/s10664-010-9152-6

2. Ahmed, A., Ahmad, S., Ehsan, N., et al.: Agile software development: impact on productivity and quality. In: Anonymous 2010 IEEE International Conference on Management of Innovation & Technology, pp. 287–291. IEEE (2010)
3. Akinnuwesi, B.A., Uzoka, F., Olabiyisi, S.O., et al.: An empirical analysis of end-user participation in software development projects in a developing country context. Electron. J. Inf. Syst. Dev. Ctries. **58**(1), 1–25 (2013)
4. Bass, J.: Tailoring in Large Scale Agile, Interview guide (2018). https://salford.figshare.com/articles/Tailoring_in_Large-Scale_Agile_Interview_Guide/7122503
5. Bass, J.M.: Artefacts and agile method tailoring in large-scale offshore software development programmes. Inf. Softw. Technol. **75**, 1–16 (2016)
6. Bass, J.M., Haxby, A.: Tailoring product ownership in large-scale agile projects: managing scale, distance, and governance. IEEE Softw. **36**(2), 58–63 (2019)
7. Bass, J.M., Nicholson, B., Subhramanian, E.: A framework using institutional analysis and the capability approach in ICT4D. Inf. Technol. Int. Dev. **9**(1), 19–35 (2013)
8. Bass, J., Rahy, S.: Agile Software Development in Lebanon (2020). https://salford.figshare.com/articles/Agile_Software_Development_in_Lebanon/11887824
9. Beck, K., Beedle, M., Van Bennekum, A., et al.: Manifesto for agile software development (2001)
10. Blake, E., Tucker, W.: Socially aware software engineering for the developing world (2006)
11. Dingsøyr, T., Falessi, D., Power, K.: Agile development at scale: the next frontier. IEEE Softw. **36**(2), 30–38 (2019)
12. Dyba, T., Dingsoyr, T.: What do we know about agile software development? IEEE Softw. **26**(5) (2009). https://doi.org/10.1109/ms.2009.145
13. Feghali, T., Ahmed, Z.U., Halawani, S.: Determinants of Lebanon's ICT export competitiveness: evaluating a country's readiness to export ICT. J. Transnatl. Manage. **12**(3), 3–23 (2007)
14. Hoda, R., Noble, J., Marshall, S.: Self-organizing roles on agile software development teams. IEEE Trans. on Softw. Eng. **39**(3), 422–444 (2013). https://doi.org/10.1109/TSE.2012.30
15. IDAL: Technology Sector in Lebanon Factbook 2018 (2018)
16. Mohallel, Amr A., Bass, Julian M.: Agile software development practices in Egypt SMEs: a grounded theory investigation. In: Nielsen, P., Kimaro, H.C. (eds.) ICT4D 2019. IAICT, vol. 551, pp. 355–365. Springer, Cham (2019). https://doi.org/10.1007/978-3-030-18400-1_29
17. Rahy, S., Bass, J.: Information Flows at inter-team boundaries in agile information systems development. In: Anonymous European, Mediterranean, and Middle Eastern Conference on Information Systems, Limassol, Cyprus, 4–5 October (2019)
18. Regassa, Z., Bass, Julian M., Midekso, D.: Agile methods in Ethiopia: an empirical study. In: Choudrie, J., Islam, M.Sirajul, Wahid, F., Bass, Julian M., Priyatma, J.E. (eds.) ICT4D 2017. IAICT, vol. 504, pp. 367–378. Springer, Cham (2017). https://doi.org/10.1007/978-3-319-59111-7_31
19. Runeson, P., Host, M., Rainer, A., et al.: Case Study Research in Software Engineering: Guidelines and Examples. Wiley, Hoboken (2012)
20. Sommerville, I.: Software Engineering, Global Edition. Pearson Education Limited, Harlow (2016)
21. Tarhini, A., Yunis, M., El-Kassar, A.: Innovative sustainable methodology for managing in-house software development in SMEs. Benchmarking Int. J. **25**(3), 1085–1103 (2018)
22. UNDP: Mind the Gap a Labour Needs Assessment for Lebanon (2016)
23. Vaivio, J.: Interviews – learning the craft of qualitative research interviewing. Eur. Account. Rev. **21**(1), 186–189 (2012)
24. WIPO: Study on the Economic Contribution of the Software Industry in Lebnaon (2015)

Author Index

Printed in the United States
by Baker & Taylor Publisher Services

Printed in the United States
by Baker & Taylor Publisher Services